WILL POWER

WILL POWER

How to Act
SHAKESPEARE
in 21 Days

JOHN BASIL
with STEPHANIE GUNNING

Applause Theatre & Cinema Books

Will Power
How to Act Shakespeare in 21 Days
John Basil with Stephanie Gunning
Applause Theatre & Cinema Books
Copyright © 2006 John Basil

Book design by Pearl Chang; Cover photo: The American Globe Theatre's production of *A Midsummer Night's Dream* by David Laundra.

Library of Congress Cataloging-in-Publication Data:

Basil, John.
   Will power : how to act Shakespeare in 21 days / by John Basil ; with Stephanie Gunning.
        p.   cm.
   Includes bibliographical references and index.
   ISBN-13: 978-1-55783-666-3 (pbk. : alk. paper)
   ISBN-10: 1-55783-666-3 (pbk. : alk. paper)
      1. Shakespeare, William, 1564-1616--Dramatic production. 2. Acting.
I. Gunning, Stephanie, 1962-   . II. Title. III. Title: How to act Shakespeare in 21 days.
PR3091.B374   2006
792.9'5--dc22

                                                                2006010960

Applause Theatre & Cinema Books

19 West 21st Street, Suite 201
New York, NY 10010
Phone: (212) 575-9265
Fax: (212) 575-9270
Email: info@applausepub.com
Internet: www.applausepub.com

Applause books are available through your local bookstore, or you may order at www.applausepub.com or call Music Dispatch at 800-637-2852

Sales & Distribution

North America:
   Hal Leonard Corp.
   7777 West Bluemound Road
   P. O. Box 13819
   Milwaukee, WI 53213
   Phone: (414) 774-3630
   Fax: (414) 774-3259
   Email: halinfo@halleonard.com
   Internet: www.halleonard.com

Europe:
   Roundhouse Publishing Ltd.
   Millstone, Limers Lane
   Northam, North Devon EX 39 2RG
   Phone: (0) 1237-474-474
   Fax: (0) 1237-474-774
   Email:
   roundhouse.group@ukgateway.net
   Internet: www.halleonard.com

To Liz

Contents

Acknowledgements

My list of appreciations begins with my friend Stephanie Gunning without whom *Will Power* simply would not exist. When I suggested that we coauthor a book based on my "Playing Shakespeare" courses, she was encouraging and enthusiastic. She introduced me to Stephany Evans, of Imprint Agency, who agreed to represent our project and found it a good home at Applause Books. Many thanks are due for the support of both women.

A big thank you to my publisher, Michael Messina, and the entire publishing team at Applause for shepherding the book into print. You have made a dream come true.

Ideas, stories, facts, information-checking, artwork, and other support were contributed by the following people: Elizabeth Keefe, Kevin Otos, Rick Fay, Kathryn Savannah, Robert Liftig, Rainard Rachele, Paige Lussier, Galen Hoffman, Sue Bastian, Kenneth Mitchell, Nick and Erika Anselmo, John and Nancy Smith, and Christopher Frey. A special thanks to David Laundra, Dennis Turney, Kimberley McNeese, Jeanette Leslie, and Pilialoha Nathaniel.

As always, I am grateful to my wife Liz for standing beside me as my partner.

INTRODUCTION

Your 21-Day Journey with Will

In *Will Power: How to Act Shakespeare in 21 Days,* I'll be your guide on an adventure through the strange and delightful lands of Shakespeare's characters and the plots they inhabit. You'll learn how to use his remarkable language as a detailed performance map, one you may follow over a three-week period, first to scout out new and unknown territory, and then to stake your personal claim on it. As you'll discover, you needn't fear the language–it's specially designed to involve and support you.

Shakespeare wrote his plays to engage the "ear" of his audience's imagination. As a successful entrepreneur in the entertainment business of the Elizabethan era (the late 1500s to early 1600s), he was crafting dramatic, tragic, and funny stories in a way he knew would delight people of a culture more oriented to sound than ours. He intended his plays to be *heard* and *seen,* rather than read silently while sitting on the living room couch. To help his performers make the language of his plays spring to life on stage, he embedded linguistic and rhetorical clues within the scripts he provided them. These were combined by two of his colleagues after his death to form the First Folio edition of 1623. Of course, as Shakespeare was an exceptionally inventive wordsmith and a keen interpreter of human nature, his plays have become timeless classics. But he didn't write the plays to inspire awe; he wrote them to entertain a broad cross-section of people.

Elizabethan actors had only three or four days of rehearsal in which to prepare a production. They worked without formal direction, although they may have occasionally asked the playwright a few questions. As a result, they didn't have much time to learn their lines and generally had to come up with their own blocking on the spur of the moment. To get around the issues that such circumstances would raise, certain conventions were developed that actors of the day understood. A prompter sat on stage with them. Backstage, a *platt* (a chart) hung by the stage entrance indicating when the actors would go on and come off. Hence, we have the word *plot.*

Most importantly, Shakespeare supplied his actors with specific punctuation, capital letters, and other verbal clues that informed them *how* and *when* he wanted them to speak and move. He provided these basic vocal instructions and stage directions inside the lines themselves. No doubt, through years of practical experience, the actors learned to make the kinds of choices that would best fulfill these scripted opportunities.

When modern actors learn to understand the clues that Shakespeare gave to his actors, suddenly every line and scene becomes more intelligible and fun to play. Imagine what the men in Shakespeare's company must have been like. They were probably a rather motley and rambunctious crew. After all, these were guys who didn't want to become carpenters or blacksmiths, or pursue other so-called respectable trades. No. They wanted to dress up in costumes and wigs and prance or swagger around in public. They weren't graduates of the Royal Shakespeare Academy or Julliard. In fact, they probably had very little formal education. So, talented as they may have been, they were not smarter than actors of today. Acting Shakespeare was never supposed to be the daunting or even petrifying challenge it's all too frequently viewed as by the inexperienced.

How I Discovered Shakespeare

Twenty years ago, I felt electrified and inspired when I was introduced to the secrets of the Bard's language. Until then, I'd been lucky as an actor. But my discovery would lead me in an entirely new direction that I found even more intriguing.

Before graduating from Temple University's intensive graduate program in theatre in 1975, I spent several seasons working at the renowned Williamstown Summer Theatre Festival in Northern Massachusetts, after which I was eligible to join Actors' Equity, the performers' union. At Williamstown, I met and worked with professional directors and star actors, people such as Frank Langella and Blythe Danner. Once I completed my master's degree, I found an agent and was hired by regional theatres around the country. But the parts I got were all what I call "the Dicks." I played Nick and Rick and Brick—and anyone else whose name ended in an "ick." And, as I always seemed to have to take my shirt off, I basically felt as though I was playing the same role over and over again.

I decided it was time to deepen my training. I returned to New York City to study method acting with the highly respected Stella Adler, Uta Hagen, and Mira Rostova, teachers whom I mischievously referred to as the "Three Sisters" in homage to playwright Anton

Chekhov. I also explored the art of direction by working as assistant director to Bruce Paltrow at the Writer's Theatre (on a production starring Blythe Danner) and as a director at the New Playwright's Conference produced by Ensemble Studio Theatre. I felt that I definitely knew how to act. However, I was nonetheless frustrated by the sameness of the way I was playing the different roles that were offered to me. That just wasn't the way it was supposed to be. It wasn't what attracted me to the theatre. But I didn't know yet how to get out of the trap.

In the early '80s, my passion for Shakespeare was spontaneously evoked. One Wednesday morning, standing in front of the callboard at the Equity offices, I read an announcement that said that John Barton, Director of the Royal Shakespeare Company, would be giving a lecture that very evening. Frankly, I'd never heard of the man. *He's going to talk about Shakespeare? What do these Brits know?* I thought skeptically. *I mean: They don't know as much about naturalistic acting as we Americans do. We have heart, whereas they only act from the head up, right? Nevertheless,* I decided, *I'll go and listen to him just in case he says anything interesting.*

Barton's lecture was an introduction to the First Folio edition and the embedded acting clues in it that have been largely forgotten in the modern world. They've only survived in a few instances by being passed down from teacher to student. He talked about how much joy and fun we could have performing Shakespeare's plays, and made them seem much less intimidating. Several times he threw in the statement that if American actors embraced this technique for doing Shakespeare, we could be better at it than classically trained British actors. Due to our background in method acting, Americans are emotionally connected to our material; however, we tend to get bogged down by technique—which he felt was simpler to learn.

The decision to attend that talk changed my life. It was like being struck by a lightning bolt. From that moment on, I knew that I definitely wanted to be involved in what John Barton had spoken about—and immediately, if not for the rest of my life. Subsequently, I studied directing, staging, and interpreting Shakespeare with Barton and then later with Patrick Tucker, founder of the Original Shakespeare Company in London, who was formerly Barton's assistant. Their combined influence on me was life altering. Right away, I began gathering groups of actors at my kitchen table and leading them through the process. I also was given an opportunity to direct a staged reading produced by the Riverside Shakespeare Company in New York. In it, I had my actors employ the same techniques. The production was a huge hit. As a result, I was invited to become a principal director and teacher at Riverside, where I remained until 1987. At that point, I was inspired to found my own acting conservatory and theatre company to pass on these tools to students and actors much like you.

Today, I'm still committed to this incredibly dynamic and effective way of working on Shakespeare, and I still feel just as excited as I was in that first Barton workshop. These authentically Elizabethan techniques form the backbone of the rehearsal process you're going to learn while using *Will Power*.

The Importance of Preparation

To those of us who catch the acting bug, the lure of the theatre is powerful. Thousands of young (and not-so-young) actors flock to major cities every year seeking work, and the competition for parts is fierce. There's no way around the fact that it's a tough industry to break into and within which to earn a decent living on a regular basis. Actors endure long periods of unemployment and frequent rejection in auditions. To better their chances, they must develop performance skills that lift them above the average. They must have poise, stage presence, and the ability to affect an audience. Savvy actors therefore take classes regularly and thoroughly prepare for the opportunities that may come their way. They persevere, working to build an influential network of contacts that can gain them entrée to the better auditions. But it's artistic ability that ultimately helps them attract jobs. Casting directors want to be impressed—and surprised. Emerging actors who learn how to do that on a regular basis soon find they've got viable careers, rather than on-again-off-again occasional gigs.

As a professional acting coach running an independent studio in the heart of the Broadway Theatre district of New York City, and as the artistic director of American Globe Theatre (a small, resident classical theatre company in the same neighborhood), I now train, cast, and direct literally hundreds of new and seasoned actors each year. For more than 25 years, my work has centered on Shakespeare. My "Playing Shakespeare" series includes five workshops: Speaking the Text, Staging from the Text, Script Analysis, Monologues/ Soliloquies/Auditions, and the Master Class (scene study of classical plays). I'm very familiar with the challenges actors face and also with what it takes for them to begin realizing their potential. The bottom line is whether or not they can learn to speak, move, and pursue specific actions on stage in ways that engage and excite an audience.

Shakespeare's plays provide actors with incredible opportunities to explore, improve, and celebrate their craft. Understanding how to handle a piece of text well by emphasizing its strong stresses, key words, and internal logic is not only a classical technique, it's also a good approach to modern plays and advertising copy. For example, in 1994 I had a student who was a young dad type in his early 30s. He got called in for a Yuban coffee commercial. Fortunately, the night before in my Speaking the Text class we'd discussed the importance of the sounds of "un" in a monologue he was preparing (words that incorporated un-, in-, and en-). When he arrived at his audition, he was handed some cold copy and had only five minutes to prepare it. My student cleverly underlined all the capitalized words and all the sounds of "un." When he read the copy, he relished those words and made them stand out as special. The copy read:

> Untamed
> Undiluted
> All its riches intact
> Yuban
> made from 100 % Columbian beans,
> the richest coffee in the world.
> Yuban
> Unleash it and taste…
> the Spirit…
> of Coffee.

My student got the job. The director told him, "You were the only actor we saw who knew how the copy was supposed to sound." So, as you can plainly see, actors who can handle Shakespeare can also handle contemporary material with style and confidence.

Throughout his lifetime, the painter Vincent Van Gogh sent hundreds of letters to his brother Theo. In one, he wrote: "I have spent the day mixing greens and yellows with blades of grass, threads from my shirt, and sticks, and now I am beginning to feel I have found my own uniqueness in my own art."

Years ago, wandering through an exhibition of his artwork at the Metropolitan Museum of Art, I scribbled this anecdote on a piece of paper and tucked it inside my wallet for inspiration. Van Gogh's curiosity and perseverance is a model of the exacting dedication that defines an artist. He was on a journey of investigation, seeking to understand and reveal his unique self through various combinations of media.

If an actor wants to breathe fresh life into each new moment on the stage, he or she must be just as meticulous with each line of Shakespeare as Van Gogh was with his pigments. Subtle details matter. Shakespeare understood that the best way to make audiences pay attention was to surprise them with shifts of direction. He was aware that dramatic tension comes from conflict, questions, contrasts, problem solving, and resolution. Therefore, every line he wrote–every moment–is distinct from the ones that precede and follow it. Each has its own special meaning and its own actable verb. If an actors stick to the specifics of the lines, as Shakespeare wrote them, and don't allow themselves to get lazy by playing generalities, they seem more exciting and imaginative than other actors.

Shakespeare's language is unparalleled by any other playwright's, even that of his contemporaries, and his plays have become classics for good reason. Although 70 percent of his texts are in the form of poetry, the verse makes sense to the audience when it's properly performed. They can apprehend the meaning, even when they do not necessarily comprehend individual words. As an educated man of his era, Shakespeare knew and admired the works of the Ancient Greek and Roman dramatists and orators. His characters are constantly engaging in debates with each other and within themselves. Thus, he structured his plays along various rules of rhetoric: the art of verbal persuasion.

Prepared actors who make bold, unique choices and follow through on the rhetorical impulses of their characters impress casting directors. They're also able to connect with audiences on a much more heartfelt level. When they've done their homework, actors may stand behind the decisions they've made about a role without apology. By the time Ian McKellen brought Richard the Third to the screen, I guarantee you that he'd explored every possible angle and aspect of his character and the language. No one would have debated his authority to personify Richard as he saw fit. Taking responsibility for the performance is always the actors' ultimate key to freedom.

Well-prepared Shakespearean actors must learn to embody the seven *C*s of acting:

1. *Commitment:* The willingness to do whatever it takes to get the job done to your greatest satisfaction–to dig deeper, spend the necessary time, and aim to fly higher. There is a degree of effort involved in rehearsing, thus it requires discipline. Commitment is the decision to pursue a course of preparation from which all of your subsequent choices will emerge.

2. *Concentration:* Once you've committed yourself, you need to gather your mental faculties and focus them on the task at hand—solving the equation of a speech, a scene, or an entire play, or receiving the greatest benefit from a day's rehearsal. Your objective may change every day, yet you will always need to concentrate. Concentration is how you draw in your scattered energy and stream it into the more powerful form of a laser beam that is targeted and specific.

3. *Conditioning:* Tuning your instrument (your breath, tongue, vocal cords, muscles, tendons, mental focus, memory, vocabulary, nervous system, and "heart"), so you will be flexible, connected, alert, energized, and physically able to perform when the time comes. If you're a well-conditioned actor, the number and range of possibilities available to you in a performance increases. If you're poorly conditioned, you are limited. Doing Shakespeare demands a certain degree of verbal gymnastics. It demands mental acuity and emotional responsiveness. Rehearsal is primarily, although not exclusively, a conditioning process.

4. *Control:* The ability to flow and succeed under pressure, and in the face of challenges and obstacles. Acting is a high-pressure occupation that puts you under certain stresses such as auditions and live appearances. Rehearsing is a process of developing self-mastery at the same time that you are mastering your material. While you can never hope to control external events, you can learn to control yourself.

5. *Confidence:* An ever-increasing degree of trust in your ability

to make strong, positive, and appropriate acting choices and bring them all to fruition. Although you may not have much confidence on the first day of rehearsal, and wouldn't necessarily want to stand up and perform your monologue or scene in an audition then, you can anticipate being full of confidence on the last day of rehearsal.

6. *Courage*: Boldness and heart–the ultimate leap to fly or to fall without a net–giving 150 percent of your self to every performance. As an actor, you must be willing to take risks. You must put your abilities in the service of your art form. After rehearsing, you will have developed more confidence, conditioning, and control. You'll have strengthened your commitment, or resolve. You'll also have made a specific plan for your performance and thoroughly memorized and integrated its nuances on every level of your being. Courage enables you to put your work out in public, whether for a friend, a casting director, or an audience.

7. *Clarity*: Does your work make sense to the listener/viewer? Are you impacting your fellow actors on stage? Is your delivery affecting the audience? Is it reaching the last row? The ultimate and ongoing measure of every acting choice must be whether or not it adds or subtracts from the moment. Clarity is the bottom line. It's the function of Shakespeare's characters to try to win the debate they're engaged in during a particular line, scene, or act; so you must be clear about your character's point of view and communicate his or her argument persuasively.

How to Use This Book

Featuring a four-phase rehearsal process that leads up to the day of an actual audition or performance, *Will Power* will guide you through three weeks of daily rehearsals that condition you to perform the musicality of the Bard's language and assist you in bringing his inimitable characters to life. Part of the reason that playing Shakespeare is so incredibly fun is that he never wrote the same personality twice. While most actors would love to play Shakespeare because it is such rich, delicious material, many fear the heightened, poetic language. Or they simply don't know where or how to begin working on the texts in order to make them come to life. These need no longer be your dilemmas.

Thomas Edison spent more than a decade heading a team that was researching and building prototypes of the car battery. In the tenth year, when they still hadn't created a viable model, his lead scientist gave up and quit the project. In the eleventh year, a newspaper reporter came up and asked the famed inventor, "How does it feel to fail?" "I haven't," responded Edison. "I am the only person in the world who knows 22,000 ways *not* to make a car battery."

In the twelfth year, Edison's team succeeded. Within another year, they'd made back all the money spent during the research and development phase of the project and more. Today, all car batteries still use that same basic design.

A rehearsal process may be likened to scientific research and development, although of a character rather than of a marketable product. Whether you are a beginning actor or a seasoned professional, you'll be the inventor of a character and a performance that are uniquely your own. You'll know what works and what doesn't work. Be willing to "fail" in rehearsal. Pushing your language and actions to various extremes can help you discover opportunities you wouldn't have otherwise considered.

In *Will Power*, I'm going to walk you, step by step, through 21 sets of activities designed to help you make discoveries and add distinctive layers to your performance. Like a journey into a foreign land, these steps form a *repeatable* process–a map. After you've finished the book, you'll be able to apply the steps on your own to any scene or monologue. You'll also know which of these tools contribute the most to your own artistic process. *Will Power* will lay clear stepping-stones before you.

Remember, however, that this book is neither Shake 'n' Bake-style instant Shakespeare, nor is it easy Shakespeare. Performing Shakespeare demands much from an actor. Though you've got plenty of hard work ahead, once you complete this book, you'll no longer have to overcome the obstacle of strategizing how to prepare for your audition or performance. You'll simply have to dig in and move forward. Freedom and joy come hand in hand with responsibility. As a result of your perseverance and commitment, you're certain to take much more satisfaction in your performances in the near future.

Break a leg!

The
SHAKESPEARE
Rehearsal

PHASE 1

Map Reading

Secrets of Your Script Unfolded

As an actor, you're on book in the first phase of rehearsal. Your aim is to discover as much about the text and character as possible, allowing room to be surprised. The process of working through a script is to go line-by-line, then sentence-by-sentence, and finally to put together the whole speech or scene. As you experiment in making the language crystal clear, you'll form impressions and establish a unique relationship to your role.

In Phase 1, you won't concern yourself with memorization. No matter how eager you feel to be free of holding the script, it's important not to commit to specific acting choices too early, as they can rapidly become stale. It is incredibly difficult to unlearn memorized choices. An important distinction between an exploratory learning process and rote memorization is that exploratory learning engages the right hemisphere of the brain. It is creative, expressive, and imaginative. By contrast, rote memorization is left-brain and linear. It rarely leads to unanticipated associations and emotional richness, because it stays on the surface level of the text. Exploration is three-dimensional. It's a heart, soul, and spirit process that gives you much richer, evolving line readings. Memorization is flatter–afterward lines tend to always come out the same way.

In Map Reading, we'll explore the acting clues that are embedded in the text of the First Folio edition of 1623. Shakespeare wrote in an era attuned to sound, so his scripts—due to their idiosyncrasies—serve as musical scores for how to speak and what to do on stage. People in his day used to say, "Let's go hear a play!"

For the next several chapters, your goal is to learn as much as possible about the peculiarities of your character's speech patterns. Shakespeare's characters are problem-solvers, and they harness language to reason, to persuade, and to resolve conflicts. Demystifying the text clarifies their rhetoric.

DAY 1

Revealing Your Repetitions

Welcome to your first day of rehearsal. Over the next three weeks we will venture deeper and deeper into the strange and wondrous territory created by playwright William Shakespeare whose plays have been studied and celebrated for over four centuries. You will discover new and exciting ways to bring his subtly crafted words to life–to put flesh on his characters. Step by step, I promise that you will quickly become able to craft a reliable map for your unique stage performance.

One of the primary tools of rhetoric is repetition. Repeating a consonant, a vowel, a word, or a phrase is a way of reinforcing what you're saying, leading you to the meat of your argument and indicating to the audience what's important. Clarity is your primary goal. But there's a trick to repetition. You have to say repeat a sound, word, or phrase the second time because it sounded good the first time. And you have to learn to repeat it the third time because it sounded so good the first and second times. This invites the audience to listen. Done properly, repetition builds the strength and impact of a speech or scene. It is one of Shakespeare's favorite verbal devices.

Act 2, Scene 1 from *The Taming of the Shrew* is a perfect example. Katherine is a spirited young woman whose father is so eager to marry her off that he has promised to give her future husband a large dowry. Despite the income for her potential bridegroom, local suitors keep allowing her to maliciously drive them away. None can stand up to her rejection and ridicule. That's when Petruchio (pronounced Puh-true-key-oh) arrives on the scene. A man of the world and not so easily stymied, he sets his designs on marrying Katherine and claiming the dowry—no matter how poorly she behaves. Our scene is their first face-to-face meeting.

To begin today's rehearsal, take a close look at the 19 lines below, which compose about a third of the scene. Read the lines silently on the page one at a time, scanning for any repeated sounds and words.

Then, read the lines again slowly, this time aloud, listening for any repeated sounds and words. You may hear more repetitions than you see, because some letters are spoken hard at times and soft at others. Take the letter *C*, for example. At the beginning of a word, a *C* may sound hard like a *K* (e.g., **c**up). Near the end of a word, a *C* may sound soft like an *S* (e.g., ni**c**e). In the process you're learning, it's important to be always concerned with how the language sounds, rather than how it looks.

On a procedural note, if you're preparing a monologue, work on the whole monologue as a unit. If you're preparing a scene, however, consider dividing it into smaller, more manageable chunks of text—as I've done with the Kate and Petruchio scene here—and then proceeding through each piece separately.

Now, go ahead and read the scene.

1 PETRUCHIO But heere she comes, and now *Petruchio* speake.
       <Enter Katerina>
2   Good morrow *Kate*, for that's your name I heare.

KATE	Well have you heard, but something hard of hearing:	3
	They call me *Katerine*, that do talke of me.	4
PETRUCHIO	You lye infaith, for you are call'd plaine *Kate*,	5
	And bony *Kate*, and sometimes *Kate* the curst:	6
	But *Kate*, the prettiest *Kate* in Christendome,	7
	Kate of *Kate* -hall, my super-daintie *Kate*,	8
	For dainties are all *Kates*, and therefore *Kate*	9
	Take this of me, *Kate* of my consolation,	10
	Hearing thy mildnesse prais'd in every Towne,	11
	Thy vertues spoke of, and thy beautie sounded,	12
	Yet not so deepely as to thee belongs,	13
	My selfe am moov'd to woo thee for my wife.	14
KATE	Mov'd, in good time, let him that mov'd you hether	15
	Remove you hence: I knew you at the first	16
	You were a movable.	17
PETRUCHIO	Why, what's a movable?	18
KATE	A joyn'd stoole.	19

What did you notice about the repeated sounds? No doubt you caught a plethora of *K*s and certain words, such as *Kate*, *hear*, and *move*. As we break down the text for the Day 2 rehearsal, you'll become aware of even more. Most importantly, get comfortable putting the sounds you discover to work for you.

How do you get comfortable? The same way a pole-vaulter gets comfortable with running and flying 16 feet into the air: by repetition and exercise. Saying your lines is like working a muscle. It's athletic conditioning. The tip of your tongue gets more facile as you perform these feats. In the process of developing strength and dexterity, you also discover rhythm, clarity, and action. This doesn't happen in a single day.

One of the main purposes of repetition is to draw in the audience. When they notice that you're repeating yourself, they lean forward in their seats with anticipation. What are you going to do with the next repetition, they wonder? How many times can you do it? And they especially want to know, how clever and witty are you?

Repeated Consonant Sounds (a.k.a. Alliteration)

In Shakespeare's plays, a character's thoughts and intellect are generally revealed on consonants. As Neil Simon wrote in the first scene of *The Sunshine Boys*, *K* is the funniest letter in the alphabet. "If it doesn't have a 'K,' it's not funny," old vaudevillian Willie tells his nephew. According to him, words that are funny include: cupcake, cookie, cucumber, car keys, and Cleveland.

On *The Tonight Show*, a couple of decades ago, Johnny Carson and Jack Webb did a sketch satirizing detective Joe Friday, Webb's lead character from *Dragnet*, in which they put this comedic philosophy into action. After building *K* sounds through two pages of dialogue, the punch line ultimately was: "If I ever catch kleptomaniac Claude Cooper from Cleveland who copped my clean copper clappers kept in the closet...I'll clobber him!"

Shakespeare understood the power of alliteration, which is one term for repeating consonant sounds. He repeatedly used *K*s, *P*s, and *B*s for humor ("Boiling bloody breast" causes an actors cheeks to puff out comically) and *F*s and *T*s for emphasis ("Farewell fair cruelty" is Viola's way of telling off Olivia in *Twelfth Night*). As he placed at least

17 *K* sounds into this part of the scene, we can be certain that Petruchio is having fun teasing and sparring with Kate right from the get-go.

In line 3, Kate opens the verbal joust by repeating the *H* sound four times: "Well **have** you **heard**, but something **hard** of **hearing**..." In essence, she's laughing at Petruchio—"Ha ha ha ha"—before correcting him.

Petruchio responds with a veritable machine gun of *K* sounds: "...**c**alled...**K**ate...**K**ate...**K**ate...**c**urst..." and so on. At line 11, he adds some *M*s: "**m**ildnesse...**m**y...**m**ov'd..." These send her a different message: He likes what he sees in her. Mmm-mmm-mmm.

Although she seems to reject him, as she basically retorts, "Move away, Bucko," we know that on some level she likes him, because she picks up on his *M* sounds and adds a few of her own ("**m**ov'd...time...hi**m**...**m**ov'd..."), and she continues laughing ("**h**im...**h**ether...**h**ence...").

It's now time to apply this information to your own monologue or scene. First, scan your lines on the page. Then, read them slowly and carefully out loud. Whenever you discover a series of repeated consonants, please do the following task.

—— Your Task—Rising Up for Consonants——

Develop heightened awareness of consonant sounds by going up on tiptoe every time you say a certain one, such as a *K*, *S*, or *T* sound. In line 1, for instance, if you were tracking *K* sounds in our scene from *Shrew*, you would rise once during each of the words *come*, *Petruchio*, and *speake*. Your own monologue or scene may contain a different series of alliterations.

The purpose of this task is to make sure that you won't pass by repeated consonant sounds, and will make a commitment to articulating them. Your goal here is to deliver your lines with clarity, not speed. See if you can bring to life the hissing of the *S*, the lasciviousness of the *L*, the warmth and satisfaction of the *M*. Listen. Make note of how you sound and feel as you do.

An actress in my class was excited by a discovery she made using this exercise for *T* sounds while rehearsing the role of Phebe from *As You Like It*. Her line was:

Youth, you have done me much ungentlenesse,

To shew the letter that I writ to you.

When she stopped suddenly, I wasn't sure exactly what had happened. Then, with her eyes as wide open as saucers, she exclaimed, "Oh! I'm spitting at him!" Characters who repeat are being clever, witty, or mwah-ha-ha mad (like the evil queen in the animated version of *Snow White and the Seven Dwarfs* or a crazy arch villain hiding in a dungeon in a 1920s black-and-white movie). Which of these three approaches to take is left open to the individual actor's imagination. We'll talk more about these distinctions in the Day 15 rehearsal, "Surely, You Jest." In this instance, the actress decided that, by spitting, Phebe is being clever. Making this decision subtly altered her behavior.

Before the significance of the alliteration in Shakespeare is pointed out, most actors will decrescendo on the repetitions and otherwise diminish or flatten them out. Once they go up on tiptoe, their whole bodies begin to resonate with these sounds. Among other benefits, their vocal variety increases, they stop thinking and start doing, and their behavior becomes more imaginative and playful. Many students have even told me that awareness of repeated consonants ultimately helps them memorize their lines.

Repeated Vowel Sounds (a.k.a. Assonance)

A character's feelings tend to be revealed on vowel sounds (*a, e, i, o, u, y*) and diphthongs (combination vowels like *–ae*). Feelings are fleeting, of course, and can change from moment to moment, line to line. You can ferret out repeated vowels in the same way you ferreted out the repeated consonants: first, scan the lines on the page. Then, read the lines aloud and listen to yourself.

In lines 11 through 14 Petruchio provides a clear example of the repeated *E* sound: "every…beaut**ie**…d**ee**pely…th**ee**…th**ee**…" Whereas, our protagonists share the -oo sound in lines 14 through 18: "m**o**v'd…w**oo**…m**o**v'd…m**o**v'd…rem**o**ve…m**o**vable…m**o**vable."

So what can you do to take advantage of repeated vowel sounds? Or, put another way, what was Shakespeare indicating he wanted you to do?

Remember the basic rule. Say the sound the second time because it sounded good the first time. Say it the third time because it sounded so good the first and the second time. In other words, you need to find a way to say the sound that indicates to the audience how much your character is relishing it. To determine an appropriate way to relish a sound, you'll benefit from answering questions about it. Is Kate being clever, witty, or mwah-ha-ha mad when she uses that sound? Is she being ironic, sarcastic, or perhaps even literal?

Another reason Shakespeare might have added repeated sounds is to reveal the hidden message beneath the words, the real meaning of what's going on. The character may not know that Ah-ah-ah or Buh-buh-buh sounds funny. But we do. There is no subtext in Shakespeare. The words themselves contain both "text" and "subtext."

Since breath is released on vowel sounds, one of the easiest ways to change them is by elongating them. This is called adjusting the *weight* of a word–a topic we'll cover in greater depth on Day 15. Technically, this is what I'm asking you to do: The first time, say "–oo" for one count (move). The second time, stretch "–oo" for three counts (mooove). The third time, sit on "–oo" for six counts (moooooove).

Now, explore this task while working on your own monologue or scene.

———— Your Task—Playing with Accents ————

Practice elongating your vowels and diphthongs by speaking your lines using three different dialects: an Italian accent, an Irish brogue, and a Southern drawl. Each of these dialects has a characteristic upward inflection and so naturally "lifts the line," which is one of our most important rhetorical objectives. Don't necessarily strive for accuracy (although you're welcome to be accurate if you have the ability), but rather aim for a stereotypically lazy and drawn-out mode of speech. Ham it up and have as much fun with your lines as possible. Also, listen and make note of how you sound and feel in the process.

Rehearsing the Kate and Petruchio scene with an Italian accent has produced tremendous results in my classes. Students naturally find physical aspects of character they can work with, such as postures, gestures, and other body language. I've noticed that the men, in particular, become more demonstratively seductive. As budding Rudolph Valentinos, you could say they pour olive oil all over the scene and slither around Kate.

Repeated Words and Phrases

When repeated, whole words and phrases provide the audience with an even stronger sense of rhetoric building than repeated sounds do. Whereas sounds have an almost subliminal impact on the listener, words carry direct meanings. As an actor, you can use the repetition of whole words and phrases to build emphasis. If you fail to do something exciting with a repeated word or phrase, the audience disconnects from you. They notice your lack of relish and give up on you. Your job here is to avoid plateauing. You will only stimulate the audience's imagination and draw them in by creating vocal variety.

By line 10 in our sample scene from *The Taming of the Shrew*, Petruchio has already made 12 repetitions of the word *Kate*. Fortunately, most of these are modified by an adjective, such as *bony* or *dainty* or *curst*, and these adjectives are clues to possible tones you might assume and body language that might demonstrate your point of view.

In addition to relishing repetitions, your job as an actor is to increase the meaning of repeated words and phrases. Petruchio, like a good lawyer, is providing Kate with the evidence to prove his point (i.e., "Your name is Kate") after she disagrees with him. That's his side of their rhetorical debate. And he's apparently so confident in his argument that he goes on to propose to her ("My selfe am moov'd to woo thee for my wife"). If it had worked the way he wanted it to, at the end she would immediately say, "You're right! My name is Kate–and I'll marry you!" But, of course, she doesn't.

If you're working on a scene with a partner and your character repeats what the other character says, the same rules apply. Imagine that your character likes how a word or phrase sounds when the other character said it and so repeats it back to build emphasis. This is a tennis match with two people lobbing the verbal ball back and forth over a net. For example, when Petruchio says, "Good morrow *Kate*, for that's your name I heare," Kate replies, "Well have you heard, but something hard of hearing." They love the game. They don't want it to stop; they want to prolong it. Variety includes and involves the audience in the joke, because the dynamic can be seen unfolding.

How should you apply this information to the monologue or scene you're rehearsing?

—— Your Task–Seeking Variety——

As you read your lines, make extreme and distinct vocal and physical choices on each repetition of a word or of a phrase. Repeat that word or phrase the second time because you, as the character, like how it sounded the first time. Sing one repetition, for example, and then whisper the next. Savor that language. Or, if you're standing up on one repetition, sit down on the next.

Be bold with your exploration. Reserve judgment for later.

Let me be clear. In this phase of rehearsal, I neither encourage nor expect you to concern yourself with giving a polished perform-ance. I don't want you to try to get it right. You are only beginning the process of "tuning your instrument" (acting jargon for your unified body-mind-spirit) to play Shakespeare's intricate and vibrant language, so it's best to remove all limits. Even if you supposedly do it wrong or miss the clues, as my students sometimes tell me that they believe they have, you may discover a contrary choice that you couldn't have planned and otherwise would have missed.

As you read your lines aloud and follow through on this task, pay attention. Make note of any interesting vocal or behavioral choices you discover for future reference.

In a production of *Richard the Third* that I directed several years ago, my Lady Anne had a rather quiet style of delivery, so I instructed the actors playing pallbearers in Act 1, Scene 2 not to set down the corpse of her father-in-law that they were carrying until she repeated herself. I wanted to see if we could get more out of the moment. As she didn't know they'd received this directorial note, the first time she said her phrase, "Set down," she said it as calmly as usual. When they didn't respond, she yelled the second repetition and scared the stuffing out of them. "SET DOWN YOUR HONORABLE LOAD!" she said, and they promptly did.

Simple Lines

If you scan a line and read it aloud and you're certain it has no repetitions in it, just deliver the line simply. Line 19, "A joyn'd stoole," is a simple line, for example. Simple lines provide contrast to complex lines, and often serve to keep events flowing. In this case, the line is a set up for another series of jokes. There's no need for hoopla and fanfare on simple lines. Be straightforward and clear. Just say them.

Trust the Repetitions

Have you ever watched a skyscraper being built? I live in New York City, where new high rises are constantly being erected. It's an amazing process. The first step the construction crews take is digging a gigantic hole in the bedrock into which they pour a foundation. Next, they erect a steel skeleton of upright girders and crossbeams. If there were no such concrete foundation or metal framework, the final structure would topple under relatively little pressure. So when I'm walking by an existing building, I know those layers have been placed underneath its edifice.

Shakespeare's repetitions are the foundation of his speeches and make them strong. Not long ago, when one of my students was learning about this aspect of the material, he kept asking me the same question after each of his appearances before the class. "Is this *right?*" he would ask. My answer? "Stop attempting to create a performance so soon." Repetition is only one of the many layers that add up to a fleshed out performance. Just as a builder would never stop at the layer of the steel understructure during construction, you must keep adding new layers to your scene or monologue. Don't expect to get it right on Day 1, or even Day 10 for that matter.

Today, I encourage you to explore the logic of any repeated sounds, words, and phrases you notice and also to perceive your character as a master strategist—more of a verbal gymnast than a baseball homerun slugger.

Shakespeare knew exactly what he was doing. His repetitions are intentional: designed to lead the actor and the audience through specific moments, thoughts, and feelings. Trust that in the end they'll add up to a rhetorical conclusion.

Your Day 1 Rehearsal Checklist

Have you completed your tasks?

☐ Rising Up for Consonants

☐ Playing with Accents

☐ Seeking Variety on Words

☐ Seeking Variety on Phrases

What discoveries have you made?

DAY 2

Cracking the Capitalization Code

To begin work on any speech or scene, it is important to look for the most obvious clues first before attempting to penetrate the more subtle mysteries of character. In the First Folio, the capitalized words hold miniature stories, like subliminal messages, that underscore Shakespeare's plotlines. Proper names are always italicized. Technically, as an actor, you need to hit upon these words and make them sound important. (Don't club them to death vocally, just emphasize.) You need to express their deeper meaning, because they give the text extra dimension. He intended you to speak them with emphasis, feeling, or relish. The audience should recognize from your delivery that these words matter. When modern editors remove these capital letters and italics from typeset editions of Shakespeare, because they aren't grammatical, they're robbing actors and audiences of an incredible wealth of information.

Encapsulated Stories

Take a look at *Henry the Fourth, Part One* (Act 2, Scene 3). Lady Percy's capitalized words say: "O…Lord…I…Harries…Lord… Treasures…Iron Warres…Steed…Sallies…Retires; Trenches, Tents…

32

Palizadoes, Frontiers, Parapets...Basiliskes...Canon, Culverin... Prisoners...Souldiers...Warre...Brow...Streame...O...Lord." That's quite descriptive and specific, even though it lacks polish and subtle detail.

The original speech, which takes place right after Lady Percy's husband Hotspur (Lord Henry Percy) decides to join a rebellion against King Henry IV, is on one level intended to seduce him. A student in my acting class couldn't make good sense of it until she did this exercise. Then, when she had spoken the first and second "O...Lord" with emphasis, she realized it sounded as though she was sexually aroused. The word "O" or "Oh" always signifies a major release of emotional energy in Shakespeare.

Lady Percy is a clever woman, who no doubt has sensed that something is on her husband's mind. She chooses to communicate with Hotspur in military language, because she knows war stirs his passion. For him, it's like dirty talk. Furthermore, taking a clue from the fact that the text was in verse–indicating that it is emotionally heightened–my student found comedy in the speech, knowing a servant would interrupt the couple right at the end of it. With **bold** type to emphasize the capital letters, it reads:

LADY PERCY **O** my good **Lord**, why are you thus alone?	1
For what offence have I this fortnight bin	2
A banish'd woman from my **Harries** bed?	3
Tell me (sweet **Lord**) what is't that takes from thee	4
Thy stomacke, pleasure, and thy golden sleepe?	5
Why dost thou bend thine eyes upon the earth?	6
And start so often when thou sitt'st alone?	7
Why hast thou lost the fresh blood in thy cheekes?	8

9	And given my **Treasures** and my rights of thee,
10	To thicke-ey'd musing, and curst melancholly?
11	In my faint-slumbers, I by thee have watcht,
12	And heard thee murmore tales of **Iron Warres**:
13	Speake tearmes of manage to thy bounding **Steed**,
14	Cry courage to the field. And thou hast talk'd
15	Of **Sallies**, and **Retires**; **Trenches**, **Tents**,
16	Of **Palizadoes**, **Frontiers**, **Parapets**,
17	Of **Basiliskes**, of **Canon**, **Culverin**,
18	Of **Prisoners** ransome, and of **Souldiers** slaine,
19	And all the current of a headdy fight.
20	Thy spirit within thee hath beene so at **Warre**,
21	And thus hath so bestirr'd thee in thy sleepe,
22	That beds of sweate hath stood upon thy **Brow**,
23	Like bubbles in a late-disturbed **Streame**;
24	And in thy face strange motions have appear'd,
25	Such as we see when men restraine their breath
26	On some great sodaine hast. **O** what portents are these?
27	Some heavie businesse hath my **Lord** in hand,
28	And I must know it: else he loves me not.

Please, take a few moments to read the speech aloud in full, listening for the presence and impact of the capitalized words. Then, read it again slowly, but this time vocalizing *only* the capitalized words. Leave pauses for the duration of unspoken text.

What did you notice? No doubt you experienced how much distance there is between the early capitalized words, and how their frequency increases after line 12. Of course, the frequency also decreases after line 18. Perhaps you felt a sense of building intensity or pressure in the middle section that was relieved by the speech's end?

Most speeches have beginnings, middles, and ends that are significantly different. Cracking the capitalization code may be an approach that helps you create variety.

Acting on the Capitalized Word

Capitalized words can also be used to generate insights about your blocking and gestures, and how you might work off the presence of other actors. Let's consider the following speech from *As You Like It* (Act 2, Scene 7). Special words are in **bold** type.

JACQUES	All the world's a stage,	1
	And all the men and women, meerely **Players**;	2
	They have their **Exits** and their **Entrances**,	3
	And one man in his time playes many parts,	4
	His **Acts** being seven ages. At first the **Infant**,	5
	Mewling, and puking in the **Nurses** armes:	6
	Then, the whining **Schoole**-boy with his **Satchell**	7
	And shining morning face, creeping like snaile	8
	Unwillingly to schoole. And then the **Lover**,	9
	Sighing like **Furnace**, with a wofull ballad	10
	Made to his **Mistresse** eye-brow. Then, a **Soldier**,	11
	Full of strange oaths, and bearded like the **Pard**,	12
	Jelous in honor, sodaine, and quicke in quarrell,	13
	Seeking the bubble **Reputation**	14
	Even in the **Canons** mouth: **And** then, the **Justice**	15

16	In faire round belly, with good **Capon** lin'd,
17	With eyes severe, and beard of formall cut,
18	Full of wise sawes, and moderne instances,
19	And so he playes his part. The sixt age shifts
20	Into the leane and slipper'd **Pantaloone**,
21	With spectacles on nose, and pouch on side,
22	His youthfull hose well sav'd, a world too wide,
23	For his shrunke shanke, and his bigge manly voice,
24	Turning againe toward childish trebble pipes,
25	And whistles in his sound. **Last Scene** of all,
26	That ends this strange eventfull historie,
27	Is second childishnesse, and meere oblivion,
28	Sans teeth, sans eyes, sans taste, sans every thing.

Several years ago, I directed *As You Like It* and was impressed with the choices made by the actor playing Jacques in his delivery of this monologue, which occurs during a scene in the Forest of Arden. As a role, Jacques functions as an emotional counterpoint to the other characters. When they're sad, he's happy. When he's melancholy, they're happy. He's a bit of a philosopher. Here, he is standing amidst a group of people that the Duke has banished for unknown reasons. The speech is a journey through the seven ages of the life span, beginning in infancy and ending in old age.

On each of the capitalized words, the actor stopped and turned his attention to a different cast member on stage, using that character as a focal point to serve as an example of his meaning. He chose the youngest actor for "Infant" (line 5). He had a couple serve as his "Lover" (line 9) and "Mistresse" (line 11). He patted the stomach of a portly older man on "Justice" (line 15) and "Capon" (line 16). For "Pantaloone" (the name of a stock character taken from the Comedia del Arte, the archetype of a doddering old man), he gestured towards a guy taking a nap off to one side (line 20). My Jacques' delivery seemed natural and changed subtly each night in performance depending on what kind of responses the other characters gave him.

Capitals as Spoken Bombs

A third model of the power of capitalized words comes from a speech Paulina directs at the King in *The Winter's Tale* (Act 3, Scene 2). Her words are like bombs going off, an incitement to riot. Calling the King a tyrant to his face is treasonous and punishable by death. What she says shocks him into silence. Many of her capitalized words are also set in parentheses, adding even more force. The repetition of the letter *T* (Tyrant, Torture, Tyranny) is dramatic. Here is a brief sample of the text, which goes on for another 23 lines.

PAULINA	What studied torments (**Tyrant**) hast for me?	1
	What **Wheeles**? **Racks**? **Fires**? What flaying? boyling	2
	In **Leads**, or **Oyles**? What old, or newer **Torture**	3
	Must I receive? whose every word deserves	4
	To taste of thy most worst. **Thy Tyranny**...	5

——— Your Task—Targeting the Capitalized Words———

Once or twice, read only the capitalized and italicized words in the speech you are working on (excluding the first words of the verse lines, which are always capitalized). Hear their impact and resonance. Were the capitalized words a cryptic encapsulation of the entire speech?

Write down these words on a sheet of paper. Put the literal meanings of the words next to each. For example, if the word is "run," you might jot down: "run in the park," "run in the stock market," "run in your pantyhose," "run of the house," "run a blender." Even the most seemingly ordinary words have multiple meanings.

Ask: Is this word the most important word in the sentence where it appears? Why? Those questions may guide you to a powerful insight.

—— Your Task—Adding Significance——

Next, add another dimension to the speech by asking yourself: "If this word meant *more*, what more could it mean?" In Jacques' speech above, for instance, the words "Last Scene" hold an implication of mortality. For when the play is over, the curtain falls and there is no more life on stage.

Try to identify an ironic or ambiguous alternative to the literal meaning of each capitalized word you've found. Take a look at Mark Antony's capitalized words—printed in **bold** type below—from *Julius Caesar* (Act 3, Scene 2). In part, the original speech, which takes place after Caesar's murder and is intended to shame Brutus among his peers, reads:

1 MARK ANTONY …**The Noble Brutus,**

2 　　　　　　　Hath told you **Caesar** was **Ambitious**:

3 　　　　　　　If it were so, it was a greevous **Fault**.

4 　　　　　　　And greevously hath **Caesar** answer'd it.

5 　　　　　　　Heere, under leave of **Brutus**, and the rest

6 　　　　　　　(For **Brutus** is an **Honourable** man,

7 　　　　　　　So are they all; all **Honourable** men)

Come I to speake in **Caesars Funerall**.   8

He was my **Friend**, faithfull, and just to me;   9

But **Brutus** sayes, he was **Ambitious**,   10

And **Brutus** is an **Honourable** man.   11

He hath brought many **Captives** home to **Rome**,   12

Whose **Ransomes**, did the generall **Coffers** fill: 13

Did this in **Caesar** seeme **Ambitious**?   14

When that the poore have cry'de, **Caesar** hath wept: 15

Ambition should be made of sterner stuffe,   16

Yet **Brutus** sayes, he was **Ambitious**:   17

And **Brutus** is an **Honourable** man.   18

An ironic meaning in this speech might be using the word honorable to suggest you mean "dishonorable." Ambiguity occurs when you put an implication on the table—like a question—and leave it up to the audience to decide. Is Brutus honorable or dishonorable, what do you think? This engages the audience in a thought process.

Can you add that nuance to your tone when you read the speech aloud?

—— Your Task—Relishing Your Speech ——

Next, read your entire speech aloud while saying every capitalized and italicized word with feeling or verbal relish. Make a bold choice for each one—not necessarily the safest and most literal choice. Listen to the sound.

Panning for Gold

Today's rehearsal is relatively straightforward. But you should watch out for a common mistake that many of my students make. At first, there's a tendency to want to raise the volume. Later, as the deeper meanings become clearer, the more essential meaning emerges. So the correction, or note, is to do more with the capitalized words than merely say them loudly. You need to do these tasks several times to let the deeper meanings percolate up from your subconscious mind into your conscious mind. Imagine that you are panning for gold. As you sift the loose soil through your filter, precious nuggets begin to appear.

Your Day 2 Rehearsal Checklist

Have you completed your tasks?

☐ Targeting the Capitalized Words

☐ Adding Significance

☐ Relishing Your Speech

What discoveries have you made?

DAY 3

Verse or Prose?

Everyday speech patterns are not the ideal mirror in which to evaluate the performance of a Shakespearean role, because the words in Shakespeare's plays are strange and remarkable. Almost two-thirds of the scripts are written in blank verse, a flexible type of non-rhyming poetry popular among playwrights in the Elizabethan era, as it approximates the natural rhythms of English speech. That's why his characters don't sound the way we do when we're talking to our friends. Point of fact, blank verse also wasn't how Elizabethans sounded when they were conversing. As an actor, your challenge is to identify the nature of the language your character uses, begin to trust your instincts about its qualities, and find a way to communicate its nuances so that the audience clearly understands both what you say and your portrayal of an individual human being.

Many actors experience a sense of approach-avoidance with Shakespeare. We want to love his language, because we can see he was a clever and insightful writer, but then the language seems strange and difficult. We worry because it makes us feel unnatural–and yet it is unnatural! That's part of what is so awesome about these plays.

Today you will learn to recognize the rhythmical performance clues that Shakespeare embedded in his scripts. We'll explore blank verse (with special emphasis on a form known as *iambic pentameter*) and rhyming verse (*couplets*), as well as prose. By the end of rehearsal, hopefully you'll have a new appreciation for the music of the verse.

Let's begin with some basic definitions.

Basic Definitions of Verse and Prose

What is verse and how can you recognize it? Verse is another name for poetry, language that follows a specific meter–a rhythm of weak and strong sounds (called stresses)–and has a consistent number of syllables per line (usually ten). For Shakespeare, verse represented truth under pressure. In other words, the more intensely a character feels or the greater a challenge he confronts, the more poetically that character speaks.

In the First Folio edition of Shakespeare's plays (1623), the first word of every line of verse is capitalized and the right-hand margin is uneven. When you see those two signs upon first examination of your script, it's a clue that you're acting verse.

A Brief Explanation of Blank Verse

In speech, a strong stress is the piece of a word that is emphasized to make it more understandable to listeners. Practically, this means you strive to emphasize the correct **SYL**-la-ble in every word you say. You don't want to stress the wrong Syl-**LA**-ble or else you'll sound like an extraterrestrial that has just landed on Earth for a visit. Everyone already naturally adds stresses to their spontaneous utterances.

In classical plays, the building block of verse is the metric foot, a pattern of strong and weak syllables that is repeated a specific number of times in order to form a complete line of verse. Some feet are two syllables long. Others are three syllables long. According to Vince Gotera, poetry editor of *North American Review* and professor of creative writing and poetics at the University of Iowa, "Blank verse can be composed in any meter and with any amount of feet per line (any line length), though the iamb is generally the predominant foot." Along with the *iamb*, there are other variations of metric feet composed of different combinations of strong and weak stresses. Types include:

- *Iamb*:   – /   One weak (unstressed) followed by one strong (stressed) syllable.

- *Trochee*:   / –   One strong syllable followed by one weak syllable.

- *Spondee*:   – –   Two strong syllables together.

- *Anapest*:   – – /   Two weak syllables followed by one strong syllable.

- *Dactyl*:   / – –   One strong syllable followed by two weak syllables.

- *Amphibrach*:   – / –   One strong syllable between two weak syllables.

When metric feet are grouped in specific numbers per line, we get the name of the form of verse. For example, four trochees would make up *trochaic quadrimeter*. Five iambs would make up *iambic pentameter*. We see both of these types of verse in the plays by Shakespeare, as well as other forms of verse, including verse that rhymes.

What is prose and how can you recognize it? Although prose is not our typical on-the-street or at-home style of communication, it is nonetheless the closest thing to normal speaking that can be found in Shakespeare's plays. Prose neither conforms to the rules of any particular rhyme scheme nor to a standard meter (rhythm). As it affords characters more freedom than verse, Shakespeare employed prose for the exposition of information, for disguises, and to make jokes.

In the First Folio you can recognize prose because the first word of every line is *not* capitalized and the text extends from margin to margin on the page. When you see those two signs upon first examination of your script, it's a clue that you're acting prose.

——— Your Task—Surfing Your Lines——— for Poetry and Prose

Quickly scan the script you're working on (a monologue or a scene) to see if your lines are written in prose or verse. Are all the letters in the left-hand margin capitalized or are letters only capitalized at the beginning of sentences? Do the lines extend from margin to margin or are the right-hand margins uneven? If your lines switch from verse to prose anywhere, make a note.

Why Did Shakespeare Choose Verse or Prose?

The question of why Shakespeare has written a particular speech in a particular format—verse or prose—is perhaps most intriguing when a character suddenly switches between the two modes of expression, such as Beatrice does in *Much Ado About Nothing* when she falls in love with Benedick. Up until this moment, her every utterance has been in prose (indicating, possibly, that she is rational and in control of her emotional state). The following dialogue (Act 2, Scene 3) is an example of one of her prose speeches.

BEATRICE	Against my wil I am sent to bid you come in to	1
	dinner.	2
BENEDICK	Faire *Beatrice*, I thanke you for your paines.	3
BEATRICE	I tooke no more paines for those thankes, then	4
	you take paines to thanke me, if it had been painefull, I	5
	would not have come.	6
BENEDICK	You take pleasure then in the message.	7
BEATRICE	Yea just so much as you may take upon a knives	8
	point, and choake a daw withall: you have no stomacke	9
	signior, fare you well.	10

Then, as Beatrice overhears a conversation about her relationship with Benedick (Act 3, Scene 2), she discovers that she has special feelings for him and switches to verse (indicating that she is excited and surprised). The shift in her mode of expression indicates that her overall state of being has changed.

BEATRICE	What fire is in mine eares? can this be true?	1
	Stand I condemn'd for pride and scorne so much?	2
	Contempt, farewell, and maiden pride, adew,	3
	No glory lives behinde the backe of such.	4
	And *Benedicke*, love on, I will requite thee,	5
	Taming my wilde heart to thy loving hand:	6
	If thou dost love, my kindnesse shall incite thee	7
	To binde our loves up in a holy band.	8

9   For others say thou dost deserve, and I
10   Beleeve it better then reportingly.

As you continue your rehearsals, you should return to the questions:
"*Why* is this verse? *Why* is this prose? What *specifically* is my character doing *here* in this passage that does or does not require verse, or
language under pressure?" You'll need to answer these questions for
yourself, but remember a general rule of thumb: The more regiment-
ed and formal the verse, the more heightened the emotional life it
expresses.

Suggestions for Performing Iambic Pentameter

Handling poetic language is an aspect of stagecraft that has long
established conventions. While Shakespeare is notoriously inconsis-
tent–in everything–even he adhered to the standards of his
era...mostly. Once you understand the principles underlying his
iambic pentameter, your ability to act Shakespeare will skyrocket.

A few pages ago you learned that an iamb is an unstressed (weak)
syllable followed by a stressed (strong) syllable, as we find in the
words ful**fill**, be**hind**, there**fore**, and sur**vive**. To produce iambic
pentameter, five iambs are run together in a single line.

Read the following line aloud and listen. Strong stresses are
printed in **bold**.

What **fire** is **in** mine **eares**? can this be **true**?

When you spoke those ten counts (five iambs), did they remind you
of anything? Perhaps the human heartbeat? Read the line again to see
if you can truly locate the pulse.

The first sound we heard in our mother's womb was her two-part heartbeat: da-dum, da-dum, da-dum, da-dum, da-dum. This pulsing rhythm pervaded our atmosphere for nine months and so it retains a powerful subconscious effect on us for the rest of our lives. Most actors don't grasp that the iambic pentameter beat matches their own hearts' beating. However, the sound of the heartbeat represents the life force: blood and energy being driven forward and circulated throughout our bodies.

Iambic pentameter has a powerful, organic effect on an audience because they recognize the same sound of the life force. If the rhythm stops, stalls, or changes it makes them uncomfortable, but if it keeps pumping regularly they merge with the sound. In my experience, actors often fear iambic pentameter because they don't grasp its nature and organic impact. But once its elements are broken down, they are electrified by how much iambic pentameter supports and enhances their efforts.

If you want to perform Shakespeare's plays well, it is a good idea to familiarize yourself with basic terms for counting lines. The following items are referenced throughout this book.

MASCULINE ENDINGS

A ten-beat line is considered "masculine" for ending on a strong stress (dum), which tells you that the emphasis is supposed to be placed on the last syllable. Here are two masculine lines taken from different scenes in *Romeo and Juliet.*

JULIET	Gall**op** a**pace** you **fie**ry **foot**ed **steeds**.
ROMEO	But **soft**, what **light** through **yon**der **win**dow **breaks**?

Both are regular ten-count lines with masculine endings, which demonstrate the same organic da-dum pulsing of a heartbeat, and yet there are distinctions. The second feels gentle and pure, like a steady pulse of a calm person, whereas the first feels excited like a heart pounding after a long run or in someone inflamed with lust. That proves an important point: Just because meter is regular, doesn't mean there is no freedom in it.

FEMININE ENDINGS

An 11-beat line is considered "feminine" for ending on a weak stress (da). The stress is placed on the next to last syllable. You can see several examples in the following speech given by Ariel in *The Tempest* (Act 1, Scene 2), which is almost entirely composed of feminine lines. Only two of her lines here are masculine.

1	ARIEL	I boorded the Kings ship: now on the Beake,
2		Now in the Waste, the Decke, in every Cabyn, [11]
3		I flam'd amazement, sometime I'ld divide
4		And burne in many places; on the Top-mast, [11]
5		The Yards and Bore-spritt, would I flame distinctly, [11]
6		Then meete, and joyne. Joues Lightning, the precursors [11]
7		O'th dreadfull Thunder-claps more momentary [11]
8		And sight out-running were not; the fire, and cracks [11]
9		Of sulphurous roaring, the most mighty Neptune [11/12]
10		Seeme to besiege, and make his bold waves tremble, [11]
11		Yea, his dread Trident shake.

When performing a feminine line your emphasis should be on keeping your thought moving forward. There may be exceptions, such as when the line ends with two single syllable words and one of those words is more meaningful than the other. In line 8 of Ariel's monologue *cracks* offers more substance to the listener than the word *and*.

Did you notice that line 9 can be counted either as an 11-count or a 12-count line depending on how you pronounce the word *sulphurous*? It's more likely that sulphurous is pronounced here as two syllables (sulf-RUS) than three syllables (sul-FER-us) so that the strong stress in the last word, *Neptune*, falls on the first rather than the last syllable (NEP-tune versus nep-TUNE).

Line 11 is an incomplete line, a phenomenon we'll talk about later in this chapter.

ALEXANDRINE LINES

Every so often, you'll encounter a 12-count line. Ariel has one in her very next speech:

ARIEL   Then **all** a **fire** with **me** the **Kings** sonne **Ferd**inand [12]

This type of line is known as an Alexandrine (named after Alexander the Great). Like a masculine line, it ends on a strong stress (dum). To pronounce it properly, you either have to pick up the pace or make an effort to cram the words into the line. This feels out of place, constipated and uncomfortable, which is a definite indication that you must change your rhythm. Here we know that there's something special about Ferdinand from this first mention of his name.

Feminine alexandrines: A feminine alexandrine is a rare 13-count line that ends on a weak stress (da). Such lines indicate that the character is in a state of heightened emotion. For an example, consider the famous "Oh what a Rogue and Pesant slave am I?" soliloquy, in which Hamlet is plotting revenge. He is enraged at his father's murder (by his uncle) and at his mother's deceit, and both feels and expresses his self-loathing because he hasn't taken action to revenge his father sooner.

1 HAMLET   With this Slaves Offall, bloudy: a Bawdy villaine, [12]
2   Remorselesse, Treacherous, Letcherous, kindles villaine![13]
3   Oh Vengeance! [3]
4   Who? What an Asse am I? I sure, this is most brave [12]

Mid-speech is a sequence of 12-count, 13-count, 3-count (a half-line– very special!), and 12-count lines. Hamlet's thoughts are rushing out of him faster than he can speak them. In line 2, he is coming up with fantastic and ever more virulent ways of describing himself, and he draws out the line for extraordinary emphasis. An actor should relish, or give special vocal color, to these lines.

By making lines pop out at us, Shakespeare is telling actors: Do something special with them! For example, in *The Comedy of Errors* (Act 2, Scene 2), Adriana delivers a speech in regular iambic pen-tameter–except for a few lines that jump to 11 or 12 counts. Those lines carry extra significance. See if you can identify them by count-ing the beats.

1 ADRIANA   I, I, *Antipholus*, looke strange and frowne,
2   Some other Mistresse hath thy sweet aspects:
3   I am not *Adriana*, nor thy wife.
4   The time was once, when thou un-urg'd wouldst vow,
5   That never words were musicke to thine eare,
6   That never object pleasing in thine eye,
7   That never touch well welcome to thy hand,

That never meat sweet-savour'd in thy taste,	8
Unlesse I spake, or look'd, or touch'd, or carv'd to thee. [12]	9
How comes it now, my Husband, oh how comes it, [11]	10
That thou art then estranged from thy selfe?	11

Caution: If a line has more than 13 beats, stop counting! You're probably speaking prose. In poetry it is extremely rare for counts to go above 12, or 13 at the most. I know of only one poetic 15-count line, which is in *All's Well That Ends Well* (Act 1, Scene 3). Contact me at **www.willpowerthebook.com** if you find another.

HELEN	Then I confesse	1
	Here on my knee, before high heaven and you,	2
	That before you, and next unto high heaven, I love	3
	your Sonne:	

Lifting Your Lines

In order for an airplane to lift off the ground, it has to have forward momentum, or thrust. The same is true when speaking a line. Each line is like the flight of a different bird or airplane. To fly until you come to the end of your thought–your destination–you need the right breath and enough of it. Your breath is your fuel. Every time you exhale and say your lines you are propelled forward, until you gain the requisite amount of momentum to achieve flight and eventually arrive at your destination.

Perhaps there is turbulence on your flight. Perhaps the flight is smooth. Rhythm is intimately connected to the quality of how the line flies. The da-dum rhythm of your words contributes to pushing you forward in a specific manner and keeps you aloft until you are ready to land. With momentum, you are lifted up–thrust forward and up–and with rhythm your meaning is suspended–sustained in flight.

Incomplete Lines

Every so often in Shakespeare we encounter lines that scan at less than ten counts. *Incomplete lines* are occasions when one character concludes a line of poetry for another, as with the exchange between Claudio and his sister Isabella in Act 3, Scene 1 of *Measure for Measure*. Both halves of these incomplete pairings are marked in **bold**.

1	ISABELLA	Yes brother, you may live;
2		There is a divellish mercie in the Judge,
3		If you'l implore it, that will free your life,
4		**But fetter you till death.** [6 counts]
5	CLAUDIO	**Perpetuall durance?** [5 counts]
6	ISABELLA	I just, perpetuall durance, a restraint
7		Through all the worlds vastiditie you had
8		**To a determin'd scope.** [6 counts]
9	CLAUDIO	**But in what nature?** [5 counts]
10	ISABELLA	In such a one, as you consenting too't,
11		Would barke your honor from that trunke you beare,
12		**And leave you naked.** [5 counts]
13	CLAUDIO	**Let me know the point.** [5 counts]
14	ISABELLA	Oh, I do feare thee *Claudio*, and I quake,

	Least thou a feavorous life shouldst entertaine,	15
	And six or seven winters more respect	16
	Then a perpetuall Honor. Dar'st thou die?	17
	The sence of death is most in apprehension,	18
	And the poore Beetle that we treade upon	19
	In corporall sufferance, finds a pang as great,	20
	As when a Giant dies. [6 counts]	21
CLAUDIO	**Why give you me this shame?** [6 counts]	22
	Thinke you I can a resolution fetch	23
	From flowrie tendernesse? If I must die,	24
	I will encounter darknesse as a bride,	25
	And hugge it in mine armes.	26

Performance-wise, an incomplete line signals one important thing: the actor who completes the line must pick up the other's slack immediately! Jump right in. The first actor plays the line exactly the same as he or she would play a regular, full-length line.

You may have noticed that the last line in this exchange (line 26) is less than ten counts. And yet it must be handled in a different technical manner than the others, as Isabella does not complete it. At American Globe Theatre we call such lines *half-lines*. Let's take a look at half-lines right now.

Half-Lines

Half-lines are subtly different than incomplete lines. When a character reaches an end stop before the tenth beat of a standard line of poetry has been reached–and no one else picks up the count–you can be confident that room has been created either for the actor to insert a dramatic pause or to do some specific stage business. That's a half-line.

Lady Macbeth's dialogue in Act 1, Scene 7 of *Macbeth* offers a powerful example of a half-line ending. Her husband, Macbeth, is in the process of deciding whether or not to murder King Duncan. Whenever he's alone, Macbeth's resolve weakens–doubts creep over him. Lady Macbeth is more ambitious and single-minded. She's using every tactic she knows to manipulate him into the evil act. In the following exchange, first the conspirators share a line (half the counts are hers, and half his), and then she has a half-line ending followed by eight empty counts–a void many directors fill with a kiss.

1 LADY MACBETH As you have done to this. **[6 counts–shared]**

2 MACBETH If we should faile? **[4 counts–achieving ten]**

3 LADY MACBETH We faile? **[Only 2 counts spoken]**

4 But screw your courage to the sticking place,

5 And wee'le not fayle: when Duncan is asleepe…

——— Your Task–Scanning Your Lines:———

Counting syllables is one of your first tasks in addressing any piece of text, whether from a monologue or a scene. Break down the counts of your individual lines so you can zero in on and play specific choices later. Use your fingers (most of us have ten) or your toes, or drum the rhythm out on a desk in our mother's two-part heartbeat rhythm: da-dum, da-dum, da-dum, da-dum, da-dum.

If you find you have extra counts–more than ten–make note of how many. Does the line have a feminine ending, or is it an alexandrine or a feminine alexandrine? If you have less than ten counts in a line, also make note of that. How many counts are there? Is it an incomplete line? Is it a half-line? Where has the norm been broken? Asking these questions helps you find out if there is an emotional change of some kind going on in the character. Look for rhythm shifts. When you're satisfied that you've accurately counted the number of syllables in your lines, continue reading this chapter.

Making the Lines Fit?

In England, the acting community wouldn't think it weird to elongate a word like "ocean" to three syllables in order to establish a regular, masculine ten-foot rhyme scheme (Oh-She-ANN). An American director would probably instruct you to keep it at two syllables (OHSH-Ann), even if the count of your line doesn't add up to the regular ten-foot meter. This is because American audiences generally cannot hear meaning in the former example. Elongation distances the audience from the actor's reality by presenting the word as an abstraction. This puts the audience into a state of confusion or mental evaluation. As a performer you must make the choice to elongate or not.

The same is true for small clues like words that end in *ed*. You can pronounce the word *worked* as "workT" (one syllable) or "work-ED" (two syllables). If you find nine counts in a line like "That thou art then estranged from thy selfe?" and notice that a word in the line ends with an *ed* you can choose to extend the word estranged by an extra syllable and thus make the line regular (e.g., estranged, pronounced estrange-ED). Or you may have an 11-count line that you would prefer came out as a regular ten-count line. In that case, you can elide a word—not just *any* word, but an *appropriate* word, like *sulphurous*, which could be pronounced "sul-FER-ous" or "sulf-RUS," as we saw a few pages ago in Ariel's speech.

Shakespeare played with sounds in word endings like these in order to make his meter flow regularly. Sometimes you'll see a word on the page, add up the line count, and decide to go for it anyway. "This is weird, but I'll make it work for the sake of the meter," you say. Elongating or eliding the words may be strange, but it makes them scan correctly—and it makes a point, because different strong and weak stresses are emphasized.

The British definitely do this. My first teacher in this method, John Barton, knew where to elide his words and where to contract them to make them fit the meter. But use your common sense. You'll lose the audience if they can't understand you. I once took a directing seminar in which it was noted that after losing the audience's attention and involvement it takes an average of seven minutes to get them back. Meanwhile they try to figure out what confused them.

Your rule: If the audience doesn't get it, forget it.

Check out Diana's speech from Act 4, Scene 1 of *All's Well That Ends Well.* Lines 2, 4, and 7 are elided. Line 5 has a count expansion, which is intended to keep the internal rhyme scheme going (i.e., *dead* rhymes with *buri-ED*).

1	DIANA	My mother told me just how he would woo,
2		As if she sate **in's** heart. She sayes, all men
3		Have the like oathes: He had sworne to marrie me
4		When his **wife's** dead: therfore Ile lye with him

When I am **buried**. Since Frenchmen are so braide,	5
Marry that will, I live and die a Maid:	6
Onely in this disguise, I **think't** no sinne,	7
To cosen him that would unjustly winne.	8

Well, it is evident that Shakespeare is eliding words to suit iambic pentameter, but as an actor you have to wonder *why* your character is doing this. There are at least two possible reasons. First, the character could be thinking and speaking faster than normal because events demand it, emotions are running high, or scheming is going on and ideas are sparking like dried brush in a wildfire. Second, it could simply be a character's character trait. Perhaps the person speaks poorly. Perhaps he or she isn't well educated. Or perhaps the character speaks with some sort of regionalism. Historians believe that some of Shakespeare's plays, such as *The Merry Wives of Windsor*, took advantage of regional dialects (Welsh, Irish brogues, and so on) for humor. A modern actor would not be able to pull this off without intensive research.

When I was growing up, a few of the guys working in the local gas station, Eddie, Vincent, and Frank, had a sloppy way of talking among themselves that I loved listening to. They had a friendly way of greeting everyone at the pumps that always came out as one long word: "Howbouditwaddayasay?" It certainly would have been out of character for them to slow down and articulate more clearly. For instance I would have been shocked if they had greeted me by saying, "How about it? What do you say?"

King Henry's famous speech from *Henry the Fifth*, Act 2, Scene 2, is composed of perfectly normal iambic pentameter, until we reach line 7, which contains 11 counts. (Use your common sense and combine lines 1 and 2. Don't stop at the end of line 1.) It is also irregular on lines 12 and 14 (see **bold** words). If you stretch the word *ocean* to three syllables in line 15 it is irregular. To handle line 7, I suggest placing an emphasis on *TY* in the word Tyger.

1	KING HENRY	Once more unto the Breach,
2		Deare friends, once more;
3		Or close the Wall Up with our English dead:
4		In Peace, there's nothing so becomes a man,
5		As modest stillnesse, and humilitie:
6		But when the blast of Warre blowes in our eares,
7		**Then imitate the action of the Tyger:**
8		Stiffen the sinewes, commune up the blood,
9		Disguise faire Nature with hard-favour'd Rage:
10		Then lend the Eye a terrible aspect:
11		Let it pry through the portage of the Head,
12		Like the Brasse Cannon: let the Brow **o'rewhelme** it,
13		As fearefully, as doth a galled Rocke
14		**O're**-hang and jutty his confounded Base,
15		Swill'd with the wild and wastfull **Ocean.**

Rhyming Couplets

Rhymes at the ends of lines in iambic pentameter usually mean "the end." They show that the character is wrapping up a thought, a speech, a scene–or even the entire play. You can perform them to make them sound as if your character is drawing a conclusion, as that's probably what's going on. The worst thing you can do is to try to ignore them. Audiences will notice that you are pretending.

Here's an example drawn from *All's Well That Ends Well* (Act 1, Scene 3).

COUNTESSE	Begon to morrow, and be sure of **this,**	1
	What I can helpe thee to, thou shalt not **misse.**	2

Rhyming couplets also can be romantic, indicating great harmony and heightened feeling between two people or within a single individual. We see an example of this in a speech from *The Comedy of Errors* (Act 3, Scene 1). (**Bold** type shows rhymes.)

LUCIANA	Why call you me love? Call my sister so.	1
ANTIPHOLUS V.	Thy sisters **sister.**	2
LUCIANA	That's my **sister.**	3
ANTIPHOLUS V.	No: it is thy selfe, mine owne selfes better **part:**	4
	Mine eies cleere eie, my deere hearts deerer **heart;**	5
	My foode, my fortune, and my sweet hopes **aime;**	6
	My sole earths heaven, and my heavens **claime.**	7
LUCIANA	All this my sister is, or else should **be.**	8
ANTIPHOLUS V.	Call thy selfe sister sweet, for I am **thee:**	9
	Thee will I love, and with thee lead my **life;**	10
	Thou hast no husband yet, nor I no **wife:**	11
	Give me thy hand.	12
LUCIANA	Oh soft sir, hold you **still:**	13
	Ile fetch my sister to get her good **will.**	14

Although not always comical, rhyming couplets are often very funny. Berowne's bad rhyming couplet at the end of a lovesick speech he gives in Act 3, Scene 1 of *Love's Labours Lost* always gets a laugh because, among other things, there is no character in the play named Joan. You may also notice that the word "grone" in line 1 has the potential to be elongated into a true groan because the line runs one count short of the regular ten in iambic pentameter. Some especially astute actors make this choice.

1	BEROWNE	Well, I will love, write, sigh, pray, shue, **grone,**
2		Some men must love my Lady, and some **Jone.**

Magical Rhythms

When you locate a bunch of seven- and eight-count lines in a row, guess what? Your speech is not iambic pentameter, even if the lines rhyme. Shakespeare uses alternative rhythms for his own magical purposes. One example is *Macbeth* Act 4, Scene 1, written in the verse form known properly as *trochaic quadrimeter*. Remember, a trochee is the opposite of an iamb. It consists of a strong syllable followed by a weak one.

1	FIRST WITCH	Thrice the brinded Cat hath mew'd.
2	SECOND WITCH	Thrice, and once the Hedge-Pigge whin'd.
3	THIRD WITCH	Harpier cries, 'tis time, 'tis time.
4	FIRST WITCH	Round about the Caldron go:
5		In the poysond Entrailes throw
6		Toad, that under cold stone,
7		Dayes and Nights, ha's thirty one:
8		Sweltred Venom sleeping got,

	Boyle thou first i'th' charmed pot.	9
ALL WITCHES	Double, double, toile and trouble;	10
	Fire burne, and Cauldron bubble.	11

At the end of *A Midsummer Night's Dream* (Act 5, Scene 1), when the audience recognizes that the sound of Puck's speech has a different rhythm, they know the play is over. Puck is telling his listeners that they've been dreaming, and that it is time to wake up now and get back to reality. Like the witches, Puck also uses trochees.

PUCK	Now the hungry Lyons rores,	1
	And the Wolfe beholds the Moone:	2
	Whilest the heavy ploughman snores,	3
	All with weary taske fore-done.	4

Meter Is Your Gateway to Shakespeare

As the method in this book primarily involves the sound of the language, please use this Day 3 rehearsal as a foundation for other, later rehearsals. Come back to this information again and again. Scanning your lines for rhythm changes is going to make Shakespeare more accessible to you and less of a mystery than it may seem right now.

If you're ever wondering where to begin working on a speech or a scene, or even a single line of text, turn to the rhythm of the line— it's poetic form—for insights. Remember, you've just entered a new and marvelous foreign land. Meter is the soil of the country you are visiting. Although you don't have a map of this land yet, you'll be drafting your own as you take a few steps during each day's rehearsal.

By the end of the mapping process, you'll have a clearly defined route through your speech: a way to perform each step—each line or each line fragment. Then you can develop freedom with your role, and can allow your performance to be silly, big, and risky.

Memorizing the words and discovering their meaning are not important tasks yet. At first, you can gain confidence and clarity just by learning how to use your breath and voice in patterns of rhythm. That's what the meter of the language gives you. Meaning and emotion will reveal themselves in time. Later rehearsals in this 21-day rehearsal process will help you make specific choices about meaning.

—— Your Task—Can-Do Kazoo ——

If you're feeling as though you'll never be able to deliver a speech clearly and effectively or that you are locked into a single way of performing it, here is one playful activity that can help you feel more free and spontaneous. All you need is an inexpensive musical instrument: a kazoo. Saying your lines through this children's toy will open your throat and allow you to act your lines on your breath. This task will also instigate laughter, help you to drop your guard, and get your creative juices flowing. I highly recommend this task as a warm-up for the beginning of your daily rehearsal sessions.

The kazoo exercise is especially helpful for actors who are self-conscious about pronunciation and tend to flatten out their lines. Words are unintelligible spoken through a kazoo, so you can let go of worrying about articulation and other technical qualities of words when you train on a kazoo. Verse speaking should be anything but flat. The most you can get from playing a kazoo is changing intonations, so focus on this "music.

Your Day 3 Rehearsal
Checklist

Have you completed your tasks?

- ☐ Surfing Your Lines for Poetry and Prose
- ☐ Scanning Your Lines
- ☐ Can-do Kazoo

What discoveries have you made?

DAY 4

Picking Out Punctuation

In the Elizabethan era, there was no such thing as English grammar. Shakespeare would have studied Latin and Ancient Greek in school. Therefore, we can assume that Shakespeare didn't employ punctuation for the purpose of literary clarity. Rather it was for theatricality, intended to make the audience believe they were observing real human beings living through fresh and original moments on stage. Actors must learn to approach Shakespeare's punctuation as *acting* punctuation rather than *grammatical* punctuation.

This isn't such a weird idea. Notes often appear in modern scripts as instructions for the professionals who stage plays, or shoot films and television programs. When I used to direct the soap opera *Another World,* for instance, there could be a note next to a line in the script reading "V.O." TV viewers never saw or knew this note existed. But they would hear that particular line delivered as a "voice over." It was purely intended for the actor, director, and crew. Similarly, punctuation in Shakespeare is for the actor's eyes only.

As a rule of thumb, assume that every piece of punctuation in the First Folio has a purpose and reason for being where it is. Shakespeare knew very well what he was doing.

Why Do Actors Need Punctuation?

Punctuation is a remarkable tool. On the page, as a writer, it assists you in being clear with your readers. It is how you tell them to group your words–and the ideas the words are intended to convey–in their minds. In stage performance, just as in routine daily conversation, punctuation is an intangible element of speech. The audience is only aware of its presence through your breaths and pauses.

Consider the following sentence: "A woman without her man is nothing." There are two possible meanings, which are revealed when we add punctuation.

1. A woman, without her man, is nothing.
2. A woman, without her, man is nothing.

In the first version, the woman needs the man. In the second, the man needs the woman. The meaning of the sentence is dramatically changed by the addition of two carefully placed commas.

Read both versions aloud and listen to the sound of your voice as it makes sense of the phrasing. There is a slight hesitation at the commas, but not a true pause. The first phrase, "A woman," sounds pretty much the same in both readings. But chances are that the second and third phrases sound quite a bit different. Interesting, right?

So punctuation helps actors establish their phraseology. By *phraseology* I mean how they group their words together so listeners can comprehend a whole thought. How words are grouped provides a rhythm. That rhythm provides motion. Motion leads to emotion. Finally, all these elements form a character, a recognizable personality. One of the greatest aspects of Shakespeare's plays, a quality that makes his writing fascinating, is that each of his characters speaks with a special rhythm. Find it and they come to life.

Today's rehearsal may give you an edge over the other actors in your community. Why? In acting, a main purpose of punctuation is to give you a physiological anchor that assists you in your emotional build. It causes you to pause here and there to breathe. Done correctly, the listener hangs suspended in those brief instants, willingly awaiting your thought's conclusion–participating. In an audition or performance, this is very compelling. Literally, since you need to talk on an outward stream of air, when you breathe in you increase your life force. Your breath sparks your emotions.

Phrasing is the music of language. You could say that the distance between every set of punctuation marks is a measure of thought. Even if that measure is only a partial sentence, you'll need to know the total thought it is contributing to. The sentence will begin and then move from part to part, measure to measure, until the complete thought is built. Evolution of thought, like the emotion, is therefore anchored on the breath.

As a director, I believe the proper use of punctuation separates the pros from the amateurs. After all, characters are what they say and what they do. That's really all that an audience can perceive. When actors find the right rhythms in different speeches, they embody the characters that Shakespeare wrote. Then the plays come to life. Of course, no one speaks in poetry unless they're acting in a play. However, when actors find the intended rhythm they know it, because they sound like real people would if they normally speak in poetry. Unless their speeches sound that natural, they clearly haven't done enough work on the material. Professionals put in the necessary effort. Using punctuation well generates energy, emotion, specificity, and forward momentum, whereas using punctuation poorly only causes confusion.

As a matter of fact, if you breathe incorrectly and begin to run out of air, the audience will worry. They can see everything happening in your body. It reads on stage.

Basic Acting Punctuation

Let's explore a few simple rules about Shakespeare's idiosyncratic punctuation.

END STOPS [. ? !]

Shakespearean thoughts are not complete until they reach an end stop: a period, a question mark, or an exclamation point. In some cases, a 20-line speech contains only a single end stop, though it will have lots of other punctuation that enables you to breathe and build along the way. In order to arrive at the intended finish line, actors must always arc their lines rhetorically towards the end stop, rather than sounding as though they intend to stop sooner.

Rhythm changes always illustrate character development, a shift to a new thought or a new permutation of an idea. The importance of an end stop is that it indicates where such a gearshift must occur. Like driving a car that has to switch gears to handle different terrain, an actor has to switch gears when there's a need for an emotional change, a physical change, or both. A genuine entertainer, Shakespeare wrote his plays line by line. He wanted his actors to play a completely new action on each new thought, so the audience would often experience startling variety. He expected actors to theatricalize those shifts.

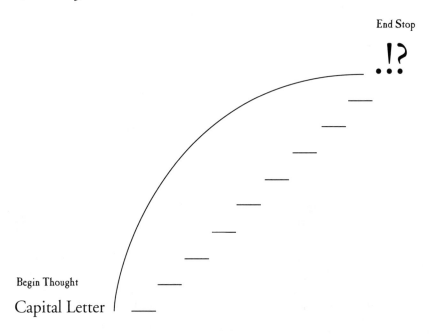

End Stop

Begin Thought

Capital Letter

We find many arcs in nature: a rainbow, a palm tree bending in the wind, the C-curve of a wave just before it crashes against the shore. Waves always get to shore, and actors must be just as committed to reaching their ultimate destination. Each line, each thought, is a wave heading for shore. Interestingly, there's a second arc underneath the wave, the undertow, pulling its energy back to the sea despite forward momentum. In a performance or a scene, after your "wave" has reached shore, the counterforce or undertow of the scene is the response to your line. You receive someone else's line, or a new thought or impulse bubbles up inside you. And then you send out a new wave.

Consider the following monologue delivered by the character Hotspur in *Henry the Fourth, Part One* (Act 1, Scene 3). Here he is addressing the King with a grievance about a man who came to the battlefield and wanted to leave with the prisoners that Hotspur captured. In that era, captured soldiers could be ransomed and were a source of income. The disagreement being articulated in this speech ultimately sparks a civil war. The end stops and the final words in each sentence are highlighted in **bold** type.

HOTSPUR	My Liege, I did deny no **Prisoners.**	1
	But, I remember when the fight was done,	2
	When I was dry with Rage, and extreame Toyle,	3
	Breathlesse, and Faint, leaning upon my Sword,	4
	Came there a certaine Lord, neat and trimly drest;	5
	Fresh as a Bride-groome, and his Chin new reapt,	6
	Shew'd like a stubble Land at Harvest **home.**	7
	He was perfumed like a Milliner,	8
	And 'twixt his Finger and his Thumbe, he held	9
	A Pouncet-box: which ever and anon	10
	He gave his Nose, and took't away againe:	11
	Who therewith angry, when it next came there,	12
	Tooke it in Snuffe: And still he smil'd and talk'd:	13
	And as the Souldiers bare dead bodies by,	14
	He call'd them untaught Knaves, Unmannerly,	15
	To bring a slovenly unhandsome Coarse	16
	Betwixt the Winde, and his **Nobility.**	17
	With many Holiday and Lady tearme	18
	He question'd me: Among the rest, demanded	19
	My Prisoners, in your Majesties **behalfe.**	20

21   I then, all-smarting, with my wounds being cold,

22   (To be so pestered with a Popingay)

23   Out of my Greefe, and my Impatience,

24   Answer'd (neglectingly) I know not what,

25   He should, or should not: For he made me mad,

26   To see him shine so briske, and smell so sweet,

27   To talk so like a Waiting Gentlewoman,

28   Of Guns, & Drums, and Wounds: God save the marke;

29   And telling me, the Soveraign'st thing on earth

30   Was Parmacity, for an inward bruise:

31   And that it was great pitty, so it was,

32   That villainous Salt-peter should be digg'd

33   Out of the Bowels of the harmlesse Earth,

34   Which many a good Tall Fellow had destroy'd

35   So **Cowardly**. And but for these vile Gunnes,

36   He would himselfe have beene a **Souldier.**

37   This bald, unjoynted Chat of his (my Lord)

38   Made me to answer indirectly (as I **said.**)

39   And I beseech you, let not this report

40   Come currant for an Accusation,

41   Betwixt my Love, and your high **Majesty.**

As you read Hotspur's speech, did you notice the mental and emotional shifts that took place following the end stops? Basically, the plot here is that Hotspur has been accused of withholding the king's prisoners. His first thought (line 1) states his respectful disagreement with this position. In lines 2 through 7, he begins to explain his version of the events that took place. He is recreating the scene. From line 8 to line 13, he describes the annoying man who showed up and made the outrageous request. He is commenting on the man's non-warrior-like demeanor. In the middle of line 13, right after the colon following the word snuffe, he escalates with another condemning comment.

The sentence that runs from line 18 to line 20 articulates the injustice. From line 21 to the middle of line 35, he explains his personal reaction to this affront. Then, in two short sentences, he lays out his evidence of other "offenses" of the man he dislikes. The speech ends with his request, respectfully delivered to the king, for peace.

No doubt, you can already see how each one of these complete thoughts must be presented with a different flavor, tone, tempo, pitch, volume, or urgency. Later rehearsals will assist you in establishing those internal and technical distinctions. For now, the idea is to get as clear as possible about where the gearshifts are indicated–even though you haven't made any decisions yet about how to play each moment.

Exclamation points appear infrequently in the First Folio of 1623, though modern editors sprinkle them liberally through their typeset editions. So when you do locate an exclamation mark in the Folio, get excited! *Exclaim* means "to shout" or "cry out." An exclamation indicates an excited, dramatic outburst.

Question marks are a very significant element in punctuation–and in persuasion. On Day 8, we'll present a highly detailed explanation of how best to handle questions.

COMMAS [,]

Commas are places for quick breaths, but they aren't just inserted for the actor's comfort. Rather they are springboards–like miniature trampolines–to keep your thoughts moving forward. If you take in a breath on a comma, you will have more energy to build. Commas don't indicate places to pause and think, or to slow down, so please remember to keep the idea moving briskly toward its destination, a conclusion.

Sometimes, Shakespeare puts a comma after a single word. If he does, you need to find a good acting reason for it to be there. For instance, in *The Taming of the Shrew* (Act 2, Scene 1), when Petruchio tells Kate that he plans to woo her, she responds:

1 KATE   Mov'd, in good time, let him that mov'd you hether

2   Remove you hence: I knew you at the first

3   You were a movable.

Here, the actress playing Kate could choose to elongate the word before the comma ("Mov'd"), expending most of her breath on it. Her reason might be the need to think of a clever retort. Kate doesn't stop after "mov'd." She could take another measure to buy time ("in good time") and then launch a sarcastic barb back to Petruchio off of that phrase. Another actress might do it differently.

If you miss the commas and run all the words in a sentence together without dividing the words in some way (it's your choice how), you'll be missing an opportunity to find the rhythm of your character. You'll be overlooking the individuality of the moment, and failing to take advantage of Shakespeare's moment-to-moment shifts.

Go back to Hotspur's speech and notice that in the sentence that extends from line 2 to line 7, there are ten commas. Each phrase, between two commas, has its own sense and also contributes to the overall picture Hotspur's painting of what happened when the battle he's describing was over. He's explaining why he's rebelling against the king. By line 24, Hotspur begins to speak mostly in monosyllables. The commas break up the speech so that it sounds almost like a drum beat: "Of Guns, and Drums, and Wounds…" As his name implies, he has spurts of hotness and then calms down again.

SEMICOLONS [;]

A semicolon indicates that the character's thoughts are rushing and gushing forward. The next turn of thought is more impassioned. Whenever you see a semicolon, take a quick breath, as on a comma, and internally think "and." Keep your speech moving forward, just the same as you would with a comma.

Semicolons are rare in Shakespeare's plays. When the Duchess of York has one in *Richard the Third* (Act 4, Scene 4), it's as if he's telling her, "Pick up the pace!" See the bold type in line 6 of the following speech excerpt.

DUCHESS	A greevous burthen was thy Birth to me,	1
	Tetchy and wayward was thy Infancie.	2
	Thy School-daies frightfull, desp'rate, wilde, and furious,	3
	Thy prime of Manhood, daring, bold, and venturous:	4
	Thy Age confirm'd, proud, subtle, slye, and bloody,	5
	More milde, but yet more **harmfull;** Kinde in hatred:	6
	What comfortable houre canst thou name,	7
	That ever grac'd me with thy company?	8

Macbeth also has two semicolons in his famous soliloquy ("If it were done, when 'tis done, then 'twer well/It were done quickly") at the end of Act 1 of *Macbeth*, wherein he contemplates murdering

Duncan, the king. The actor playing this speech must keep its momentum going. See the **bold** type in lines 6 and 11 of the following excerpt.

1	MACBETH	…But in these Cases,
2		We still have judgement heere, that we but teach
3		Bloody Instructions, which being taught, returne
4		To plague th' Inventer, this even-handed Justice
5		Commends th' Ingredience of our poyson'd Challice
6		To our owne lips. Hee's heere in double **trust;**
7		First, as I am his Kinsman, and his Subject,
8		Strong both against the Deed: Then, as his Host,
9		Who should against his Murtherer shut the doore,
10		Not beare the knife my selfe. Besides, this *Duncane*
11		Hath borne his Faculties so **meeke;** hath bin
12		So cleere in his great Office, that his Vertues
13		Will pleade like Angels…

COLONS [:]

A colon indicates that the character's next turn of thought is going to be more articulate, a better version of the same thought or a new twist. The character is honing in on the logic. As an actor, internally you need to think "therefore" whenever you see a colon. It's an opportunity for a big breath. This is as close as you can come to an end stop without actually stopping the flow of your speech.

In Act 4, Scene 3 of *Othello,* Amelia works hard to persuade Desdemona that she has done nothing to warrant her husband's anger. Colons reveal the evolution of Amelia's thought process, and perhaps also her growing sense of outrage.

See the **bold** type in the following excerpt.

Yes, a **dozen:** and as many to'th'vantage, as	1
Would store the world they plaid for.	2
But I do thinke it is their Husbands faults	3
If Wives do **fall:** (Say, that they slacke their duties,	4
And powre our Treasures into forraigne laps;	5
Or else break out in peevish Jealousies,	6
Throwing restraint upon **us:** Or say they strike us,	7
Or scant our former having in despight)	8
Why we have **galles:** and though we have some Grace,	9
Yet have we some Revenge. Let Husbands know,	10
Their wives have sense like **them:** They see, and smell,	11
And have their Palats both for sweet, and sowre,	12
As Husbands have. What is it that they do,	13
When they change us for others? Is it Sport?	14
I thinke it **is:** and doth Affection breed it?	15
I thinke it doth. Is't Frailty that thus erres?	16
It is so too. And have we not Affections?	17
Desires for Sport? and Frailty, as men have?	18
Then let them use us **well:** else let them know,	19
The illes we do, their illes instruct us so.	20

A colon also gives an actor the opportunity to make a physical choice. Here's a chance to make a bold cross or do a false exit. Or you could shift your focus–if you're looking left switch your gaze to the right. (We'll do a full rehearsal on focus in Day 14.) In Act 4, Scene 2 of *Much Ado About Nothing*, Benedick has been approached by Beatrice to defend her cousin Hero's honor. Claudio stood up the

ingénue at the altar, because he mistook something he overheard.
Beatrice wants Benedick to duel Claudio. Finally, Benedick agrees,
saying:

1   Enough, I am engaged, I will challenge him, I
2   will kisse your hand, and so leave **you:** by this hand *Claudio*
3   shall render me a deere **account:** as you heare of me,
4   so thinke of **me:** goe comfort your coosin, I must say she
5   is dead, and so **farewell**.

An actor could pretend to leave the stage three times, essentially
dragging out Benedick's conversation with his beloved, before he
makes a final, true exit on "farewell." Why would he delay? Perhaps
Benedick is hoping Beatrice will change her mind and won't ask him
to go kill Claudio. Perhaps he has another reason. Most importantly,
the actor needs to develop the ability to see that clue and embrace all
the possibilities to which it might lead him. Different imaginations
will come up with different scenarios and justifications.

PARENTHESES ( )

Whenever a phrase is set aside between parentheses (like this), you're
given a terrific opportunity to do something dramatically different
with the text. A contrast could involve changing your:

- *Tempo*: from fast to slow, or slow to fast.

- *Volume*: from loud to soft, or soft to loud.

- *Emotional affect*: from happy to sad, or sad to happy.

- *Pitch*: from low to high, or high to low.

Of course, don't go wacko-crazy on that segment of the line, unless your character is supposed to be nuts. But do make a clear new choice, so your point is made. Anything you do must be backed up imaginatively by an acting purpose: the character's reason.

Often a parenthetical remark indicates that a character is working to figure something out, a problem that has several steps to it. In lines 4 through 8 in the scene from *Othello*, Amelia gives a good example of this kind of remark. Clearly she is attempting to explain why men, in her opinion, are responsible for their wives' betrayals. Other times, a parenthetical remark follows an *Aha!* moment. It's as if a light bulb goes off and a character realizes he or she needs to be more tactful or pointed at that moment to get through to someone, for instance, in *Othello* when Bianca says: "Save you (friend Cassio)."

In other instances, a parenthetical remark may be a way to make a joke at another character's expense, sort of like holding rabbit ears behind someone's head when a photograph is being taken. Everyone else sees it, yet the butt of the joke doesn't. Or the remark may be a way of cluing the audience in to secret information.

Frankly, the list of reasons why parentheses are used may be endless. Technically, you need to change your delivery so the audience gets how different the moment is.

Another way you can create an energetic shift on a parenthetical remark is by performing it as an aside. An *aside* is a stop action moment in which the character comments on events or reveals special information to the listener. Imagine a kid in class who's whispering to a friend behind the teacher's back. On stage, the other actors will help you out and make the moment seem real by pretending not to hear you.

Technically, an aside would be performed in a lower pitched voice. There are three possible targets of this type of uttterance. You may speak an aside to:

- Another character on stage

- Your audience

- Yourself (rarely, if ever!)

Once again, in Amelia's speech above, she has a five-line long parenthetical remark. As an actor, you have to consider where it's being directed. There's only one other character on stage–Desdemona–so it's not an aside to someone else in the play. This leaves the audience or herself as its target. Which would be a stronger choice? Since audience involvement is the key to successful theatre, I'd personally choose to break the illusionary fourth wall and speak directly to the audience. But you, the actor, need to make up your own mind in cases such as this one. In the interest of discovery, you could always try it several different ways in your rehearsal process and observe the results.

——— Your Task—Locating the Punctuation———

Figure out which punctuation marks Shakespeare used in your speech or scene, and where they're located. Look for end stops, commas, semicolons, colons, and the occasional parentheses. If it seems helpful, consider highlighting them on your script with different colored pens.

Shakespeare's Special Poetic Endings

While you were marking your punctuation in the last task, you may have noticed that end stops don't always fall at the end of a ten-beat line. Sometimes they fall in the middle of the line. You may also have noticed that while most lines have punctuation at the end, in many cases they do not. How did Shakespeare want those end words to sound?

Let's consider Shakespeare's poetic endings: midline endings, half-line endings, and over-runs. (You may recall reading about half-line endings on Day 3.) By the way, there are no such things as poetic endings in prose, as there is no meter. These clues can only found by looking closely at speeches drafted in verse.

MIDLINE ENDINGS

When an end stop occurs in the middle of a line, such as in line 35 of Hotspur's speech above, the next thought should come crashing in like a tidal wave. In Shakespeare, this is a way that characters can interrupt themselves. Here, Hotspur may be thinking so fast that a new thought is entering his mind before he's done with the old one.

Similarly, in Amelia's speech above, after nine lines and after reaching the conclusion of two full thoughts, her pace quickens. There are eleven end stops in the second half of the speech, and six are midline endings (see lines 10, 13, 14, 16, 17, and 18). When you examine a midline ending closely, doesn't it draw your attention either to the last word of the sentence that's ending or to the first word, or couple of words, in the new sentence?

Yet we have some Revenge. Let Husbands know,...   10
As Husbands have. What is it that they do,...   13

14	…Is it Sport?
16	…Is't Frailty that thus erres?
17	…And have we not Affections?
18	Desires for Sport? And Frailty, as men have?

Amelia is asking a lot of questions, and she also really wants men to know how it is with their women: "Let Husbands know." Why? So they'll treat their wives better. She is instructing the audience as much as she is initiating Desdemona to her point of view.

When you come across a midline ending, ask an important question: Why am I saying this now, when Shakespeare could have given me any other word to say?

As a master wordsmith, Shakespeare was capable of ending lines however he pleased, for effect. If the particular speech you're rehearsing is full of midline endings, your character is probably making discoveries and speaking without forethought. It's not a mistake, or a failure to reach the "normal" stopping place at the end of the line. Rather it's a clue that Shakespeare has given the actor. Your task is to utilize it.

HALF-LINE ENDINGS

In our Day 3 rehearsal, you learned about incomplete lines, occasions when one character concludes a ten-beat line of poetry for another. You also learned about half-line endings, occasions when a character speaking in perfect verse stops in mid-line—prior to completing ten counts—and is silent until the next line, where he or she resumes iambic pentameter. What's going on? Probably stage business.

In a highly descriptive speech from *Anthony and Cleopatra* (Act 2, Scene 2), the first line Enobarbus utters is a half-line that achieves only four counts.

ENOBARBUS	I will tell you.	1
	The Barge she sat in, like a burnisht Throne	2
	Burnt on the Water…	3

It's my conviction that Shakespeare gave Enobarbus room to build tension on his silent six counts, perhaps by crossing the stage and taking a seat where he could serve as a storyteller or somehow otherwise gathering the other people on stage around him. Half-lines are ripe opportunities for you to perform big gestures and significant movements.

END WORDS VERSUS OVER-RUNS

When a poetic line ends without a punctuation mark, the actor must make an important decision. Should you sustain the last word or should you run your character's thought over into the next line (a technique formally known as enjambment)? It is your choice, bearing in mind, of course, that any such line should sound logical when spoken.

So if you (the actor, rather than the character) view the lack of punctuation as a place to briefly suspend your speech, you must find a compelling reason why your character would sustain the last word of the line–the end word–rather than promptly going on. Possibly the character needs time to think of what to say next.

When Hermione is on trial in Act 3, Scene 2 of *The Winter's Tale,* she has reason to be very cautious. Her end words could indicate her internal process of trying to figure out how best to plead her case. End words are printed in **bold** type in the following excerpt.

| HERMIONE | Since what I am to say, must be but **that** | 1 |
| | Which contradicts my Accusation, **and** | 2 |

3	The testimonie on my part, no **other**
4	But what comes from my selfe, it shall scarce boot **me**
5	To say, Not guiltie: mine **Integritie**
6	Being counted Falsehood, shall (as I expresse it)
7	Be so receiv'd...

Olivia has a similar problem in *Twelfth Night*, which is reflected in her speech to the Priest in Act 5, Scene 1. She is an unmarried woman who has just spent the night with a man named Sebastian, and therefore she urgently wants to get married. She is carefully attempting to persuade the Priest to give them a shotgun wedding. Maybe she is embarrassed at a lapse in morality or judgment. An actress must decide what's occurring. End words are printed in **bold** type.

1 OLIVIA	O welcome Father:
2	Father, I charge thee by thy **reverence**
3	Heere to unfold, though lately we **intended**
4	To keep in darknesse, what occasion **now**
5	Reveales before 'tis ripe: what thou dost **know**
6	Hath newly past, betweene this youth, and me.

Take the following example from Act 5, Scene 1 of *A Midsummer Night's Dream*, which has three unpunctuated line endings. Two young Athenian couples have told a strange, magical tale of romantic mix-ups in the nighttime forest. Here, King Theseus tells Queen Hippolita that he doesn't believe them.

Note the end words in lines 1, 4, and 11. As a simple exercise, read the speech aloud right now and suspend speaking on those words. Observe what that's like. Then, read it a second time and flow the end of those three lines into the next lines–over-run them. Again, listen carefully.

THESEUS	More strange then true. I never may **beleeve**	1
	These anticke fables, nor these Fairy toyes,	2
	Lovers and mad men have such seething braines,	3
	Such shaping phantasies, that apprehend **more**	4
	Then coole reason ever comprehends.	5
	The Lunaticke, the Lover, and the Poet,	6
	Are of imagination all compact.	7
	One sees more divels then vaste hell can hold;	8
	That is the mad man. The Lover, all as franticke,	9
	Sees *Helens* beauty in a brow of *Egipt*.	10
	The Poets eye in a fine frenzy rolling, doth **glance**	11
	From heaven to earth, from earth to heaven.	12

I believe the first and third examples (lines 1 and 11) are actually meant to be over-runs, while the second example (line 4) is a true end word. What do you think, now that you've tried them both ways?

As was previously stated, you need to explore two possible approaches to unpunctuated line endings. Should you hook up the end word with the line below–without breathing until the next comma? Or should you sustain that end word–perhaps by elongating it? As long as your pitch doesn't drop, the audience will keep listening.

Why would a character hold onto a thought? Usually, a straightforward reason is sufficient. It could be that someone is thinking on the spot, considering what's the best way to say something, doesn't know what to say next, is hesitant to speak, or is teasing. The most important thing is that you make a choice, commit to it, and make it work. You'll develop confidence after working with these principles for a while, because with each attempt you'll be gathering evidence that you can trust yourself.

—— Your Task—Arcing and Building——

Choose to say the final word before every punctuation mark with special emphasis, such as changing your volume, pitch, intonation, or inflection. Listen to how your choices affect the sound and meaning of your speech.

- Volume is loudness or softness.
- Pitch is a high or low note.
- Intonation is "staccato" (short and clipped) or "legato" (long and smooth).
- Inflection means rising or falling.

The word before an end stop is likely to be the key word in the sentence. Shakespeare always breaks his own rules, but as a rule of thumb this one is reliable. For instance, in *Twelfth Night* (Act 1, Scene 2), Olivia has a 22-line monologue with 11 end stops. These are shown in **bold** face below. Words followed by commas, semicolons, and colons are underlined and should also be emphasized.

1	OLIVIA	What is your **Parentage?**
2		Above my <u>fortunes</u>, yet my state is <u>well</u>;
3		I am a **Gentleman.** Ile be sworne thou <u>art</u>,
4		Thy <u>tongue</u>, thy <u>face</u>, thy <u>limbes</u>, <u>actions</u>, and <u>spirit</u>,
5		Do give thee five-fold <u>blazon</u>: not too <u>fast</u>: <u>soft</u>, <u>soft</u>,
6		Unlesse the Master were the **man.** How **now?**

Even so quickly may one catch the **plague**?   7
Me thinkes I feele this youths perfections   8
With an <u>invisible</u>, and subtle stealth   9
To creep in at mine **eyes**. <u>Well</u>, let it **be**.   10
What <u>hoa</u>, **Malvolio**.   11

Run after that same peevish Messenger   12
The Countes <u>man</u>: he left his Ring behinde him   13
Would <u>I</u>, or <u>not</u>: tell <u>him</u>, Ile none of **it**.   14
Desire him not to flatter with his <u>Lord</u>,   15
Nor hold him up for <u>hopes</u>, I am not for <u>him</u>:   16
If that the youth will come this way to <u>morrow</u>,   17
Ile give him reasons <u>for't</u>: hie thee **Malvolio**.   18

I do I know not <u>what</u>, and feare to finde   19
Mine eye too great a flatterer for my <u>minde</u>:   20
<u>Fate</u>, shew thy <u>force</u>, our selves we do not <u>owe</u>,   21
What is <u>decreed</u>, must <u>be</u>: and be this **so**.   22

Observe that there are midline endings in lines 3, 6, and 10. Perhaps the thoughts that directly follow these end stops represent huge gear changes for Olivia? Shakespeare has designed this speech to include many entertaining surprises for the listener.

The purpose of this next task is to assist you in finding the intended phrasing. This means finding not only your speech's meaning, but also its rhythm, which will help you find your character. Every character has a unique rhythm.

——— Your Task—Changing Directions———

Walk around the room while saying your lines, and radically shift direction every time you hit a punctuation mark in the text. Make sharp turns right and left. Spin and walk back the way you came. This task develops your "muscle memory," as it engrains the punctuation in your body as well as in the words.

How might it look in practice? Well, in Olivia's speech above you could turn immediately following the **boldface** words. On commas, you could rise up on your toes or clap your hands. On semicolons, you could jump. On colons, you could spin around or jog in place. It doesn't matter exactly what you do so long as it is something physical. Be imaginative and enjoy yourself.

Your Day 4 Rehearsal Checklist

Have you completed your tasks?

- ☐ Locating the Punctuation
- ☐ Arcing and Building
- ☐ Changing Directions

What discoveries have you made?

DAY 5

Revving Up Your Verbs

Most of the time when I coach actors to prepare them for Shakespeare auditions and performances, I hear sounds coming out of their mouths–and that's about it. I don't believe that they absolutely know what they're saying, because they're not using their words well. Words are tools that impact the listener. They are thoughts *in action*. When words travel through space and hit their intended targets, they should explode and cause something to happen. But if actors don't have a clear idea of what they're doing, or how, or the meaning of what they're saying, then nothing occurs. As a result, the audience gets bored and stops paying attention.

Like a powder charge, a verb can give the impact of a bullet to your speech. As the part of speech that asserts, declares, galvanizes, or predicates, verbs give you power. They are the catalysts that can bring a sentence to life and make your speech electric.

In your performance, there must be alignment in what you say and what you do. As Shakespeare wrote in *Hamlet* (Act 3, Scene 2): "Suit the Action to the Word, the Word to the Action." Elizabethan plays were produced without benefit of direction, so the Bard purposefully embedded stage directions in his text for actors to follow.

Picking out your verbs from Shakespeare's text helps you know what you're supposed to do on stage.

Thoughts in Action

I have a pet peeve. It's something many actors do that saps the energy from their verbs and also makes them miss the targets at which Shakespeare intended them to aim. They don't act *on* their verbs. Instead, they either move too soon or too late. To execute a scene properly, however, actions must happen simultaneously to the words spoken.

Here's a simple example. In *Twelfth Night* (Act 1, Scene 5), Olivia and Viola play a game of pass-the-purse. Viola, after disguising herself as a teenage boy named Cesario, is now employed by the Duke, who sends her to woo the Lady Olivia. Creating a funny plot twist, Olivia develops a crush on Viola. Here she tries to entice "Cesario" to come back and give her a report on how the Duke takes her rejection. She offers "him" a purse filled with coins as a fee for the service. Viola (as Cesario) gives the purse back. Stage business is marked in **boldface** type in the following excerpt.

1	OLIVIA	Get you to your Lord:
2		I cannot love him: let him send no more,
3		Unlesse (perchance) you come to me againe,
4		To tell me how he takes it: Fare you well:
5		I thanke you for your paines: **spend this for mee.**
6	VIOLA	I am no feede poast, Lady; **keepe your purse,**
7		My Master, not my selfe, lacks recompence.

I cannot tell you how many times I've seen actresses playing Olivia take out the purse and hand it over to Viola *before* saying "spend this for me" (line 5). They jump the gun. If they hand over the purse too soon, it gives away the most significant moment in the two characters' interaction, and the visual impression made by Viola's literal physical rejection of the purse (line 6) falls flat. If Viola fails to take the purse–or to give it back–the audience doesn't get to see the purse offered and rejected, which is comparable to the subject of Olivia's affection for "Cesario." How you demonstrate this exchange is up to you. Olivia might place it in Viola's hand and then not let go. To linger is a flirtatious move. How would Viola react to that? She can't let her mask down.

For her part, Viola can see more of what's going on than Olivia (because she knows she's running around in disguise), and therefore many actresses choose to play the moment as though she's annoyed on behalf of her employer, the Duke, a man with whom Viola herself is in love. If she doesn't hand the purse back on her line "keepe your purse," we don't hear the full meaning of "My Master, not my selfe, lacks recompence."

A general rule of thumb: Don't get ahead of your words. You must not play the end at the beginning. Stay in the present. The joy of Shakespeare is its immediacy.

THE ENERGY OF VERBS

Verbs are the motors, or propellers, of your speeches. They put "muscle" behind your energy language. For instance, in *Macbeth* (Act 2, Scene 1), Macbeth says:

> Is this a Dagger, which I see before me,　　　　1

| 2 | The Handle toward my Hand? Come, let me **clutch** thee: |
| 3 | I have thee not, and yet I see thee still. |

When we're discussing the feeling of words, we're talking about energy language and its varying degrees of intensity. The sound and the meaning of a word affect both the speaker and the listener. *Clutch* has a very different energetic quality than *touch, hold,* or *grasp* would. When I directed the play, at first my lead actor gave a bland line reading and I had to point out that he wasn't communicating the primitive feeling of the word "clutch." He tried several different ways of saying it, before settling on a dangerous tone of voice. Similarly, "The bell *invites* me," a few lines later, feels much different than "the bell *commands* me" or "the bell *beckons* me" would. (Author's italics)

Never forget that Shakespeare was a poet who loved making sound pictures. He innovated words and word-combinations in order to produce strong emotions. We may not always know a word's definition, yet its sound informs us of its meaning. He was a master of onomatopoeia, which *The Oxford American Dictionary* defines as a "formation of words that imitate or suggest what they stand for, as *cuckoo, plop,* and *sizzle.*"

Lear's speech taken from *King Lear* (Act 3, Scene 2) perfectly illustrates the force of verb imagery. The aging monarch Lear has bequeathed his kingdom to two ungrateful daughters, who subsequently refuse him the hospitality of their homes. Outraged, he delivers these lines outdoors in the midst of an equally furious lightning storm, preferring to combat the unruly elements than his treacherous daughters.

To begin today's rehearsal, read the seven lines below silently on the page, scanning for any verbs you may find. Then, read the lines again slowly, this time aloud, listening for the sounds of the verbs.

Make a mental note of any discoveries, such as repeated verbs, verbs that have similar meanings, and verbs that have similar sounds.

Go ahead and read the lines now.

KING LEAR	Blow windes, & crack your cheeks; Rage, blow	1
	You Cataracts, and Hyrricano's spout,	2
	Till you have drench'd our Steeples, drowne the Cockes.	3
	You Sulph'rous and Thought-executing fires,	4
	Vaunt-curriors of Oake-cleaving Thunder-bolts,	5
	Sindge my white head. And thou all-shaking Thunder,	6
	Strike flat the thicke Rotundity o'th'world...	7

What did you experience? What tense are the verbs—past, present, future? I'm sure you noticed that Lear mostly draws upon the imperative voice: *Blow, crack, blow, spout, sindge,* and *strike.* How did Lear's commanding tone affect you as a listener? How did it affect you as a speaker?

In line 3, he switches to a future tense: "Till you *have drench'd* our Steeples..." Would you agree that this line brings to mind a powerful image of natural destruction, perhaps similar to a catastrophic tsunami? Or is it more reminiscent of a Californian mudslide or a hurricane in the Gulf of Mexico? Consider what Lear is commanding Nature to do with his verbs: "*Strike* flat the thicke Rotundity o'th'world." He demands that everything be demolished.

You may have noticed two inventive adjectives that contain –ing verb forms: "Thought-executing" (line 4) and "Oake-cleaving" (line 5). Although they aren't actually verbs in this context, *executing* and *cleaving* serve to activate the destructive imagery of fire and thunder. You'll get the chance to explore adjectives in your Day 6 rehearsal.

For an actor, the purpose of your verbs is to put images into action. Ideas are energy that rises up inside of you. Energy jumps from character to character, and out into the audience. When you use verbs well, you are energizing, or electrifying, Shakespeare's metaphors: a raging lightning storm is symbolic of the storm of emotions raging in Lear. The verbs call the action of the storm to life in the audience's imagination.

Hidden Stage Directions

As I mentioned at the top of the chapter, verbs should also be considered a literal source of stage directions. We know that Shakespeare's actors didn't have long rehearsal periods, so their blocking was probably largely improvisational. It may even have been different every night. Although there were swordfights and dancing, which may have been choreographed, most of the action comes either from painting a word-picture, as we explored above, or from the general activities, or stage business, taking place between characters. Let's look at a couple of speeches.

An opportunity for loads of stage business is the clown Launce's speech in *Two Gentlemen of Verona* (Act 2, Scene 3), which is written in prose. Several summers ago, I saw the celebrated clown Bill Irwin play this role at the Delacorte Theatre in Central Park. He entered the stage carrying a small stuffed dog to which he often referred during the speech. In the midst of a very funny production, the monologue stood out because his work was so specific and so physical. He made bold choices. As he revealed Launce's pain with physical gestures, he uncorked the audience's sympathetic pain by making us laugh hard. (The verbs in the speech are printed in bold type.)

DAY 5

LAUNCE	I **thinke** *Crab* my dog, **be** the sowrest natured	1
	dogge that **lives**: My Mother **weeping**: My Father	2
	wayling: My Sister **crying**: our Maid **howling**: our	3
	Catte **wringing** her hands, and all our house in a great	4
	perplexitie, yet **did** not this cruell-hearted Curre **shedde**	5
	one teare: he **is** a stone, a very pibble stone, and **has** no	6
	more pitty in him then a dogge...	7

The energy of *weeping, wayling, crying,* and *howling* are distinct, although the words mean much the same thing. The repetitive nature of this verb series is reminiscent of the humor found in repeated consonant sounds. The audience wonders, "How long can this actor sustain them? Can he do it any differently the next time?" This character repeats himself the second time because he liked it so much the first time. He repeats it the third time because he liked it so much the first and second time. And so on.

Since there are colons in this piece of text–meaning that an actor can truly take his time to develop this imagery thoroughly–there's room to do physical shtick. As you'll recall from your Day 4 rehearsal, a colon means that the next thought will be more articulate. Launce is elaborating on his central theme. Colons are so close to being the end of a thought that each implies that you need to shift direction–take a new tack–by changing your rhythm. We'll talk about pace in detail on Day 13.

Done well, Launce's dog speech can be a superb audition piece. It requires a high degree of conditioning to be as flexible as Launce must be to move so dynamically from segment to segment of this long single sentence. But that's why Shakespeare has offered so much support in his verbs. If you play the verbs wholeheartedly, you'll unlock the humor.

——— Your Task—Finding Your Hidden——— Stage Directions

First, examine the text of the scene or speech you are working on, and highlight the verbs that your character mentions. Then, literally perform each verb with a specific gesture. Do so whether or not this technique makes you feel as though you're "hamming it up." After having tried a poor choice for a stage direction at least once, you'll be able to move forward confidently and make a better choice. You won't be acting upon a lack of knowledge.

Remember, always do an action on the word it matches. Not sooner.

As an example, let's take a portion of Adriana's verse speech in *The Comedy of Errors* (Act 2, Scene 2). (Her verbs are in **bold** type.)

1	ADRIANA	How deerely **would** it **touch** thee to the quicke,
2		Shouldst thou but **heare** I **were** licencious?
3		And that this body **consecrate** to thee,
4		By Ruffian Lust should **be** contaminate?
5		**Wouldst** thou not **spit** at me, and **spurne** at me,
6		And **hurle** the name of husband in my face,
7		And **teare** the stain'd skin of my Harlot brow,
8		And from my false hand **cut** the wedding ring,
9		And **breake** it with a deepe-**divorcing** vow?...

When I gave this task to an actress in one of my classes, asking her to ham it up, she put a hand to her ear on *heare*, joined her hands together as if to pray on *consecrate,* turned away from her fellow actor on *spurne,* mimed throwing something on *hurle,* and pretended to saw off her left ring finger on *cut.* While not all of those choices could be considered "keepers," by physicalizing the speech she was conditioning her body.

—— Your Task—Playing the —— Antithetical Action

Now that you've performed each verb in your speech or scene as literally as you can, emoting them like crazy and without subtlety, try doing the opposite of what a verb means. If Shakespeare says, "Come close," move far away. If he says, "Laugh," then cry. While you may not find an actual gesture to use in performance, there's always the possibility that you might.

There's irony in saying no and behaving yes; it's a very human thing to have competing desires and to behave inconsistently. We say we want to lose weight, but then we eat French fries or chocolate layer cake. We say we don't want to argue, and then we try to get in the last word. I know that you know what I mean. It's funny on stage.

During the rehearsal process, it is important always to look for the possibility of creating a surprise in the moment. To surprise someone, you may need to do something that's the opposite of the social norm. Here are two places where this might work well; both scenarios involve malicious intentions.

In Act 2, Scene 3 of *Measure for Measure,* when the villain Angelo considers blackmailing Isabella to sleep with him, knowing full well that she is a virgin and intends to become a nun, he utters the following lines:

1 ANGELO   Can it be,

2   That Modesty may more betray our Sence

3   Then womans lightnesse? having waste ground enough,

4   Shall we desire to raze the Sanctuary

5   And pitch our evils there? oh fie, fie, fie:

6   What dost thou? or what art thou *Angelo?*

Spoken angrily or with a tone of self-disgust would be a conventional take on the phrase "Oh fie, fie, fie." Done giggling and rubbing his hands together or with other signs of obvious delight, they are much creepier.

Let's compare that to a speech delivered by Posthumus' in Act 2, Scene 5 of *Cymbeline*. With a name like that–a word usually reserved to describe corpses–you can be assured that this guy is not a quick-witted Speedy Gonzalez. Mentally, he's always "after" (in Latin: *post*) everyone else. In this part of the play, Iachimo has come to Posthumus claiming that he's slept with Posthumus' wife. They had a bet, so Iachimo has brought proof, a bracelet he stole from her. In fact, his story is a lie. Nonetheless, Posthumus is very angry and goes off on a tirade.

1 POSTHUMUS …We are all Bastards,

2   And that most venerable man, which I

3   Did call my Father, was, I know not where

4   When I was stampt. Some Coyner with his Tooles

5   Made me a Counterfeit: yet my Mother seem'd

6   The *Dian* of that time: so doth my Wife

7   The Non-pareill of this. Oh Vengeance, Vengeance!

In this case, if the actor playing Posthumus laughed on the line "Oh Vengeance, Vengeance!" the audience would be likely to perceive him as a madman, a formerly innocuous fool who might have been tipped far enough over the edge of reason by the news of his wife's supposed infidelity that he has become capable of anything. Laughter would make the character seem dangerous–and that surprise would be entertaining.

Degrees of Intensity

Some movements that you try out in rehearsal will surely go beyond the intended meaning, or beyond an intensity that would play well on stage. On the other hand, some of your movements and gestures won't go far enough. In fact, that's more likely. American actors especially are conditioned for film acting, which can be subtle because a camera can be placed practically up your nose. Stage acting must read from the back row of the balcony.

It is also easy to make ineffective choices because you're making assumptions about your character and the limits of what he or she would do, or should do. Therefore, be sure to experiment with degrees of intensity. Watch human beings on the street. They do some pretty big, bizarre, and wild things. Embrace the intensity of real life.

Degree of intensity is an acting choice, but you need to consider the context in which the expression is occurring. We'll talk more about context, or given circumstances, on Day 18, but partly this is common sense. For instance, if you say to someone, "Run, run," because that person might be caught and killed, it's high intensity, isn't it? But if you just want them to run for fun, it's low intensity. Here are two differing examples.

In Act 3, Scene 2 of *Macbeth*, as three murderers sent by Macbeth to kill him and his family approach, Banquo warns his son, Fleans:

1	O, Treacherie!
2	Flye good Fleans, flye, flye, flye,
3	Though must revenge. O Slave!

We know from the prophecy of the three witches in an earlier scene that Banquo's sons will ultimately inherit the throne. Banquo poses a threat to Macbeth, and he also stands in contrast to Macbeth, representing the better choice that Macbeth did not take. And here Banquo dies. Line 2 above is a truly high intensity utterance.

By contrast, Orlando has a soliloquy, or dialogue with himself, in Act 3, Scene 2 of *As You Like It*, in which he races around the forest like a lovesick puppy, smitten with his affection for Rosalind. His speech would be considered moderate intensity.

1	Run, run, Orlando, carve on every Tree,
2	The faire, the chaste, and unexpressive shee.

———— Your Task—Acknowledging the Verbs————

To locate the muscle of your verbs, clap your hands whenever you come to one in the text. Clap hard and explosively for high-intensity verbs. Clap softly for low-intensity verbs. Notice how frequently or rarely you are stimulated to clap. Some speeches are more dynamic than others.

I know of an Australian stage actress who was so technically proficient that she regularly played three levels in her auditions–that is, if she was given the chance to exhibit her work. The first go-round, she'd hit the level she thought was naturalistic. The second time, she'd boost her energy to the level of a rocket. She'd eat the scenery. By the way, that didn't mean yelling, it meant being big and bold–intense. Then, if asked to go again, she'd ask, "Would you like me to take it down for you?" Most directors are interested to know a performer's range, so they usually would say yes. Then she'd bring it down. She'd move less, and let her eyes speak for her. Very subtle, low intensity acting of this kind often works better on film than on stage. That style of auditioning gave directors three views of her abilities, and three views of how their pieces might work. As a result, she frequently got hired to do the parts for which she auditioned.

Remember, boldness gives you the authority to act. Trying gestures out teaches you the reality of what will fly and can help you feel more confident about your choices. So always ask: Have I gone too far? Not far enough? This next task is a great way to practice degrees of intensity.

—— Your Task—The Slap-Stroke Exercise ——

Put a cushion on a table in front of you. Then, either slap or stroke the cushion whenever you feel stimulated to action by a verb. This is especially useful when working on scenes with other actors.

My student tapped into the energy of her character by using the Slap-Stroke Exercise to rehearse the following 27-line speech taken from *Henry the Sixth, Part Three* (Act 1, Scene 1). It made the scene come to life and stimulated her scene partners to boost their energy.

Here, Queen Margaret has just found out that the Duke of York has challenged her husband's crown, and that her son Henry, the Prince, has been disinherited as a result. In the bargain, she has also lost some of her status, because women in that period of history had no property or status of their own. Their fate was almost entirely linked to that of the men in their lives. She's upset because Henry is acting like an accommodating wimp. Although Henry supposedly gets to keep his throne, because the Duke has promised to wait until Henry's death to succeed him, Henry has basically given up without a fight. He naïvely believes that York will wait to ascend, and leave him be.

The speech is part of a confrontation between the King and Queen in which she chastises him and then leaves him. Because this interchange occurs at the beginning of the play, it sets up the significance of the plot, which revolves around the succession to the throne. A war will commence and who the combatants are is made clear. (Verbs are set in **bold** type.)

QUEEN MARGARET

1	**Enforc't** thee? **Art** thou King, and wilt **be forc't?**
2	I **shame** to **heare** thee **speake**: ah timorous Wretch,
3	Thou **hast undone** thy selfe, thy Sonne, and me,
4	And **giv'n** unto the House of *Yorke* such head,
5	As thou **shalt reigne** but by their sufferance.
6	To **entayle** him and his Heires unto the Crowne,
7	What **is** it, but to **make** thy Sepulcher,
8	And **creepe** into it farre before thy time?
9	*Warwick* **is** Chancelor, and the Lord of Callice,

Sterne *Falconbridge* **commands** the Narrow Seas, 10

The Duke **is** made Protector of the Realme, 11

And yet **shalt** thou **be** safe? Such safetie **findes** 12

The trembling Lambe, **invironned** with Wolves. 13

Had I **beene** there, which **am** a silly Woman, 14

The Souldiers **should have toss'd** me on their Pikes, 15

Before I **would have granted** to that Act. 16

But thou **preferr'st** thy Life, before thine Honor. 17

And **seeing** thou **do'st**, I here **divorce** my selfe, 18

Both from thy Table *Henry*, and thy Bed, 19

Untill that Act of Parliament **be repeal'd**, 20

Whereby my Sonne **is dis-inherited**. 21

The Northerne Lords, that **have forsworne** thy Colours, 22

Will **follow** mine, if once they **see** them **spread**: 23

And **spread** thy **shall be**, to thy foule disgrace, 24

And utter ruine of the House of *Yorke*. 25

Thus **doe** I **leave** thee: **Come** Sonne, let's **away**, 26

Our Army **is** ready; **come**, wee'le after them. 27

Do you see and hear how in the first five lines of Queen Margaret's speech she repeats *F* and *S* sounds, basically spitting and hissing in Henry's face? Her verbs activate the energy of venomous spite as much as the sounds of her words do: *Enforc't, forc't,* and *shame* (a noun used in this context as a verb). The book-ending repetition of *forc't* in the first line, composed of two complete thoughts—questions—is like an electric shock.

See if delivering the verbs in your own speech or scene with varying degrees of intensity opens up a new vocal or physical choice for you. An actress could really get a lot of mileage and variation out of an unconventional choice, such as saying, "I hate you," while stroking rather than slapping. This technique can vastly enhance the clarity of your rhetoric and assist the audience in understanding the plot.

Remember to alternate, however. If you find that you're only doing one of these gestures—a slap or a stroke—you are missing the point of this exercise, which is yet another way to create variety and identify new, original, and exciting acting choices.

Putting It All Together in Your Blocking

Among other things, please remember to review all the earlier steps in this book before you make any ultimate decision about your blocking. Consider the matter of prose versus poetry, as well as your repetitions, your capitalized words, and your punctuation. Right about now, the steps should begin to work in unison. Combine your verbal clues with all your other clues before making a final choice of what to do on a particular line, speech, or section of a scene.

A couple of years ago, one of my students decided to put these few foundational steps together in preparing her blocking for a monologue from *As You Like It* for an audition at my small theatre company, American Globe Theatre in New York City. She chose Phebe the shepherdess' speech from Act 3, Scene 5, in which Phebe wrestles with her emerging infatuation for "Ganymede" (Rosalind in disguise as a young man, like Viola was in the pass-the-purse scene from *Twelfth Night* we looked at earlier). Forming a comedic love triangle, Phebe is addressing Silvius, a shepherd in love with her!

Every time my student found a reversal of meaning—a denial or disagreement, as it were–in Phebe's utterances, she took a huge step forward (downstage) or backward (upstage), or to her right (stage right) or her left (stage left). The ten places where she remembers doing so are marked in bold in the text below: "yet," "but," "yet," "not," "and yet," "yet," "and yet," "but," "and yet" –and a final "but" in line 25.

PHEBE	Thinke not I love him, though I ask for him,	1
	'Tis but a peevish boy, **yet** he talkes well,	2
	But what care I for words? **yet** words do well	3
	When he that speakes them pleases those that heare:	4
	It is a pretty youth, **not** very prettie,	5
	But sure hee's proud, **and yet** his pride becomes him;	6
	Hee'll make a proper man: the best thing in him	7
	Is his complexion: and faster then his tongue	8
	Did make offence, his eye did heale it up:	9
	He is not very tall, **yet** for his yeeres hee's tall:	10
	His leg is but so so, **and yet** 'tis well:	11
	There was a pretty rednesse in his lip,	12
	A little riper, and more lustie red	13
	Then that mixt in his cheeke: 'twas just the difference	14
	Betwixt the constant red, and mingled Damaske.	15
	There be some women *Silvius*, had they markt him	16
	In parcells as I did, would have gone neere	17
	To fall in love with him: **but** for my part	18
	I love him not, nor hate him not: **and yet**	19
	Have more cause to hate him then to love him,	20
	For what had he to doe to chide at me?	21
	He said mine eyes were black, and my haire blacke,	22
	And now I am remembred, scorn'd at me:	23

24	I marvell why I answer'd not againe,
25	**But** that's all one: omittance is no quittance:
26	Ile write to him a very tanting Letter,
27	And thou shalt beare it, wilt thou *Silvius*?

I asked the actress, "How did it feel to make such bold choices in your blocking?" She replied, "It was strange. While it seemed unnatural–sort of abrupt–to take such large, specific steps in the middle of my speech, it also felt wonderful and liberating first to make a clear decision and then to execute it. I didn't want the audience to have to guess where Phebe was changing her mind or aiming to cover up her feelings. To me, she's not a shy girl or a particularly complex personality, which I think made her mental and physical shifts in direction funnier."

She added, "Interestingly, once I chose to move on certain lines I also committed to *not* moving on the other lines. I wanted there to be the biggest possible contrast." Her decisions worked well for her in this audition. She got the part.

Your Day 5 Rehearsal Checklist

Have you completed your tasks?

☐ Finding Your Hidden Stage Directions

☐ Playing the Antithetical Action

☐ Acknowledging the Verbs

☐ The Slap-Stroke Exercise

What discoveries have you made?

DAY 6

Amiable Adjectives, Saucy Similes, and Merry Metaphors

Let's use reading a book as an analogy for the function of descriptive words on stage. When you read English, you scan the page from left to right. The type on the page is two-dimensional. But when you reach a descriptive word or phrase, it stops the language from flowing by you for a moment, opening up another dimension (or several) of texture and color. On stage, descriptive words and phrases reorganize the flow of sound as if to pull the action backward, making room. You, the actor, must fill in this extra space with meaning. Adjectives, similes, and metaphors are the character's choices and so these images define the character's personality. If you don't make good use of them as an actor, your character will seem bland and less interesting to watch.

There's a Bright Palette of Possibilities

Lines are often most memorable when they are visual. But all of the senses can be engaged by the imagination. What did something look, smell, taste, and feel like? Most people are curious to know. Audiences adore being surprised by unusual juxtapositions of previously unrelated concepts and images. As in poetry, assigning symbolic meaning to people, places, things, and events has the power to uncork your own bottled up emotions—as well as the emotions of your audience members. Let's look at the parts of speech that offer listeners a world of quality and connotation.

ADJECTIVES

An adjective is a word that's added to a noun to describe a quality it possesses or to modify its meaning in some fashion. For instance, a man can be *tall* or *short*, *old* or *young*. Those are adjectives. *My* hat is different than *your* hat. Those possessive words are also considered adjectives. Adjectives span the full range of sensory input. They give us a means to talk about and describe direct, tangible experiences.

In *A Midsummer Night's Dream* (Act 2, Scene 1), Oberon describes to Puck the spot in the woods where Titania is asleep and dreaming. His adjectives (printed in bold type below) bring it to life. They give us a feeling for the wind, privacy, color, and fragrance.

1   I know a banke where the **wilde** time blowes,

2   Where Oxslips and the **nodding** Violet growes,

3   Quite **over-cannoped** with **luscious** woodbine,

4   With **sweet muske** roses, and with Eglantine…

ADVERBS

Whereas *gentle* is an adjective, *gently* is an adverb. *Loving* could be an adjective (or also a verb). *Lovingly* is an adverb, because it describes how an action is done. The –ly ending is often a dead giveaway. Adverbs are words that qualify or modify verbs, and that indicate how, when, and where. The sentence "He ate *voraciously*" has quite a different flavor than "He ate *calmly*." *Soon* and *later* are adverbs, too.

Let's be clear. In the phrases "cowardly knave" and "godly company" *cowardly* and *godly* are adjectives (not adverbs) because they modify the nouns *knave* and *company*. In the phrase "to freely marry" *freely* is an adverb since it describes a quality of the verb *marry*. It would be very different to say someone has *reluctantly* or *expediently* married. We don't find too many adverbs in Shakespeare, but they appear in lines such as the following from *Merry Wives of Windsor* (adverbs are in bold face type):

- No, I thank you forsooth, **hartely;** I am very well.

- Ile rather be **unmannerly,** then troublesome...

- Looke where my ranting-Host of the Garter
  comes: there is eyther liquor in his pate, or mony in his
  purse, when hee lookes so **merrily**...

Time Words

"Now." With this first word in a play devoted to his corrupt rise to power, Richard, younger brother of King Edward, indicates to listeners that events are already unfolding under pressure. "Now is the Winter of our Discontent," not later. He means this 1/100th of a second. This instant. Now. He is utterly present with his unhappiness.

Time is a character. It either works for you or against you. If it is on your side, you can go at a normal to leisurely pace in a speech. You're not under pressure. If it is against you, your character has to think and act economically. You have to be bull's eye specific, as one false move could ruin everything. For instance, Iago knows that anyone could come around the corner and catch him as he delivers every monologue describing his evil schemes. Time pressure doesn't mean that you should rush, rather that you take care.

Here are some of the time words that appear over and over in Shakespeare's plays. Keep an eye out for them, as they are clues to your degree of urgency.

Anon	Often
Ere/Before	Sometimes
Finally	Soon
Later	Suddenly
Ne'er/Never	Then
Now	When
Occasionally	

Similes

A simile is a comparison that includes the words "as" or "like." On a third date, a man might say to a woman, "I love you." But on the 15th date, he might turn to her and say, "I love you *as* a honeybee loves flowers." He's made a choice that tells us about his character and perceptions. If I said, "My love is *like* a doorknob; it turns and turns," you'd probably guess that my character was fickle.

Othello at one point (Act 3, Scene 3) describes his vengeful mindset as:

1	**...Like to the Ponticke Sea,**
2	Whose Icie Current, and compulsive course,
3	Nev'r keepes retyring ebbe, but keepes due on...

➳ DAY 6 ➳

METAPHORS

Metaphors are highfalutin similes. How can you recognize them? In my classes, I frequently tell my students, "If you went up to a cop on a horse in Central Park and spoke to him only in metaphors he might think you were raving mad and take you to Bellevue Hospital for observation." Phrases such as "marble-breasted tyrant," which Duke Orsino says in *Twelfth Night* to describe his beloved's hardheartedness towards him, cannot be taken literally. But when you hear metaphors, such as this one, they stand out and add texture to what is being communicated.

When metaphors are spoken, we know we're in the territory of poetry. Emotions are heightened. Thoughts have special, added significance. For example, when Juliet is eagerly waiting for Romeo in Act 3, Scene 2 of *Romeo and Juliet*, she says:

Come night, come Romeo, come thou day in night,	1
For thou wilt lie upon the wings of night	2
Whiter then new Snow upon a Ravens backe...	3

Although we may not understand 100 percent of what we hear, a delicious aspect of this particular speech is its contrasts of dark and light, white and black, day and night. "Whiter than new snow upon a raven's back" is a terrifically poetic image of something clean in the air that's so fresh it hasn't even reached the ground yet. Perhaps Shakespeare intended us to think of new love or young love or first love as fresh. The insinuation of the raven into the picture of freshness is a subtle harbinger of the tragic deaths to come. Is youth day? Is death night? As with most symbols, meaning is in the eye of the beholder.

The beauty of a metaphor is that every audience member will create his or her own picture of it. No two people see exactly the same thing. Shakespeare understood this, and it plays a big part in his ability to capture our attention. He was very persuasive, a terrific salesman. He knew what made people happy and he delivered the goods.

Descriptive Words Can Establish Character

Character is not found in a false nose, hat, or cane. It is created in the audience's imagination. When the audience hears the type of vocabulary that a character habitually employs they make personal associations with it. How many women would feel flattered at being called "plain" or "bony"? What about "pretty"? When Petruchio says his 17 *K* sounds in *The Taming of the Shrew* (Act 2, Scene 1), they're always modified by adjectives such as these. Onlookers know that his wordplay is clever and flirtatious, so we assume that he's mischievous, a bit of a conman, and—perhaps—foolhardy. For sure, he's an optimist. Wouldn't he have to be if he's aiming to seduce a foul tempered woman such as Kate? But we believe he's playing to win the game of love as much as is to win her dowry. That is, we believe it if the actor is using Shakespeare's words effectively.

As an actor, in order to establish character you must look for the adjectives and adverbs, similes and metaphors that color your speech. It also is useful to look for the phrases that other characters use to describe you. These are significant clues.

In *Othello* (Act 3, Scene 3), the evil Iago falsely insinuates that Othello's wife Desdemona has been having an affair with one of his lieutenants, the good Cassio. It's a setup. As a result, jealousy begins to spread through Othello's mind like a virus. Adjectives are shown in **bold** in the following excerpt.

I had beene **happy**, if the **generall** Campe,	1
Pyoners and all, had tasted her **sweet** Body,	2
So I had nothing knowne. Oh now, for ever	3
Farewell the **Tranquill** minde; farewell Content;	4
Farewell the **plumed** Troopes, and the **bigge** Warres,	5
That makes Ambition, Vertue! Oh farewell,	6
Farewell the **neighing** Steed, and the **shrill** Trumpe,	7
The **Spirit-stirring** Drum, th' **Eare-piercing** Fife,	8
The **Royall** Banner, and all Qualitie,	9
Pride, Pompe, and Circumstance of **glorious** Warre:	10
And O you **mortall** Engines, whose **rude** throates	11
Th' **immortall** Joves **dread** Clamours, **counterfet**,	12
Farewell: Othello's Occupation's gone.	13

When Othello delivers this monologue filled with military paraphernalia and images, we are reminded that above all else he's a career soldier. That's his "character." We imagine that we know what this means: he's a man of honor and conviction, rough around the edges, competitive, dominant, and ready to take on a battle and destroy his enemy. In war, those may be the necessary qualities of a leader. In love, they turn out to be his Achilles' heel.

Descriptive Words Can Establish a Scene

In *Anthony and Cleopatra* (Act 2, Scene 2), Enobarbus has a colorful speech, full of descriptive words and phrases, that paints a vivid portrait of the play's female protagonist: her beauty, wealth, and influence. His speech sets an incredible visual scene before the mind's eye. In this section of the play, Anthony's associate Enobarbus becomes a master storyteller and we, along with the characters he is addressing in the play, cannot help but be riveted by the details he fleshes out for us. He could have said, "She sailed down the river on a barge," but instead he says:

1	I will tell you,
2	The Barge she sat in, like a burnisht Throne
3	Burnt on the water: the Poope was beaten Gold,
4	Purple the Sailes: and so perfumed that
5	The Windes were Love-sicke.
6	With them the Owers were Silver,
7	Which to the tune of flutes kept stroke, and made
8	The water which they beate, to follow faster;
9	As amorous of their strokes. For her owne person,
10	It beggerd all discription, she did lye
11	In her Pavillion, cloth of Gold, of Tissue,
12	O're-picturing that Venus, where we see
13	The fancie out-worke Nature. On each side her,
14	Stood pretty Dimpled Boyes, like smiling Cupids,
15	With divers coulour'd Fannes whose winde did seeme,
16	To glove the delicate cheeks which they did coole,
17	And what they undid did.

Notice the similes in line 2 "like a burnisht Throne," line 9 "As amorous of their strokes," and line 14 "like smiling Cupids."

The phrase "whose winde did seeme, to glove the delicate cheeks" has the flavor of metaphor in it. A wind cannot be a literal glove, as it has no tangible mass; it is only symbolic of a glove.

In *Playing Shakespeare,* a British Broadcasting Company (BBC) television series from the 1980s, renowned director John Barton hosts discussions on various topics with famous Royal Shakespeare Company actors. The strength of this program, which I highly recommend viewing, comes from hearing these superbly polished actors do different line readings from the plays. Patrick Stewart, celebrated in America for his role as Captain Jean-Luc Picard in *Star Trek: The Next Generation,* spoke Enobarbus' speech as though it were an oil painting. He used phrases such as "The Windes were Love-Sicke" to create an extraordinary number of dimensions by varying pitch, tempo, volume, and emotional affect. The recording is luscious to hear. Without that diversity, it could have been flat.

When we listen to Stewart and other actors who use their words well, we become emotionally involved in the imagery. We wonder: Are we ever going to see Cleopatra like this? It's titillating, as if we're watching *Lifestyles of the Rich and Famous* on TV, or reading *People* magazine. She's a celebrity. Her life is an epic love story, and the audience finds the description as compelling as a romance novel.

—— Your Task—Locating Descriptive Words——

Go through your own speech or scene, and highlight all the descriptive words and phrases (adjectives, adverbs, similes, and metaphors) it contains.

Highlighted, a portion of Enobarbus' speech above might look as follows:

1	I will tell you,
2	The Barge she sat in, like a **burnisht** Throne
3	**Burnt** on the water: the Poope was **beaten** Gold,
4	Purple the Sailes: and so **perfumed** that
5	The Windes were **Love-sicke**.
6	With them the Owers were Silver,
7	Which to the tune of Flutes kept stroke, and made
8	The water which they beate, to follow **faster**;
9	As **amorous** of their strokes...

———— Your Task—Coloring Your Performance ————

Once you have highlighted the descriptive words and phrases, read the speech aloud and consciously *choose* the descriptive words. Make them colorful. Be bold. Go to extremes. Discover. Adjectives such as *burnt, beaten, perfumed,* and *amorous* are potent opportunities for you, as an actor, to savor your words and involve your listeners.

Draw upon the techniques you've learned in previous days' rehearsals. Feel free to emphasize iambic pentameter, consonant and vowel sounds, capitalized letters, and so on. Relish the words. Think about what they correspond to in your world. When you have a real picture in your mind, audience members perceive real pictures in their minds' eyes.

The Power of Personal Imagery and Memories

Pictures that live within an actor's mind always result in more detailed and colorful line readings. So it is tremendously worthwhile to find personal parallels for your character's circumstances to envision while you're delivering your speeches. In future rehearsals, we will do more of this kind of imaging work, as it produces beautiful results.

A few years ago, I had a student, a man originally from Atlanta, who did Enobarbus' barge speech in my class. Part of what made his delivery incredibly effective and involving was how everyone listening to him could feel the sultry sensation of a hot summer day in Georgia layered beneath his words. He embraced his personal memories of the Deep South so well that he made our classroom seem hot. When he described the two boys fanning Cleopatra, it was as if he was lounging on a porch back home.

This student was so committed to his descriptive words and phrases that the audience was intrigued by his speech. He brought sensuality to it, because he knew which of his five senses to draw upon. When he harnessed the power of personal substitutions–memories that let him know what "hot" means–the speech became personal. As a result, he delivered his lines with greater verbal relish and energy. He truly owned them.

Like this student, I highly encourage you to observe any memories that pop into your head as you're reading and rehearsing your speech, and then allow them to inform and color your performance. Personal associations can be enormously fruitful avenues to explore. Nearing the close of the first week in a three-week rehearsal process, most actors usually have formed connections to the material they're working on quite effortlessly. It's a good idea to continue collecting these as long in your rehearsal process as possible.

Your Day 6 Rehearsal Checklist

Have you completed your tasks?

☐ Locating Descriptive Words

☐ Coloring Your Performance

What discoveries have you made?

DAY 7

O! Thy Status Is Showing

Elizabethan England was extremely status conscious and this was reflected in the vocabulary people used to address one another, such as the titles Sovereign, Lord, Liege, Sir, Queen, Lady, Dame, and so on. Every title was honored with particular ritual behavior, although history has forgotten what most were. For instance, we know that saying "liege" was accompanied by kneeling. The more important the person you were addressing, the grander the gesture you made to acknowledge his or her superiority.

On stage, knowing what the different titles signify and whether you are of a higher or lower status than the character to whom you are speaking will help you craft your body language. It sometimes will help you understand the humor in a scene. Often, the choice to use (or not use) status appropriate titles illustrates a key development in the relationship between two characters, such as a shift from simple deference to extreme subordination, or abasement. Changes in status can set up meaningful plot twists, and the Bard made them actable.

So, let's take a look at some of the ranks and titles you may find in the plays.

Ranks and Titles of Lords and Other Men

The top three of the following titles and ranks can apply to women, too.

Sovereign: A person of supreme authority; someone who is dominant and excellent, and whose powers are paramount, unmitigated, and absolute.

Majesty: A sovereign authority; someone dignified, who possesses royal bearing, grandeur, greatness, or a stately character.

Highness: A member of the royal family.

King: A male monarch or paramount chief of a major territorial unit. He holds hereditary position and rules for life.

Duke: A nobleman of the highest hereditary rank who rules a duchy.

Marquis: A member of the British peerage (peers are hereditary noblemen).

Earl: A member of the British peerage.

Count: A foreign nobleman (e.g., Italian or French) whose rank corresponds to that of a British earl.

Viscount: A member of the British peerage, who is ranked below an earl.

Lord: Any of various titled men of Great Britain: a duke, marquis, earl, count, or viscount.

Baron: One of a class of tenants holding his rights and title by military or other honorable service directly from a feudal superior, such as a king.

Baronet: A member of the lowest grade or order of the peerage of Great Britain.

Knight: A military man in honorable service to a nobleman.

Sir: A man of rank or position. Used as a title before the given name of a baron, baronet, or knight. A man who has completed service as a page and squire.

Liege: A nobleman to whom a loyal subject is obligated to render allegiance.

Gentleman: A man of noble birth belonging to the landed aristocracy.

Squire: A youth being trained for knighthood.

Page: A youth in attendance of a person of rank.

Sirrah: A form of address used mainly when speaking to inferiors without titles.

Ranks and Titles of Ladies and Other Women

Property in feudal society was passed down through the eldest male child in a family. Thus, feminine ranks and titles generally indicate marital status or parentage.

Queen: A female monarch, or the wife or widow of a king. She is eminent in rank, power, or attractions. She has supremacy in a specific realm.

Duchess: Wife of a duke.

Marchioness: Wife of a marquis.

Earless: Wife of an earl.

Countess: Wife of a count.

Viscountess: Wife of a viscount.

Baroness: Wife of a baron.

Lady: A woman having proprietary rights of authority, especially as a feudal superior. Any of various titled women of Great Britain: a marchioness, earless, countess, viscountess, or baroness.

Lady-in-waiting: A woman of the court who serves the royalty.

Dame: A woman of rank, such as a wife or daughter of a lord, or a female member of an order of knighthood.

The Great Chain of Being

Shakespeare wrote his characters from within a well-established medieval hierarchy known as the Great Chain of Being. Everyone in society understood their place in this caste system, a philosophical construct that encompassed the clergy, social ranks (noble and common), the household (man, wife, children, and servants), and the individual (reason and passion). Cosmologically, at the top of the hierarchy was God. Next came the archangels and angels, then the king and queen, the noble people, the soldiers and the regular people, and the animals in the dirt. At the bottom, finally, was the Devil. The chain descended from absolute perfection to absolute corruption.

THE GREAT CHAIN OF BEING

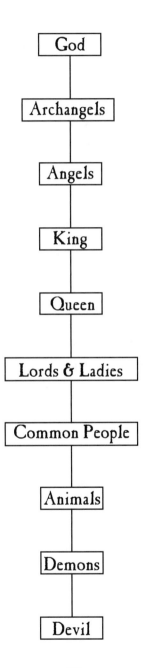

God

Archangels

Angels

King

Queen

Lords & Ladies

Common People

Animals

Demons

Devil

If everybody in a society knows their established place, it is fun for a playwright—and entertaining for the audience by extension—to start reshuffling the characters. Dramatic tension ensues whenever someone steps out of an assigned role. It can produce conflict, humor, and sometimes both. It is also a way of exploring the dimensions of a particular status level. When the Duke travels his own kingdom as a friar in *Measure for Measure,* his language undergoes the same transformation in status that his person does. People relate to him differently, and thus he gains access to information that no one wants to risk talking to a nobleman.

In a workshop with the great Shakespearean director John Barton that I attended many years ago, he pointed out that so long as everyone was in his or her proper place within the Chain of Being, the world was as it should be. Whenever the Chain is broken or disrupted, the play is about restoring order and putting people back in their proper places. After that, the people are at peace. He asserted this was a common recurring theme. For instance, after Macbeth kills King Duncan in *Macbeth,* the play centers on putting the crown back on the head of someone from the proper lineage. When Oberon and Titania are fighting in *A Midsummer Night's Dream,* the world is filled with storms, the crops are rotting, and mortals are disturbed. When the fairy king and queen reunite, the mortals are restored to harmony—men and women get along.

There's a convention in Shakespeare's plays that if a character changes his clothes, no one can recognize him. Noblemen masquerade as clergy and common soldiers. Young women masquerade as boys. The unfortunate Bottom is magically transformed into a donkey in *A Midsummer Night's Dream,* perhaps revealing his true character. However, even if the clothes change, the quality of the person does not change, and this cannot be so easily hidden. In *Twelfth Night*, for example, the aristocratic Viola has been shipwrecked in Illyria, where she disguises herself as a youth named Cesario in order to get a job. Her natural nobility shines forth.

In Act 1, Scene 5, Olivia mulls over her recent conversation with Cesario, and in the process falls for "his" charms. Note the boldface line, which indicates her confusion. "Perfection" is a euphemism for being high up on the Great Chain of Being.

OLIVIA	What is your Parentage?	1
	Above my fortunes, yet my state is well;	2
	I am a Gentleman. Ile be sworne thou art,	3
	Thy tongue, thy face, thy limbes, actions, and spirit,	4
	Do give thee five-fold blazon: not too fast: soft, soft,	5
	Unlesse the Master were the man. How now?	6
	Even so quickly may one catch the plague?	7
	Me thinkes I feele this youths perfections	8
	With an invisible, and subtle stealth	9
	To creepe in at mine eyes. Well, let it be.	10

Ordinary Versus Poetic Language

As an actor, what you need to understand is that just as Shakespeare's characters move up and down the Chain of Being, sections of his text move up and down. Prose is of a low order. A little higher is blank verse. A higher order still is rhyming couplets.

In the plays, the farther up the Chain of Being you climb, the more extraordinary the language that is used. When you find extraor-

dinary words in a speech, Shakespeare is not only speaking poetically, he is also raising the stakes for his characters. That moment is
extraordinary. For instance, *burdened* is ordinary language. It means
I'm carrying a heavy load. *Burthened* with a *th* is extraordinary.
Perhaps my soul is weighed down.

There are actually three possible levels of speech in Shakespeare's
plays: the ordinary (*please*), the poetic (*I pray you*), and the highly
poetic (*I prithee*). You could say "I think" or you could say "me
thinks." The second is the poetic expression. Here are a few more
examples contrasting ordinary and poetic speech:

In truth	In troth (highly poetic: Tro)
Taken	Tane
Forbid	Forefend

What are your perceptions in the face of the unfamiliar style of
Shakespeare's extraordinary language? Where can fancy words lead
you? As an actor, you must trust your instinct about what is truly
extraordinary and heightened, and then find a way to communicate
it so that the audience understands your interpretation.

On stage, knowing that words are common or refined (low or
high) helps you select your vocal tones and ways of relating to others. A king would speak differently than a pickpocket. Thus, when a
pickpocket uses the language of kings we know that he's putting on
airs and trying to raise his status level. Alternatively, when a king
roams the countryside as a peasant might, you can guess that the
character is living through a period of heightened emotions or circumstances, and literally not acting like himself.

If you leave your place, you disrupt the chain. That's rebellion. Someone who allows passion to control his reason gets knocked down the chain. If you usurp another's spot, you also get knocked down. On other occasions, characters choose to move down the chain. Edgar, the legitimate son of the Earl of Gloucester in *King Lear,* speaks in prose when he disguises himself as Poor Tom, a madman (Act 3, Scene 4). All of Hamlet's major speeches are in verse, except for his famous "Speech to the Players" (Act 3, Scene 2), during which he instructs a troupe of traveling actors. He comes down to their level, as if he's a friend, by joking around in prose like one of the boys. Conversely, the famous vagabond and pickpocket Autolycus, from *The Winter's Tale,* speaks in prose, but sings in verse. When he sings, his status is elevated.

——— Your Task—Locating Modes of Address———

Please begin today's rehearsal process by locating the modes of address your character uses in the script and any modes of address that other characters use when speaking to your character. This will help you identify the places where shifts in status–from high to low or from low to high–occur.

Certain information about your status is going to be evident from your name alone (e.g., Prince Hal, Sir Toby Belch, Friar Lawrence, Lady Ann, Queen Margaret, Dull, Jacquenetta). As a rule of thumb, the clown roles are mostly common people–I won't call them "ordinary" people because they're definitely not. Each is a treasure.

As an actor, these are some relevant questions to ask:

• What is your character's status?

- What is the status of your character relative to other characters in the scene?

- Does your character ever address another as a superior or an inferior?

- Is your character behaving according to the rules of his or her status?

- Is your character speaking according to the rules of his or her status?

- Is your character violating the rules of his or her status?

- Are there any shifts in status during the speech or scene?

Formality and Informality

As in modern French, Elizabethan English incorporated both informal and formal personal pronouns. *Thee* and *thy* in that era were informal synonyms for the formal words *you* and *yours,* just as *tu* and *ton* are more intimate versions of the formal words in French *vous* and *votre* today. It is a common misunderstanding that *thee* and *thy* were formal modes of address. An Elizabethan might address his family and close friends this way. But he would never address his social superiors so casually. It was a well-understood rule of conduct.

When you see an informal pronoun used in Shakespeare's plays, roughly 85 percent of the time it demonstrates friendship or love. The remaining 15 percent of the time it is being used in a derogatory fashion, with the intent to demonstrate disrespect.

For example, in Act 1, Scene 2 of *Richard the Third,* Lady Ann is walking in a procession with men carrying her father-in-law's corpse. Her husband Edward and her father-in-law King Henry VI were murdered. She blames Richard and the current king for their deaths. Suddenly, Richard arrives on the scene. He tells her that he wants to marry her. Horrified, she won't give him the reverence due a duke. She calls him "thou." She also compares him to a devil, which is the lowest order on the Chain of Being. Status words in the following text are in **bold**.

ANN	**Villaine**, thou know'st nor law of **God** nor **Man**,	1
	No **Beast** so fierce, but knowes some touch of pitty.	2
RICHARD	But I know none, and therefore am no **Beast**.	3
ANN	O wonderfull, when **divels** tell the truth!	4
RICHARD	More wonderfull, when **Angels** are so angry:	5
	Vouchsafe (divine **perfection** of a **Woman**)	6
	Of these supposed Crimes, to give me leave	7
	By circumstance, but to acquit my selfe.	8
ANN	Vouchsafe (defus'd **infection** of **man**)	9
	Of these knowne evils, but to give me leave	10
	By circumstance, to curse thy cursed Selfe.	11
RICHARD	Fairer then tongue can name thee, let me have	12
	Some patient leysure to excuse my selfe.	13
ANN	Fouler then heart can thinke thee,	14
	Thou can'st make no excuse currant,	15
	But to hang thy selfe.	16
RICHARD	By such dispaire, I should accuse my selfe.	17
ANN	And by dispairing shalt thou stand excused,	18
	That did'st unworthy slaughter upon others.	19
RICHARD	Say that I slew them not.	20

21 ANN   Then say they were not slaine:

22   But dead they are, and **divellish** slave by thee.

On stage, informality may indicate physical nearness and formality may indicate keeping a respectful distance. It is widely accepted that Shakespeare sometimes intended words like you/yours and thee/thou/thy to serve as stage directions. For instance, in *Much Ado About Nothing* (Act 4, Scene 1) Benedick asks:

> **Lady Beatrice**, have **you** wept all this while?   [**Formal status**]

He refers to her as "you," probably indicating a physical distance, until several lines later:

> By my sword **Beatrice thou** lov'st me.   [**Informal status**]

Here he also has dropped her title. And a few lines further he says:

> …I protest I love **thee**.   [**Informal status**]

As he substitutes "thee" for "you," the actor could move physically closer.

——— Your Task—Moving Near, Moving Far———

As an experiment, in just the same way you mapped your modes of address in the previous task, please now map formal and informal language. Do you ever shift from saying "you" to "thy" during your speech or scene? If so, play with moving near and far on the lines where shifts occur. Move nearer on informality. Move farther away on formality. Do this task boldly, with every fiber of your being–not halfway or timidly. Observe its impact on your physical, vocal, and emotional energy. Did it enhance your performance?

The Power of Ritual Body Language

Shakespeare's plays have a cinematic quality to them, because each theatrical moment forms a unique picture on the stage. For this reason, specificity is essential. It's the only way an audience can follow the story of a play as if they were following a movie. You simply have to make clear, specific physical choices in order to give them cinematic images that highlight the spirit of the moment. In Hermione's speech below two possible actions are shown in brackets beside the status words on which they could be performed (see lines 1 and 9).

In *The Winter's Tale,* jealous King Leontes has falsely charged his wife Queen Hermione with adultery. In Act 3, Scene 2, the righteous Hermione delivers an impassioned speech in defense of herself to the King and the Court that is a perfect example of how ritual body language and formal titles can align to highlight a dramatic moment.

Sir, spare your Threats:	[**Eye-to-eye on "Sir"**]	1
The Bugge which you would fright me with, I seeke:		2
To me can Life be no commoditie;		3
The crowne and comfort of my Life (your Favor)		4
I doe give lost, for I doe feele it gone,		5
But know not how it went...		6
...Lastly, hurried		7
Here, to this place, i'th'open ayre, before		8
I have got strength of limit. Now (my **Liege**)		
	[**Kneeling on "Liege"**]	9

10	Tell me what blessings I have here alive,
11	That I should feare to die?...

Later on in the play, Hermione's innocence is confirmed by a revelation from an oracle. Her demonstrated respect for her husband in this picture, as she so bravely faces her conviction, lingers in the mind's eye. Her submission tells us she isn't afraid of death. She honors her husband, even though he disgraces her due to his jealous fantasies.

The bolder the physical choices you make, the better, in general, the result will be. Act 1, Scene 3 of *As You Like It* is a banishment scene that takes place amidst the court of the tyrannical Duke Frederick, who usurped the throne of Rosalind's father, Duke Senior. The audience perceives a crowd on stage: the Duke and his courtiers, and Rosalind and her cousin Celia. The exchange takes place in a very public setting, where respect and formality is expected. Nonetheless, there is an informal family relationship, a closeness that stands out in contrast.

Here, if the actress playing Rosalind only makes a single choice to stand on informality but kneel and/or do another ritual gesture on formality, we know when she is in different states of being. The audience has no way of knowing what is going on inside a character except through an outward demonstration or expression. Technically, as an actor, therefore you must therefore choose an action. During today's rehearsal the suggestion is that your status language guides your actions.

Note that Rosalind begins informally on line 3 below, calling him "Uncle." Then, as soon as he threatens to punish her with death, she addresses him on line 8 as "your Grace." If she dropped to her knees on that line, where might she pop up again? Does her use of another form of address give you a clue?

DUKE	Mistris, dispatch you with your safest haste,	1
	And get you from our Court.	2
ROSALIND	Me **Uncle.**	3
DUKE	You Cosen,	4
	Within these ten daies if that thou beest found	5
	So neere our publike Court as twentie miles,	6
	Thou diest for it.	7
ROSALIND	I doe beseech **your Grace**	8
	Let me the knowledge of my fault beare with me:	9
	If with my selfe I hold intelligence,	10
	Or have acquaintance with mine owne desires,	11
	If that I doe not dreame, or be not franticke,	12
	(As I doe trust I am not) then **deere Uncle,**	13
	Never so much as in a thought unborne,	14
	Did I offend **your highnesse.**	15
DUKE	Thus doe all Traitors,	16
	If their purgation did consist in words,	17
	They are as innocent as grace it selfe;	18
	Let is suffice thee that I trust thee not.	19
ROSALIND	Yet your mistrust cannot make me a Traitor;	20
	Tell me whereon the likelihoods depends?	21
DUKE	Thou art thy Fathers daughter, there's enough.	22
ROSALIND	So was I when **your highnes** took his Dukdome,	23
	So was I when **your highnesse** banisht him;	24
	Treason is not inherited **my Lord,**	25
	Or if we did derive it from our friends,	26

27   What's that to me, my Father was no Traitor,

28   Then **good my Leige,** mistake me not so much,

29   To thinke my povertie is treacherous.

When Rosalind addresses Duke Frederick as "deere Uncle" on line 13, it's possible that she forgets herself and her situation. By line 15, she would kneel again. For the listening ears and watching eyes of the audience, Rosalind must come across as being in a heightened state of desperation. She uses the verb *beseech,* which is a poetic word, rather than *beg* or *ask,* or even *implore.* Thus, the actress' vocal, physical, and emotional energy must align with Shakespeare's intention that she is beseeching her uncle. All her acting tools must come into play. Her physicality backs up the language.

——— Your Task—Designing Ritual Body Language———

By now, you have located the modes of address, heightened language, and formal and informal expressions in your script. If you haven't done so, highlight these elements of the text now. You have also played with moving near and far from your scene partner on certain shifts. Please explore several physical possibilities for each change in status that you encounter in your speeches. Stay at it until you come up with a viable line reading. Remember to be specific.

Ritual body language is repeatable symbolism. Sometimes an entire cast does the same gesture on a certain mode of address and the impact is stunning. For instance, putting their right hands over their hearts on the words "your grace" or doing a slight bow or head nod on "my lord" or "my lady." Look at customs from around the world, in your own community, and different eras in history, and you may find some fresh ideas. These might be anything from a curtsy, to a salute, to flapping your fingers under your chin. Experiment with choices from the Marx Brothers, Jim Carrey, and the Klingons on *Star Trek*. Borrow from the Japanese. When you are rehearsing, there are no "wrong choices."

Your Day 7 Rehearsal Checklist

Have you completed your tasks?

☐ Locating Modes of Address

☐ Moving Near, Moving Far

☐ Designing Ritual Body Language

What discoveries have you made?

DAY 8

Your Secret Formula for Persuasive Rhetoric

Rhetoric is a form of argumentation that takes place either between two characters or between an actor and the audience. This type of debate doesn't imply a loud or angry confrontation. In fact, assume that points are being awarded for style! How clever can your character be? Theatre is entertainment. Since nobody likes to be around someone who is yelling, including a character from a play, loud anger is often a negative acting choice. Rhetoric is the art of persuasion. Wherever you find it in the plays, ultimately either a conclusion will be drawn or a new issue will be put on the table for discussion.

Like the mathematical formula $1 + 1 = 2$, be assured that rhetorical debate is taking place whenever characters are using Questions and Answers, Agreements and Disagreements, and Comparisons and Contrasts. Today, we'll explore these elements of debate, which occur both within monologues and soliloquies and within scenes between characters. What purpose do they serve? How do they change your vocal tones? These tools are the ingredients in your secret formula for persuasive rhetoric.

Among other things, your job as an actor–a storyteller–is to stand up for your character's point of view and persuade the audience of its rightness. To give an argument a solid foundation, you must know its internal logic. These literary devices can help you figure out how your lines add up and lead the audience to a result. Like stepping stones, they can dramatize your character's discoveries and decision-making process.

Never forget that in every speech or scene you are debating the pros and cons of an issue. You must learn to keep going vocally until you hit the part of your speech or scene that represents the equal sign (=) in your "mathematical equation," whether that means you are just adding up the total of two numbers (1 + 1 = 2) or a longer column of figures (1 + 1 + 1 + 1 + 1 = 5). Especially when the language of the play you're working on is complex and ripe with imagery, using this secret formula of rhetoric will help you establish clarity for the listeners.

Questions and Answers

Edmond's famous speech in *King Lear* (Act 1, Scene 2) is a brilliant example of the theatricality of Questions and Answers. Illegitimate son of the Earl of Gloucester, Edmond bitterly resents his half-brother Edgar for the fact that he will inherit their father's estate and noble title. Here Edmond expresses dissatisfaction with society's rules of inheritance and attitudes towards "bastard" children through a powerful series of questions.

EDMOND	Thou Nature art my Goddesse, to thy Law	1
	My services are bound, wherefore should I	2
	Stand in the plague of custome, and permit	3
	The curiosity of Nations, to deprive me? [Q]	4
	For that I am some twelve, or fourteene Moonshines	5
	Lag of a Brother? Why Bastard? Wherefore base? [3 Qs]	6

7	When my Dimensions are as well compact,
8	My minde as generous, and my shape as true
9	As honest Madams issue? Why brand they us [Q]
10	With Base? With baseness Bastardie? Base, Base? [3 Qs]

Edmond's soliloquy becomes the launching platform for a devious scheme to turn Gloucester against Edgar. Dramatically, everything Edmond does in the rest of the play is an answer to this series of questions. Although the audience may at times find him vile and deceitful, this first speech puts them inside his head. They enjoy a good piece of villainy by an anti-hero. The plot is propelled forward as a result of his vengeful decision-making process.

Although questions sometimes aren't marked with a question mark, there's usually something about the sentence structure that tips you off that a question has been posed. For instance, there's an implied question in Act 1, Scene 1 of Twelfth Night, when Duke Orsino enters and begins the play with the following statement:

1	DUKE	**If Musicke be the food of Love**, play on,
2		Give me excesse of it: that surfetting,
3		The appetite may sicken, and so dye.

The possibility that music sustains love, which is phrased as a metaphor, informs us that the Duke is lovesick. He also tells us why: he wishes his feelings of love would end or be satiated. When he says, "If…" the audience wonders for a second, "Is it?" When he says, "Give me excesse…" for another split second they wonder, "Why?"

When you play a question, it should sound like a question would in real life. It should sound as though you really want to know the answer (e.g., does $1 + 1 = 3$?). If you succeed, audience members will embrace the question in their own minds and create a response to it. (No, $1 + 1 = 2$!) Or they'll lean forward in their chairs in anticipation of a character's answer.

—— Your Task—Locating Questions and Answers——

Go through your script now and highlight all the questions and answers. As a rule, locating questions is easy. You already know where your end stops are, because you picked them out during your Day 4 rehearsal. When the punctuation is a question mark, the thought is definitely a question.

Also look for *If...Then* sentence constructions, as those are implied questions, and for the sort of words that are typically associated with questions: *Who, What, Where, Why, When,* and *How.* Incidentally, those are the basic questions in modern journalism.

President John F. Kennedy used to say to his cabinet, "You come up with the *Ifs* and I'll come up with the *Thens.*" A *Then* is an action-answer. For actors, this will be a dare or a self-imposed challenge.

Comparisons and Contrasts

Gaining insight into different characters' thought processes is fascinating. Watching them weigh alternatives and assign values adds to a play's dramatic tension, and can be riveting for the audience. As with any conflict, when we don't know what the outcome will be, we get more involved. Audiences take sides in the struggle. It's only human nature.

Comparison takes two things, puts them alongside one another, and evaluates them. Here is a train of logic–a rhetorical argument–which uses comparison.

- Thing #1 is purple. Purple is good.
- Thing #2 is orange. Orange is bad.
- Therefore, Thing #1 is better than Thing #2.

Many times, the various building blocks of rhetoric overlap. For instance, go back and take another look at Edmond's speech in the section above. Do you see how he is comparing his situation as the illegitimate son of Gloucester to his half-brother Edgar's situation as the Earl's legitimate son even as he asks his questions? He says:

7	my Dimensions are as well compact,
8	My minde is generous, and my shape as true

In a speech from Act 4, Scene 3 of *Othello,* Amelia builds a rhetorical case that men are at fault if their wives cheat on them by comparing husbands and wives. She says men and women are the same in a specific way: They like to experience variety.

1	AMELIA	…Let Husbands know,
2		Their wives have sense like them: They see, and smell,
3		And have their Palats both for sweet, and sowre,
4		As Husbands have….

Characters can even compare time frames. For instance, in *The Comedy of Errors* (Act 2, Scene 2), Adriana, mistaking her husband's twin for her husband, utters a speech contrasting the past with the present. Essentially, she is asserting, "The past was great, wasn't it?" She clearly feels that today is not as good.

ADRIANA	I, I, *Antipholus*, looke strange and frowne,	1
	Some other Mistresse hath thy sweet aspects:	2
	I am not *Adriana*, nor thy wife.	3
	The time was once, when thou un-urg'd wouldst vow,	4
	That never words were musicke to thine eare,	5
	That never object pleasing in thine eye,	6
	That never touch well welcome to thy hand,	7
	That never meat sweet-savour'd in thy taste,	8
	Unlesse I spake, or look'd, or touch'd, or carv'd to thee.	9
	How comes it now, my Husband, oh how comes it,	10
	That thou art then estranged from thy selfe?	11
	Thy selfe I call it, being strange to me:	12
	That undividable Incorporate	13
	Am better then thy deere selfes better part.	14

Contrast is subtly different from comparison. Contrasts in Shakespeare usually involve pairs of opposites: day and night, light and dark, hard and soft, up and down, and so forth. When pairs of opposites are juxtaposed in the same line, same sentence, or same speech, the second item is an "antithesis." This is one of Shakespeare's favorite devices.

Antithesis is aptly demonstrated in *Henry the Sixth, Part Three* (Act 1, Scene 4), in this excerpt from a speech made by Queen Margaret to Richard, the Duke of York, in the presence of two of her husband Henry's allies. "Him" in line 2 refers to the Duke. Contrasted items are shown in **bold** here.

1 QUEEN MARGARET

Brave Warriors, *Clifford* and *Northumberland,*

2   Come make him stand upon this **Mole-hill** here,

3   That raught at **Mountaines** with out-stretched Armes,

4   Yet parted but the **shadow** with his Hand.

You may notice that something small (a molehill) is being contrasted with something large (a mountain), and then that substantial form is subsequently contrasted with something intangible (a shadow). So we have two antitheses in a row.

——— Your Task—Locating Comparisons——— and Contrasts

Go through your speech and highlight all its comparisons and contrasts. Read the speech aloud once or twice emphasizing the distinctions your character is making. Allow your voice to be as dynamic as the language. Using our mathematical analogy, the rhetorical formula in this case should sound as though you were saying: $1 + 1 \neq 3$. Example (*Julius Caesar*):

ANTHONY   I come to bury *Caesar*, not to praise him

Formula $1 + 1$ $\neq$ 3

Of course, identifying the comparisons and contrasts isn't always an easy task. Sometimes they're *implied* rather than spelled out for you. Even well educated performers often need practice to pick them out. I once coached an actress in her late 40s, an intelligent woman of substance, who just couldn't figure out how to do this task. She was working on a monologue of Tamora's from *Titus Andronicus* (Act 2, Scene 3). Nothing was adding up and her reading was basically flat and uninteresting. Then, she got the concept that she was mentally contrasting the "detested vale" with a nicer place to be. Suddenly, her vocal tones and her phrasing shifted, and what she was saying became understandable.

TAMORA	Have I not reason thinke you to looke pale.	1
	These two have tic'd me hither to this place,	2
	A barren, detested vale you see it is.	3
	The Trees though Sommer, yet forlorne and leane,	4
	Ore-come with Mosse, and balefull Misselto.	5
	Heere never shines the Sunne, here nothing breeds,	6
	Unlesse the nightly Owle, or fatall Raven:	7
	And when they shew'd me this abhorred pit,	8
	They told me here at dead time of the night,	9
	A thousand Fiends, a thousand hissing Snakes,	10
	Ten thousand swelling Toades, as many Urchins,	11
	Would make such fearefull and confused cries,	12
	As any mortall body hearing it,	13
	Should straite fall mad, or else die suddenly.	14

I encourage you not to give up looking. Even if you don't find an explicit comparison or contrast, take a few minutes to imagine what might be an opposite of the images you're using. Having that distinction under your belt will enable you to portray your character's point of view more effectively, and take a firm stand.

Agreements and Disagreements

In *Much Ado About Nothing*, Beatrice and Benedick are often engaged in a merry war of wits. They delight in their arguments. As both have sworn never to marry, watching them suddenly fall in love with one another during the course of Act 4, Scene 1 is a delicious treat. It begins with a good example of a Question and Answer that leads into a subsequent string of Disagreements and Agreements that resolve in a singularly important Agreement. From that moment (line 24), the play's plot is pushed in a new direction.

1	BENEDICK	Lady *Beatrice*, have you wept all this while?
2	BEATRICE	Yea, and I will weepe a while longer. **[Agreement]**
3	BENEDICK	I will not desire that. **[Disagreement]**
4	BEATRICE	You have no reason, I doe it freely. **[Disagreement]**
5	BENEDICK	Surelie I do beleeve your fair cosin is wrong'd.
6	BEATRICE	Ah, how much might the man deserve of mee
7		that would right her!
8	BENEDICK	Is there any way to shew such friendship?
9	BEATRICE	A verie even way, but no such friend.
10	BENEDICK	May a man doe it?
11	BEATRICE	It is a mans office, but not yours.
12	BENEDICK	I doe love nothing in the world so well as you,
13		is not that strange?
14	BEATRICE	As strange as the thing I know not, it were as
		[Agreement]
15		possible for me to say, I loved nothing so well as you, but
16		beleeve me not, and yet I lie not, I confesse nothing, nor
17		I deny nothing, I am sorry for my cousin.

BENEDICK	By my sword *Beatrice* thou lov'st me.	18
BEATRICE	Doe not sweare by it and eat it. **[Disagreement]**	19
BENEDICK	I will sweare by it that you love mee, and I will	20
	[Disagreement]	
	make him eat it that sayes I love not you.	21
BEATRICE	Will you not eat your word?	22
BENEDICK	With no sawce that can be devised to it, I protest	23
	I love thee.	24
BEATRICE	Why then God forgive me.	25
BENEDICK	What offence sweet Beatrice?	26
BEATRICE	You have stayed me in a happy howre, I was about	27
	to protest I loved you.	28
BENEDICK	And doe it with all thy heart. **[Agreement]**	29

——— Your Task—Locating Agreements——— and Disagreements

Read through your lines and see which of them seem to be agreements and which disagreements. Highlight them with a colored marker. While characters are perfectly capable of disagreeing with themselves (and often do), it's fair to say that Agreements and Disagreements are always responses to an active assertion. For instance, when Benedick says, "By my sword *Beatrice* thou lov'st me," he is making a discovery aloud. Beatrice chooses to disagree with this assertion, saying, "Doe not sweare by it and eat it." But she could just as easily have said, "By George, you're right!" If characters were always in complete agreement, there would be no dramatic tension.

Lifting Your Lines

Plays are heightened reality. You have to find an urgent reason to say whatever you're saying. It has to matter. When you speak a line, the idea it holds must be sustained from the beginning to the end. It must all add up to a coherent thought. A listener should be able to hear this process of thought building in the sound of your voice. To sustain a meaning, you must learn how to technically "lift" your lines.

Here are a few rhetorical clues that help listeners understand what's going on. We should hear these sounds in your tone of voice and in the way your energy reaches us. If you focus on communicating these underlying concepts, your voice will reflect them.

And: You are building. Think of a mathematical plus sign.

Or: You are comparing values and weighing merits.

Unless: You are backtracking, possibly disagreeing with yourself.

Yet: You are turning in a new direction.

But: You are moving on, and possibly trying to make a decision.

Lifting a line doesn't mean that you must necessarily raise your voice or go up in pitch. Rather, you need to do something with your energy and intention. The next part of the line must come from the same or a higher plane of energy plane. A lift often occurs in mid-sentence. To hear this technique done well, go online and listen to Dr. Martin Luther King, Jr. delivering his "I Have a Dream" speech or borrow a videotape of it from the library. He was a highly persuasive orator and an expert at lifting lines.

Some actors feel self-conscious in front of an audience. They're afraid to let their voices sound as dynamic and flexible as they do in their daily lives. While poetry isn't the same thing as natural spoken language, both are truthful and poetry does not have to sound rigid or stilted. Sometimes Shakespeare will sound real, and other times it won't. That's not the exclusive determining factor in how a given line should be delivered. When you reach the end of a line of text that has no punctuation mark, be assured that it needs to lift. You may extend that last word (as if you are thinking of how best to finish your sentence), you may lilt upwards in tone, or you may solve the problem another way that you invent. Using your craftsmanship, keep that thought moving forward by thinking it and willing it toward the conclusion of your character's idea.

Unfortunately, American actors tend to swallow lines before they reach their intended target. The target of a line is a person, a place, or a thing. In a duologue, two actors are on stage and one is speaking to the other. Your scene partner is the intended target. In a soliloquy, an actor is alone on stage. The actor is usually speaking to the audience, and so the audience is the target. If the actor's words don't reach the target, the actor has failed to achieve the requisite energy. He or she fails to persuade the listener.

Here are two readings of the first line from *Twelfth Night* that illustrate where lifts could occur.

Version 1

play on.   1 = 1

If Musicke be the food of Love,

Version 2

play on.   1 + 1 = 2

be the food of Love,

　　If Musicke

Now, remember that we're talking about every script as a sort of musical score. When notes are scored, they are assigned various weights–different durations. A whole note or four one-quarter notes can fill a four-count measure. What would happen if we assigned different weights to words? What might that sound like? If a word had a vowel in it or was capitalized we could give it a longer duration, or more relish. Well, if the same line as above was written in musical notation, it might read like this:

If   Musicke   be the food of Love, play on,

———— Your Task–Speaking Terms of Endearment————

A good way to practice lifting your lines is by adding a term of endearment, such as "darling," "honey," "sweetie," or "pumpkin," to the end of each line in rehearsal. This helps you defy the American tendency to drift off at the end of the line and lose energy. You'll learn to finish each line clearly because the extra words form a definitive target.

When you're practicing solo, add the words "Honey Bunny" to the ends of lines. For example:

EDMOND   Thou Nature art my Goddesse, to thy Law **Honey Bunny**
          My services are bound, wherefore should I **Honey Bunny**

When you're practicing with a scene partner, one of you can use "Honey Bunny" and the other can use "Pootie Wootie" to do the same thing. For example:

KATE   Well have you heard, but something hard of hearing:
           Honey Bunny
           They call me *Katerine*, that do talke of me. **Honey Bunny**
PETRUCHIO You lye infaith, for you are call'd plaine *Kate*, **Pootie**
           Wootie
           And bony *Kate*, and sometimes *Kate* the curst: **Pootie**
           Wootie

Yes, this is a silly exercise. But if you genuinely commit to it and allow yourself to act silly, you'll get out of your own way and make some new discoveries about how to say and sustain your lines. When actors think too much, we tend to limit ourselves. We get self-conscious and rein in our voices. Let your voice be loose.

As you say your line with the term of endearment, be bold and shoot for a distant target. Visualize your voice as an arrow coming up and out of your solar plexus, shooting through the roof of your mouth, arcing out of your forehead, and traveling into the room next door. Or you could see it as a rocket blasting off and landing on the moon.

The Power of Persuasive Rhetoric

In *All's Well That Ends Well* (Act 4, Scene 1), Bertram attempts to persuade Diana to love him. She utters a ten and a half line speech explaining why she shouldn't agree to his request or believe his protestations of love. It is a seduction scene, and she is arguing against fulfilling his desire.

This speech is known for being tangled and difficult to unravel, but the tools you've learned in today's rehearsal should help you clarify it. Although there are different ways to approach it rhetorically, from Comparisons and Contrasts to Agreements and Disagreements, try out the style of Questions and Answers for now, as indicated in the brackets below, while remembering that you can keep adding "plus signs" until you reach your conclusion (1 + 1 + 1 + 1 = 4).

1	DIANA	Tis not the many oathes that makes the truth,[**Assertion**]
2		But the plaine single vow, that is vow'd true:
3		What is not holie, that we sweare not by,
4		But take the high'st to witnesse: then pray you tell me.
5		If I should sweare by Joves great attributes,
6		I lov'd you deerely, would you beleeve my oathes, [**Question**]
7		When I did love you ill? This ha's no holding
8		To sweare by him whom I protest to love
9		That I will worke against him. Therefore your oathes [**Answer**]
10		Are words and poore conditions, but unseal'd
11		At lest in my opinion. [**Conclusion**]

A student in my class who was assigned this scene at first blurted out this speech. Her recitation made no sense whatsoever to the audience. It had no danger in it. And her scene partner had nothing to work against. When I asked her to do the scene again, this time emphasizing the elements of rhetoric, it was as though a TV antenna had been adjusted and the static was gone from the view screen. Her meaning came into focus.

Speaking rhetorically made the actress win more laughs in the scene. It made her act in a moment-to-moment fashion. She didn't get ahead of herself. Additionally, she started to have more fun. Arguing her case brought out a devilish quality in her that was appealing to the audience. They responded with laughter in several places.

Interestingly, her newfound energy and clarity served to activate the energy in her scene partner as well. He had to work harder to seduce her, because her resistance was so clearly articulated. It upped the stakes and heightened the dramatic tension between them. Her use of the secrets of rhetoric made it easier to play off of her. Sparks flew on the stage.

Your Day 8 Rehearsal Checklist

Have you completed your tasks?

☐ Locating Comparisons and Contrasts

☐ Locating Questions and Answers

☐ Locating Agreements and Disagreements

☐ Speaking Terms of Endearment

What discoveries have you made?

PHASE 2

Scouting the Landscape

Going on Instinct, Getting Off Book

By now, if you've done every rehearsal task suggested in Map Reading, I'm sure that you're extremely close to knowing your lines by heart. It's time, therefore, to set the script aside so you can rehearse freely and cliff dive into the emotional pool. The techniques in the following four days' rehearsals represent an intermediate phase between investigating the surface and the depths of the text.

By the way, if you still haven't memorized your speech after doing all the steps I'm about to advocate in Part 2: Scouting the Landscape, I recommend going back and repeating the steps in the two preceding sections instead of memorizing your speech in an intellectual way. Rest assured that you've already accomplished a lot by rehearsing in a proactive way (rather than sitting on your butt and silently reading the play). It's as though you've already laid down 12 tracks on an album. Going through the tasks a second time will only make your ultimate performance even more detailed and entertaining. There is no good/bad or right/wrong to the rehearsal process I'm outlining, or to the speed at which you satisfactorily learn a part. The process is designed to help you make discoveries, glean insights, and identify the strongest acting choices.

When you see exceptional actors, such as Kevin Kline, Liev Schreiber, Meryl Streep, or Annette Bening, perform Shakespeare, rest assured that they are making new discoveries every night. Their professional expertise comes from knowing how to use the language as a tool to unlock their characters' thoughts and actions freshly with every performance.

DAY 9

Script Rotations

Although you never want to get stuck doing the same line reading twice when you speak a given speech, you're now going to focus on line memorization that is word-for-word exact. Paraphrasing is simply not acceptable when you're working with scripts as brilliantly crafted as Shakespeare's plays. Improvisation may be invited in filmmaking, but this is live classical theatre. The trick is performing your role perfectly–*and* freshly.

As an actor, you must be mindful to grow through a performance instead of just going through it. Your character must transform somehow. Shakespeare's scenes entertain, move the plot forward, or develop character. Where you start and where you end should be two different places with different dimensions. If you get locked into one state of being, your performance won't serve its purpose. It will come across flat and dull. You can trust that you won't give a cookie cutter performance if you continue to live moments and make discoveries in the same places as your character in the plot and in the text. Characters always change.

Shake Up the Text

As a director, I find it easy to tell if actors have done only surface memorization. When you stop them in mid-scene (perhaps to ask them to skip around the text in a rehearsal on blocking), they'll draw a blank. They only know their lines in order. The lines haven't yet been integrated with their bodies and emotions. My general practice is to set a date about three weeks into the rehearsal period for my actors to be off-book, and I've observed this common pitfall among them for years. I believe it arises from the fact that they learn their speeches from top to bottom. So they've practiced the first line 100 times, the second line 80 times, and the tenth line only 10 times. The solution to the problem of superficial knowledge of lines is the following task, which promotes integrated, or whole body, learning.

—— Your Task—Drawing a Convoluted Script Tree——

Write your lines from a particular scene or speech on a blank page in the form of a complex tree that has limbs shooting out in numerous and varied directions. As you rehearse with your newly drawn book in hand, the multidirectional nature of your lines will force you to spin the page around and around, which prevents top to bottom reciting. On a subconscious level, this will also prevent you from making a visual and cognitive connection between consecutive lines, and thus help you perceive each line as a new and differentiated moment. From now on, use this handwritten script when you need to look up a specific line.

The stings and Arrowes of outragious

Fortune, (3)

And by opposing end them:

The Heart-ake and the thousand Naturall shockes (7)

That Flesh is heyre to? (8)

that is the Question (1)

To be, or not to be,

to dye, to sleepe (5)

No more; and by a slope to say we end (6)

Or to take Armes against a Sea of troubles (4)

Whether 'tis Nobler in the minde to suffer (2)

Script rotation "tree" for speech from *Hamlet* (Act 3, Scene 1)

A speech should come across to the audience like a fountain blasting into the air or fireworks exploding. But a common acting problem is losing steam–starting strong and then fading away. Shaking up the text by reading from a chaotically written "tree" helps actors do what Shakespeare intended: build intensity. As you rehearse with your script rotation tree, deliver each subsequent line with more energy.

Another reason to handwrite your lines is that it is a sensual exercise in which your mind, hand, and eyes join forces to help you build the character. The playwright wrote his plays by hand and you can capture some of his feeling by writing rather than reading the script. Perhaps you'll develop a new respect for the writer and the text.

——— Your Task—Waking Up Your Creative Brain———

The typical top-down and from-left-to-right memorization process has an unanticipated and detrimental effect on an actor's performance. It puts the creative brain to sleep. *Automaticity* is the name brain researchers have given to the ability to do an activity without conscious participation. This ability is useful because it enables us to roll down the window while we drive a car and get home without looking at a map. But it disengages us from our learning processes, which take place in several stages. Sleeping our way through life means we never experience creative breakthroughs.

Have you ever listened to the patterns in ordinary conversation? People often interrupt themselves mid-thought to say something completely unexpected. When you're remembering your lines, it's important that you leave room for spontaneity and surprises.

Years ago, I read *Drawing on the Right Side of the Brain* by Betty Edwards, a book about drawing that is actually about seeing–perceiving visual information—the way that painters and draftsmen do. It was the first time I'd ever heard the special properties of the two hemispheres of the brain described. The left-brain is linear, logical, and verbal. The right-brain is intuitive and feeling. The author explains that when visual artists work they experience a subtle shift in consciousness, like daydreaming, that enables them to focus better. She gives exercises to help readers invoke that state of consciousness.

Since reading Edwards' book, I have assigned my students a simple task, which I ask them to explore for a day, a week, or a month, as they see fit. Many ignore my suggestion entirely. On the other hand, those who do it report a definite change in their sensibility, an opening to some exciting new possibilities. I believe it reawakens their curiosity and imagination, and heightens their focus. It activates their right brain hemisphere.

The instructions are simple: Switch hands. Do every activity that you normally do with your right hand with your left hand (or switch to your right hand, if you're a leftie.) Unlock your door holding your keys in the opposite, non-dominant hand. Reverse right and left in everything else you do as well. If you normally put on your left pant leg first, switch to putting your right pant leg on first. Brush your teeth with your left hand. Feed yourself while holding the fork in your left hand. Doodle during class with your left hand.

See what happens if you keep this up for the entire day today or tomorrow. Be diligent. It requires more conscious participation than your automatic behavior does.

Work Until You're Done

One time I noticed that most of the students in my class were doing half a scene and then their energy was fading. So I polled them: "How many of you feel as though your scene work begins strongly and ends weakly?" They all raised their hands. "Why do you believe this phenomenon is happening?" I asked.

"Well, my scene partner and I rehearsed the first half more than the second half," one student replied, "Because that's where we started."

Another said, "I know the lines at the top of the scene better than at the bottom, because I memorized them sooner."

"There just wasn't enough time this week," answered a third.

"And how many of you feel that there is a defined beginning, middle, and end to your scene?" I subsequently asked. "Do you feel as though progress is made in the course of the scene or are you trying to end where you began or begin where you plan to end?"

They told me that they were frustrated. The scenes were one-noted. They weren't sure what to do about it. I reminded them about the seven Cs of acting: commitment, concentration, conditioning, control, confidence, courage, and clarity. Commitment to the rehearsal process is essential when you are at this stage of working on the text.

You have to be diligent and do as much work as necessary to satisfy yourself and satisfy the requirements of the scene. Otherwise, you will shortchange yourself and shortchange your audience. A casting director won't care about the reasons why you weren't able to do as much work as was necessary. The amount of work one actor needs to do versus the amount of work another actor needs to do may also differ. You shouldn't be compared. If you don't take the time, find the time, make the time, and stick with it, you are the one who will ultimately suffer. Insufficient diligence is reflected in the work.

On the other hand, it is a wonderful sign of progress when an actor begins to be aware of where he or she is in the rehearsal process. When actors can feel the roughness of the work-in-progress, they can use their craft to dive back into the text and get something more out of it—more life, more juice, more color, more variety.

Set aside your preconceptions. Use this Day 9 rehearsal to shake yourself up.

Your Day 9 Rehearsal Checklist

Have you completed your tasks?

- ☐ Drawing a Convoluted Script Tree
- ☐ Waking Up Your Creative Brain

What discoveries have you made?

DAY 10

To Memorize, Physicalize

The human body is a recording device, so it's tremendously important to rehearse lines physically. Too many actors do "butt acting," meaning they sit on their butts and read their lines on the page without ever getting up and moving around. This is insufficient if you really want to ingrain a speech in your muscle memory and take advantage of the flow of energy through your nervous system. Otherwise, later, if someone startles or interrupts you, you could forget your lines. Even new impulses and discoveries sometimes can cause an actor to lose the train of thought.

The Benefits of Physical Rehearsal

During graduate school at Temple University, I studied for six weeks with the famous Polish director Jerzy Grotowski. Through his touring troupe and his book *Towards a Poor Theatre*, he popularized a style of theatre in the 1970s that was based on an extremely active rehearsal process. My classmates and I discovered that Grotowski's actors never sat down. They were always jumping, bouncing, juggling, running around, and throwing things. To rehearse inactively was considered a waste of time.

Later on, when I taught workshops and directed at the Sedona Shakespeare Festival in Arizona in 1999 and 2000, I met an accomplished British director who was a graduate of the famed Moscow Arts Theatre in Russia. In his workshops, Robert Taylor reconfirmed and reiterated for me the importance of physical rehearsals.

The benefits of active rehearsing are physical, vocal, and emotional. First, this technique helps you remain open as long as possible (at least until Phase 4) to new movements you could try out on stage. Second, you may discover an interesting sound to adopt on a given line, such as panting or breathlessness coming out of your physical exertion. Third, a strong flow of emotions will inevitably begin to surge through you, once you get physical with your lines.

This type of rehearsal is especially good if you need to become more energized, to find some fresh vocal choices, or both. It cleans the slate and allows new impulses to arise. It is also good as a warm-up done prior to a rehearsal, a performance, or an audition.

Keep Lines Fresh, Discover New Rhythms

When I directed *Macbeth*, my lead actor broke his speeches down by end stops. He then wrote each section on three-by-five index cards that he carried with him when he went out jogging. For rehearsals, we devised a plan in which he did light activities (arm circles) on simple lines and heavy activities (pushups or jumping jacks) on high pressure, emotionally charged lines. His goal was to condition himself so thoroughly that he would have control and clarity even during the most strenuous scenes. By practicing in this manner, he kept the lines fresh for himself–while knowing that he had a repertoire of three or four excellent ways to say each line that satisfied the same intention, as well as knowing the proper breath and proper energy for each line. After the physical rehearsals, he would stand and deliver the lines in new and creative ways.

Similarly, two students in my class had been working for several weeks on a scene between Richard and Lady Anne from *Richard the Third*. When they got up to do an exercise of tagging each other with Nerf balls on their lines, something spontaneously happened that replaced false yelling. The pair looked at each other and every verbal nuance and intention, as well as the energy language, had simply fallen right into place. They started playing to win. They said, "Now we finally know what the scene is about!" Before the exercise she would only scream at him. Afterward, her voice was rich and just simply speaking her lines took on more intensity than when she was flailing and pushing and pretending. Her voice was full of subtle shadings. And, as she said her lines to him, he was impacted so intensely and was so devastated by her comments that he had to work harder to persuade her that it was her fault and that he had done what he did because he loved her. The scene was much more interesting for the audience to listen to and watch.

Borrowing a concept from yoga, consider that you need to condition yourself to find the proper breath and the proper energy–the *pranayama*–for your character in every scene. *Prana* is a Sanskrit word for the life force energy that permeates everything in the universe. When we breathe in different patterns, we embody different energy. *Pranayama* are the breathing exercises that yogis use to tap the life force they need. Similarly, the acting energy that brings a character to life has a rhythm, a pattern. Once you find this proper breath of life, your rehearsals will prepare you to live it on stage.

── Your Task—Getting Physical──

Speak your speech aloud while doing a physical activity–perhaps dancing, tossing Nerf balls against a wall (or back and forth with a scene partner), hopping on one foot, jogging, and so on. As soon as you begin putting a speech into your whole body, your whole body will start resonating with it, making your emotions more accessible and expanding your range of possible acting behavior.

A lot of actors have trouble relaxing and surrendering their expectations about how their lines "should" sound and what they "should" mean. Therefore, they don't indulge in as much of a discovery process as they otherwise could. That's where physical activity also comes in handy. It helps actors who are stuck or constricted to bypass the superficial layer of meaning in a scene and get into deeper layers and possibilities. The human body is very intelligent–much more intelligent, in fact, than the judging left hemisphere of the brain is on its own. Physical rehearsing helps actors tap into the right–or everything-is-possible–hemisphere of the brain by making them sweaty, breathless, and exhausted, so they have to let go. The body begins responding more organically, and less mentally, to what is happening on stage.

── Your Task—Singing Your Lines──

Just as dancing is heightened movement, singing is heightened speaking. Singing connects you more deeply to your breath, so it grounds your lines more deeply in your body. It opens up a new pathway of memorization that is deeper than what the intellect alone can offer.

Use any tune you like, or several. Rap your lines. Chant your lines. "Happy birthday" your lines, if you can't think of something else to sing. You may even sing your lines while physicalizing them! Do them to Tchaikovsky's "Dance of the Sugar Plum Fairy" and twirl around the room. Sing them as a country-western tune while you two-step.

As you do this type of rehearsal, allow the rhythm of your activity to influence the rhythm of your speech. It's possible that you'll discover more than you already know about the strong and weak stresses that exist within the verse.

Becoming a Strategist

Are you a baseball fan? Or have you ever played in a softball league? Perhaps you've observed two types of batters. The first type is a "slugger" who will swing at any pitch and try to hit it as hard as possible. The second type is a "strategist" who waits for the right pitch and has a plan for where to place the ball in the field. Sluggers are able to bat homeruns upon occasion. But strategists more consistently help their team. If you're doing the exercises in this book, the work will transform you into a strategist rather than a slugger.

Actors who are sluggers jump into their performances without any (or much) forethought. Strategists, on the other hand, have control of their body and voice–their physical and vocal instruments. They know how to make specific, reasonable choices while allowing the energy of life to flow like lightning through their body. The difference between the two kinds of actors has its roots in the rehearsal process, which lets the body's natural intelligence guide them to a successful approach.

When I asked an actor who played *Hamlet* and how his speeches should sound. But what really helped him prepare the famous "to be or not to be" speech (Act 3, Scene 1) was when he rehearsed on his own at home holding Hamlet's dagger. On lines where Hamlet was thinking about suicide (not being), he put the dagger to his chest. On lines that were about living (being) he pointed it away. These actions made the speech very dangerous.

The actor told me, "Using the dagger gave the speech urgency. I really understood that I could die *right now*. Then, all of a sudden, I would change my mind and decide to live." Choosing an action that was a symbol of his character's mental and emotional dilemma was the physical clue that unlocked his speech.

As his director, I didn't want his soliloquy to come across as a heavy-duty serious speech where Hamlet was just griping about the unfairness of life. He didn't. It actually ended up being positive and upbeat. He made it seem like death was the only solution. The audience went along and followed his thought process. "If I'm not going to avenge my father's death, then I should die too." He persuaded the audience that it would be a correct and ethical action. In performance, it also seemed like there was a dark humor to the speech. I found this quality very refreshing, because it made the audience want to listen to him, rather than tune him out as a complaining, whiney schoolboy.

You may not understand the power of this rehearsal today. That's OK, it will add up with everything else you're doing and pay off later.

It's purpose is to open a magic door to your emotional realm-your creative side that doesn't make assumptions or judge.

Your Day 10 Rehearsal Checklist

Have you completed your tasks?

☐ Getting Physical

☐ Singing Your Lines

What discoveries have you made?

DAY 11

Now, Go Ahead and Look It Up

Shakespeare was a highly inventive wordsmith. According to *The First Folio of Shakespeare 1623*, edited by Doug Moston, Shakespeare introduced over 1,700 words into the English language, though some of the words he coined never fell into common usage. To give you a notion of how dexterous he was with language, consider this: the First Folio uses approximately 34,000 distinct words, whereas the King James version of the Bible uses only close to 8,000. Some of Shakespeare's original words are archaic in nature, based on Ancient Latin or Greek roots. Others pertain to historical figures and events that have faded from popular awareness. As Moston says: "He used words in ingenious ways, employing nouns as verbs and inventing new words, not just as a means of being clever, but for precision."

Even people of Shakespeare's own day might not have understood everything he wrote. Like a contemporary hip-hop rapper inventing new slang, he knew that the audience doesn't have to follow the exact meaning of everything you say. The audience will understand the meaning of the lines you speak so long as you do. But they won't be able to follow you if they can tell that *you* don't know what you're saying. So you must research the words in your speeches and establish meaningful definitions.

﹈ DAY 11 ﹈

An example of how audiences can apprehend words that they don't comprehend is when Iago says to Rodrigo (*Othello*, Act 1, Scene 3):

IAGO   The Food that to him now is as lushious as Locusts, 1

     shalbe to him shortly, as bitter as **Coloquintida**. 2

The audience is likely to imagine he's referring to tequila. Coloquintida was actually a bitter apple drink that people would use to purge themselves. Be clear for yourself.

Here's another example. In Act 3 of *Hamlet,* in a speech to a group of actors, Hamlet gives instructions on the worst vices of performance and how to avoid them. One of the lines he says is: "I could have such a Fellow whipt for o're-doing Termagant." What does that mean? Well, upon investigation, we discover that Termagant was a stock character used in ancient Roman plays, whose main characteristic was shrieking. Hamlet wants his actors not to overdo what is already overdone. Aha!

Did Shakespeare's contemporaries understand this reference? Possibly. But possibly not! Modern audiences certainly don't. Put into the context of the entire speech, however, modern listeners can get a sense of the point Hamlet is making. This joke is sandwiched between similar statements. An actor's job is to make it's meaning clear.

Your previous rehearsals have led to the work you'll do today, which will help you achieve full memorization of your script. With Shakespeare, it's imperative that you never substitute your own words for the playwright's. If you catch yourself stumbling over a particular line, that's a clear indication of where this day's session may benefit you most.

From more information on ancient references in Shakespeare visit the website **www.willpowerthebook.com** and receive a free handout.

Befriend Your Dictionary

For today's rehearsal, I'm going to ask you to get nitty-gritty with your word definitions. Please make friends with a good dictionary and encyclopedia. Heightened, poetic words like *alas, methought,* and *forefend* were unusual even in Elizabethan England. So it's important not to play these words as though they are normal. You can be confident that Shakespeare knew they were special. He used such vocabulary to draw our attention to what was happening on stage or to demonstrate quirks in a character's personality. Poetic words also carry us up the Chain of Being (see Day 7).

Some words that seem weird to you may not be to those who possess a large vocabulary. Or perhaps the spelling in the First Folio is odd, but the sound is the same as the modern word. Here's an example from *The Comedy of Errors* (Act 3, Scene 1).

LUCIANNA   Apparell vice like virtues harbenger

I asked students in one of my classes what they thought a "harbenger" was and several guessed it was a bird. In contemporary English, a *harbinger* (spelled with an *i* instead of an *e*) is an omen—a person, an event, or a thing that foretells the coming of another. So a robin could be a "harbinger of spring," but so could be a crocus, which isn't a bird. If my students had consulted a dictionary, they'd have understood the line better right away.

Of course, you should never make assumptions about words that seem more ordinary than those above. From now on, strive to be precise about the meaning of everything you're saying. No word should be overlooked. Each word is a clue that can help you develop your portrayal and make rhetorical sense of the play for the audience.

A line spoken by Juliet in *Romeo and Juliet* (Act 3, Scene 2) contains a fine example of an "ordinary" word that has interesting significance:

…come civill night,	1
Thou sober suted **Matron** all in blacke,	2
And learne me how to loose a winning match,	3
Plaid for a paire of stainlesse Maidenhoods,	4
Hood my unman'd blood bayting in my Cheekes,	5
With thy Blacke mantle, till strange Love grow bold,	6
Thinke true Love acted simple modestie…	7

Most people believe they know what the word *matron* means. They'll tell you a matron is an older woman, a married woman, or a mother. If you look in the dictionary, you'll learn that a matron is a woman who supervises other women or children, the chief officer of a woman's organization, or a woman of the world. But you need to begin to ask: What did Shakespeare mean by that word—and, in this place?

In the speech we're exploring, Juliet is speaking to night personified. She bids it: "Come civill night." In a longer passage within the same speech that is not shown here, where she expresses her eagerness to be with Romeo, she contrasts images of passion and modesty. Here Juliet wonders about losing her virginity. Night is described as *civil* and *sober*, perhaps like a chaperone. But then Juliet asks for night to hide signs of her desire until she feels bolder. Earlier in the speech, Juliet compared night falling to a curtain rising on a stage.

Words can be clues to character. There are subtle differences between them. As a young actor, I was cast as Brick in Tennessee Williams' play *Cat on a Hot Tin Roof.* Noticing that all of the other characters kept repeating his name, "Brick, Brick, Brick," I decided to look up how bricks are manufactured. The encyclopedia taught me that they're made of mud and straw that's tempered: heated, molded, and pressed together. Well, I believe that manufacturing process describes an aspect of Brick's character: being under pressure–in this case to decide issues of his sexuality. For me, the name Bruce wouldn't have carried the same connotation.

——— Your Task–Looking Up Word Definitions———

Only now that you've already done so much analysis of the scripts should you go and look up any words you don't understand. Turn to the *Shakespeare Lexicon and Quotation Dictionary,* then a scholarly edition of your individual play that is known as a *variorum* (meaning it compares word structure from the First Folio, the Quartos, and other original sources), then to a well-annotated acting edition, and finally to the dictionary for information–in that order of preference. Then, if you still cannot ascertain a true meaning of a word, make one up so the word at least makes sense to you. (See the bibliography to locate all these different kinds of books and other sources of information.)

To accomplish this task, be organized. Get out a clean piece of paper and a pen. Make a list of each word you don't understand and of every word you would like to understand better. Leave a couple of lines of space between these items. You will need enough room to jot down some notes and observations. Then, next to each item on your list, write down your answers to the following questions:

1. What's the literal definition?
2. If it meant more than that, what would it mean?
3. What might Shakespeare have intended for it to mean in this speech or scene?
4. What does it mean to me?
5. Why did Shakespeare use this word when he could have any other word? (This is a particularly good question to ask when you feel stuck.)

Until you purposefully give it a meaning, a word is just a word. It's general. But good acting is specific. Specificity is the way to find nuances. It's the only way to get to an exact destination. Could you find your way home if you were just driving in a general direction? No. You need to make a left at the light, drive two miles, turn right at the stop sign, and so on. Completing this task is an opportunity to be responsible and independent, to claim your creativity, and to enjoy the satisfaction of being an actor.

Is a Monarch Always a Monarch?

Let's compare two women's speeches in which the image of a crowned monarch is employed to make a point. In Act 4, Scene 3 of *Othello*, Amelia tells Desdemona that she would sleep with a man other than her husband Iago in order to help Iago advance his career. In Act 4, Scene 1 of *The Merchant of Venice*, Portia explains why mercy is admirable in an effort to persuade Shylock to spare Antonio's life.

Even though the word *monarch* is the same, its meaning in these two speeches is quite different. A man whose wife had betrayed him was called a *cuckold*, and was said to grow horns. Horns are a kind of crown, because they grow on the head. In Amelia's speech, she compares two kinds of "monarchs"—a true king and a betrayed husband. Also, she knows that her husband will never be a real king, so the idea of a monarch is an exaggeration used to signify an elevation of his status.

1	AMELIA	Introth I thinke I should, and undoo't when
2		I had done. Marry, I would not doe such a thing for a
3		joynt Ring, nor for measures of Lawne, nor for Gownes,
4		Petticoats, nor Caps, nor any petty exhibition. But for
5		all the whole world: why, who would not make her hus-
6		band a **Cuckold**, to make him a **Monarch**? I should ven-
7		ture Purgatory for't.

In Merchant of Venice, Portia uses the image of a king and his crown to acknowledge Shylocks' legal authority (sovereignty) over Antonio—the two men had a contract that now entitles Shylock to a "pound of flesh." She is also using this image in an effort to entice Shylock to follow a more ethical and humane course of action. She favorably compares mercy to a crown, as both a possession and a quality of nobility.

1	PORTIA	The quality of mercy is not strain'd,
2		It droppeth as the gentle raine from heaven
3		Upon the place beneath. It is twice blest,
4		It blesseth him that gives, and him that takes,
5		'Tis mightiest in the mightiest, it becomes
6		The throned **Monarch** better then his **Crowne**.

As you can see, actors need to understand the plot of the play, the definition of words, and the way that Shakespeare was using specific words to achieve a purpose. It can be a lot of fun to daydream about your character's words and follow the paths they lead you down in your imagination. Doing this activity will help you unlock your character and your speeches.

Your Day 11 Rehearsal Checklist

Have you completed your task?

☐ Looking Up Word Definitions

What discoveries have you made?

DAY 12

Draft Your Newspaper Headlines

As the final technique in the transitional phase that lies between being on book and off book, your character needs to become *actable*. For this, it is important to understand your character's story, needs, and doings in your own words and simple terms, and also to be able to remember them under many different circumstances and kinds of pressure (e.g., auditions, performances, the coursing flow of life on stage, technical mishaps, and so on).

To Identify the Core Essence of a Speech or Scene

It is best to play the core essence of a speech or a scene, rather than your initial or superficial assumptions about it. This understanding can serve as an anchor for you in the face of pressure and distractions. When you get down to the core idea, it is usually so simple and straightforward that it's practically unforgettable.

It is vital to play each scene or monologue from moment to moment, rather than play the end at the beginning. Today's rehearsal might be the final step in ensuring that you are not getting ahead of yourself.

How can you get at that core essence? I suggest you try the following four writing assignments. The essence (hidden and underlying meaning) can be discovered through the verbal conceits (the vowels, consonants, and metaphors) in what's being said. This technique is well illustrated in a series of lines delivered by Portia in Act 2, Scene 1 of *Julius Caesar*.

Just prior to this exchange, which takes place in the garden of Portia and Brutus' home, Brutus has met with a group of conspirators hatching a scheme to assassinate Caesar, Rome's emperor. Brutus has been swayed to participate by reason of a forged letter handed to him by a manservant at the top of the scene. He has assumed a leadership role in the plan. Yet, he still has shades of doubt about its legitimacy, which is probably why he is unwilling to admit what's going on to his beloved wife. Portia is no dummy, however. She's already figured out that something strange is afoot. She just doesn't know what! Therefore, we, the audience, are made privy to the ensuing dialogue.

PORTIA	Deare my Lord,	1
	Make me acquainted with your cause of greefe.	2
BRUTUS	I am not well in health, and that is all.	3
PORTIA	*Brutus* is wise, and were he not in health,	4
	He would embrace the meanes to come by it.	5
BRUTUS	Why so I do: good *Portia* go to bed.	6
PORTIA	Is *Brutus* sicke? And is it Physicall	7
	To walke unbraced, and sucke up the humours	8
	Of the danke Morning? What, is *Brutus* sicke?	9
	And will he steale out of his wholsome bed	10
	To dare the vile contagion of the Night?	11
	And tempt the Rhewmy, and unpurged Ayre,	12
	To adde unto his sicknesse? No my *Brutus*,	13
	You have some sicke Offence within your minde,	14

15		Which by the Right and Vertue of my place
16		I ought to know of: And upon my knees,
17		I charme you, by my once commended Beauty,
18		By all your vowes of Love, and that great Vow
19		Which did incorporate and make us one,
20		That you unfold to me, your selfe; your halfe
21		Why you are heauy: and what men to night
22		Have had resort to you: for heere have beene
23		Some sixe or seven, who did hide their faces
24		Even from darknesse.
25	BRUTUS	Kneele not gentle *Portia*.
26	PORTIA	I should not neede, if you were gentle *Brutus*.
27		Within the Bond of Marriage, tell me *Brutus*,
28		Is it excepted, I should know no Secrets
29		That appertaine to you? Am I your Selfe,
30		But as it were in sort, or limitation?
31		To keepe with you at Meales, comfort your Bed,
32		And talke to you sometimes? Dwell I but in the Suburbs
33		Of your good pleasure? If it be no more,
34		*Portia* is *Brutus* Harlot, not his Wife.
35	BRUTUS	You are my true and honourable Wife,
36		As deere to me, as are the ruddy droppes
37		That visit my sad heart.
38	PORTIA	If this were true, then should I know this secret.
39		I graunt I am a Woman; but withall,
40		A Woman that Lord *Brutus* tooke to Wife:
41		I graunt I am a Woman; but withall,
42		A Woman well reputed: *Cato's* Daughter.

Thinke you, I am no stronger then my Sex	43
Being so Father'd, and so Husbanded?	44
Tell me your Counsels, I will not disclose 'em:	45
I have made strong proofe of my Constancie,	46
Giving my selfe a voluntary wound	47
Heere, in the Thigh: Can I beare that with patience,	48
And not my Husbands Secrets?	49

——— Your Task—Drafting Your——— Newspaper Headlines

First, write three sentences that explain your speech or dialogue. For our example:

1. Portia comes out in the middle of the night and finds Brutus, whom she cajoles and seduces in an efffort to get him to tell her what happened, who was involved, and any other secrets he may be hiding from her.
2. Then, she tells him off.
3. Lastly, she proclaims her uniqueness as his wife in order to force his hand.

Second, write two sentences about your speech telling what you need. For our example:

1. Portia comes out and sees her husband in trouble, upset and suffering.
2. She needs to know what happened in order to help him.

Third, write one sentence that tells you what you're doing. For our example:

1. Portia interrogates Brutus by every method (e.g., feminine wiles, yelling, reasoning).

And, fourth, write a banner headline for a sensational newspaper like *The New York Post* (e.g., "Ivana Dumps Trump"). This gives you the core essence. For our example:

PORTIA PRODS! BRUTUS BLABS?

After you've finished this fourth step of script evaluation, please go back to your lines. Say them aloud–while listening carefully–and notice if they are now colored differently by your new understanding. Do your lines have more clarity? Are you more committed? Do you feel more confident? Later on, when you're selecting internal actions to pursue, I suspect you'll be grateful to be carrying this information in your pocket.

The Beginning, the Middle, and the End

In class, I asked my students, "How many of you feel as though you are playing the end of the scene at the beginning?" Without hesitation they all raised their hands. It was clear to me and to them that they had not yet mastered this process. But I didn't want them to be discouraged, and you shouldn't be either. Today's rehearsal cannot help but make your work more specific and clear. The simple act of writing down a definition of the scene on paper will show you how much variety there is from moment to moment. Endeavor to play the moment in front of you honestly, and the scene will divide naturally.

Your Day 12 Rehearsal
Checklist

Have you completed your task?

☐ Drafting Your Newspaper Headlines

What discoveries have you made today?

PHASE 3

Charting Your Course

Moments of Variety and Nuance

Your goal in Phase Three of the rehearsal process is to find the unique and special clues that bring your character to a brilliant focus. Now that you're off book, your work process is going to become more subjective. However, you are still going to be exploring your character as Shakespeare wrote it. The variety and nuance you develop here will help you to locate and tap the core of your character, and to embody the character's humanity. Every single role in Shakespeare's canon is an individual with an individual rhythm. Rhythm equals motion, and motion equals emotion. Once you find that rhythm, your character will come across as completely different from every other one, as intended.

Most actors stop long before this phase of rehearsal. But if you stick with the process, this is an opportunity for you to be special and shine brightly. Of course, every exercise won't pertain to every character you'll play, but it is definitely worth experimenting. Mix and match techniques. Use one technique to develop a favored way to speak one sentence and use another technique to handle another sentence. At this point, you've thoroughly memorized your script and you're off book, so life, energy, and emotions are flowing through you. Nonetheless, it's important not to make these next six steps an intellectual exercise. Keep aiming for greater clarity. Be open-minded.

DAY 13

Playing with the Pace

Drawing upon the clues that Shakespeare provided in the First Folio text for members of his acting company, you will learn to recognize which types of lines sound better if they are spoken quickly, slowly, or at an average conversational pace. Settling upon your character's rhythms–and picking special places to change tempo–can keep the script fresh and surprising. Many actors have a tendency to speak Shakespeare's lines too slowly and choppily, perhaps because the plays are poetically written and that's intimidating. Or maybe their tongues stumble over the unfamiliar words and sentence constructions. Picking up the pace is not only a matter of speeding nimbly through individual words, however. It's also about matching the speed of your character's thought patterns. Most of Shakespeare's characters think fast, and therefore they speak economically–meaning with no stutters, chopping, or extra sounds, like *uh*, *um*, and *er*. Whether the speaker is a clown or a prince, he says what he means to say.

So let's play. To begin today's rehearsal, take a close look at the three lines below from *Anthony and Cleopatra* (Act 5, Scene 2). Read them silently on the page, scanning for punctuation, line counts, repeated vowel and consonant sounds, capital letters, verbs, images, and any other clues that spontaneously come to mind from previous rehearsals.

1 CLEOPATRA   I dreamt there was an Emperor Anthony.
2   Oh such another sleepe, that I might see
3   But such another man.

Then, read the lines aloud, at a quick pace. Listen. How does it make you feel?

Wouldn't you agree that it seems entirely wrong? Cleopatra is reflecting upon a glorious dream in a highly emotional (vowel-laden) manner. Are dreams rapid? Is sleep rapid? Is desire rapid? No. She's fantasizing, so a more appropriate pace would be slow–slow and smooth–relishing "Emperor Anthony" and the sound of "Oh."

Now, go ahead and read Cleopatra's lines one more time at that new pace. Better?

To be sure, speed of delivery (the aspect of performance that's known as pace, tempo, and rhythm) is different from the quality with which you're speaking. Smoothness and sharpness are two polar opposite qualities that often influence an actor's tempo. When you are speaking in a legato manner, your words are velvety smooth and flow one into the next–a style that's commonly associated with a slower pace. When you are speaking in a staccato manner, your words are clipped, abrupt, and separate–a style that's commonly associated with a quicker pace. There are instances where either sounds ridiculous. So staccato and legato should be used selectively.

Consider this brief exchange from Act 5, Scene 1 of *The Merchant of Venice*. First read the lines aloud slowly. Then read them aloud quickly.

MESSENGER	I pray you is my Master yet return'd?	1
LORENZO	He is not, nor we have not heard from him…	2

When you read the Messenger's question and Lorenzo's answer in either one of those two ways (quickly or slowly) didn't it seem as though it was necessary to add an emotional or circumstantial spin on them, like extreme haste or depression? Neither was plotted for that scene. Remember to use an average pace to handle straightforward lines that simply communicate information, such as this snatch of dialogue.

You can also recognize an average-paced line because it isn't heightened poetry. Anyone you met on the street today could say it and it wouldn't sound weird. A little later in the same scene from *The Merchant of Venice*, Lorenzo's wife Jessica says:

JESSICA   I am never merry when I heare sweet musique.

That's straightforward communication if I ever heard it. Said slowly it would come across as melodrama–making a mountain out of a molehill. Said fast, the audience would furrow their brows and respond, "Huh? What did she say?"

Quick-paced lines might include the following example from Act 1, Scene 5 of *Macbeth*. Here the Scotsman is contemplating an assassination. Read the lines out loud at a conversational speed. Don't put any spin on them yet.

MACBETH	If it were done, when 'tis done, then 'twere well,	1
	It were done quickly…	2

What did you notice when you read the words? No doubt you observed that the words are monosyllabic, except for "quickly" in line 2. What could this tell you about the appropriate pace? Most times when a character uses simple words, the lines may be said rapidly. But in lines composed of monosyllabic words like these, all the words should be given equal emphasis, slowing down your pace a bit. When words are polysyllabic, the character (and the actor) is usually struggling to articulate more complex ideas and therefore the words may need extra airtime. But think about it logically: Should *quickly* be said slowly? I wouldn't do that because of the meaning. *Quickly* indicates speed!

An additional clue about the pace here is that Macbeth is eliding his words. Instead of saying "It is" he says "'Tis," and rather than "It were" he says "'Twere." As you may recall from Day 3, elision is a clue to think, speak, and act faster.

Now, these two lines almost form a tongue twister, which calls for extra care in articulation–perhaps a staccato style. When you spoke the speech, I am sure you heard the numerous *W* sounds (*were, when, were, well,* and *were*), *T* sounds (*it, 'tis, 'twere,* and *it*), and the three repetitions of the word *done*. Back on Day 1, we noted how consonants reveal a character's state of mind. If Macbeth wants this task to be done, finished, over, complete, resolved, behind him, and so forth, would he lollygag and loiter in saying so? Probably not. That's another clue in favor of a quick, possibly staccato, delivery.

Clues for Determining Shakespeare's Intended Pace

Are there general rules of thumb about pace in Shakespeare or should an actor's decision about tempo be primarily based on common sense? Let's take a closer look.

EXTRA COUNTS (METER)

Sometimes the number of counts per line, a characteristic of the Bard's poetic language that you learned to scan on Day 3, is helpful in determining pace. Regular iambic pentameter (a masculine rhythm) often indicates an average rate of speed. But when a character is cramming eleven counts (a feminine rhythm) and twelve counts (an Alexandrine rhythm) into ten-count lines, especially if done frequently, he or she may be excited and in a rush. In such instances Shakespeare probably meant, "Speed up!" It's as though the character's mouth can barely keep up with the thoughts, which are flowing faster than normal. Use the extra count at the end of a feminine line (the weak-stressed syllable) to keep propelling a thought forward.

REPEATED SOUNDS

If you are conditioned to handle the sounds embedded in your script, you can almost hear their onomatopoetic implications when you speak them, and that's a clue to pace. *Onomatopoeia* is when a word sounds like what it means, such as *sizzle* or *hum*. Repeated sounds contribute to the sensation they give us.

In Act 3, Scene 2 of *Romeo and Juliet,* Juliet has an onomatopoetic line that gives the listener the feeling of horses running speedily, with burning urgency, "immediately." "Gallop apace" sounds like a horse galloping, doesn't it? "Whip to the west" implies the crack of a whip over the horses' backs commanding them to run faster. Juliet is eager!

JULIET	Gallop apace, you fiery footed steedes,	1
	Towards *Phoebus* lodging, such a Wagoner	2
	And bring in Cloudie night immediately.	3

CAPITALIZED WORDS

By way of contrast with Macbeth's line that we previously evaluated ("If it were done, when 'tis done…"), here's a more slowly paced line composed of single-syllable words from *Othello* (Act 5, Scene 1):

OTHELLO   Put out the Light, and then put out the Light…

Wouldn't you agree that the line requires a slow delivery, one that's probably legato? When you say it too fast it sounds as though you're about to break out into a Vaudeville song and dance routine. What's most important is the repetition of "Light." The first statement "Put out the Light" may mean something mundane, such as, "Blow out the candle." The repetition of that phrase means, "Kill Desdemona." You want to let the audience see your characters' realization of that strong distinction and the true import of "Light."

PUNCTUATION

From Act 3, Scene 2 of *Hamlet*, let's look at another line of single-syllable words. In my opinion, this one would sound like a Chipmunks' song if it were spoken too fast. Fortunately, the commas interrupt an otherwise breakneck tempo.

HAMLET   Go too, I'le no more on't, it hath made me mad.

Here, as elsewhere, the commas indicate no blending of the words they separate. It leads to better phrasing. A comma is not a complete stop, like a period would be. The line is still lifting and the thought it communicates is still moving forward.

VERBS

In most of the examples given so far in today's rehearsal the verbs have held important clues for us about the character's mental and emotional pace. Let's review a few. Cleopatra's verb was *to dream* (slow). Macbeth repeated *done, done, done* (quick). And Juliet's verbs were *to gallop, to whip,* and *to bring* (quick). Always keep an eye peeled for verbs and their implication for the pace.

IMAGERY

Like verbs, descriptive words, such as adjectives and adverbs, and descriptive concepts, such as metaphors and analogies, offer us mental pictures that are accompanied by pace. For instance, take this speech from Act 1, Scene 2 of *Julius Caesar*:

CASSIUS	He had a Feaver when he was in Spaine,	1
	And when the Fit was on him, I did marke	2
	How he did shake: 'Tis true, this God did shake,	3
	His Coward lippes did from their colour flye,	4
	And that same Eye, whose bend doth awe the World,	5
	Did loose his Lustre...	6

The image of someone so wracked by fever that he is shaking with chills and possibly a seizure (a fit) is a fast-paced image. But Shakespeare changes it up soon enough: by line 6, with "loose his Lustre," the tempo is already shifting and being drawn out more.

CLARITY

Pace must always be determined by clarity. Without clarity, any scene is dead, flat, and essentially lifeless. Heart pumping rhythms– da-dum da-dum da-dum da-dum da-dum–are a way to find the flow of the energy and the rhetoric, so that the character comes to life. But iambic pentameter alone falls short of indicating the pace–and so do the other grammatical clues we've explored. To determine an appropriate pace you have to look at the words and their meaning. If you don't understand the text, neither will the listener. That's why I saved this step for Phase Three.

Pace is an aspect of energy language. When you breathe fully and correctly, and you commit to the musicality of Shakespeare's sounds, you can communicate the words he wrote at an appropriate speed. Don't just pick any pace–use Shakespeare's built-in pace. He's given his characters a range of possibilities in different moments.

As Enobarbus describes Cleopatra's barge in *Anthony and Cleopatra* (Act 2, Scene 2), the actor could begin to pick up a rhythm that resembles the rhythm of oarsmen rowing in unison. The speech also contains images of lovemaking and slowly heightening arousal. Throughout, an irregular rhythm interrupted by commas and a semi-colon near the end of the thought (conclusion of line 3) provides many creative dramatic options.

1 ENOBARBUS With them the Owers were Silver,
2   Which to the tune of Flutes kept stroke, and made
3   The water which they beate, to follow faster;
4   As amorous of their strokes.

You could do a lot with that speech just by varying the tempo.

The Power of Pace

Working to find the built-in shifts in the pace of a scene can be an incredibly effective performance strategy. For example, in Act 3, Scene 4 of *Othello*, Cassio meets his lover Bianca in the street. She hasn't seen him lately and is either on her way to find him or accidentally spies him going about his business. The trouble is that Bianca feels jealous and neglected by Cassio. She yearns for his affection. The scene begins:

BIANCA	'Save you (Friend *Cassio*.)	1

Bianca's elision of the standard Elizabethan greeting "God save you" to "Save you" indicates she is in a rush–a fast pace. Probably she spotted Cassio and is trying to catch up to him. When she gets his attention midline, her pace can change–probably it slows down. This is indicated by the parentheses around "Friend Cassio." He responds:

CASSIO	What make you from home?	2
	How is't with you, my most faire *Bianca*?	3
	Indeed (sweet Love) I was comming to your house.	4

Line 2 might be of average speed, since it's a straightforward question. Or, in this case he may be abrupt because he is surprised to see Bianca. But then he shifts gears–probably slowing down like she did halfway through line 1. He realizes that what he just said is no way to talk to the woman he loves, so he pours on some sugar. He's backtracking from a bad first impression. Then, the scene shows two entranced lovers making goo-goo eyes at each other in the moonlight. Bianca is slowly paced, until she suddenly remembers on line 6 that she's been neglected. Her delivery could then become rapidly paced, as she plies Cassio with a sequence of accusatory questions.

BIANCA	And I was going to your Lodging, *Cassio*.	5
	What? keepe a weeke away? Seven dayes, and Nights?	6
	Eight score eight houres? And Lovers absent howres	7

8	More tedious then the Diall, eight score times?
9	Oh weary reck'ning.

Perhaps she slows down on "weary," as she has an incomplete line there that Cassio finishes with a comparable "leaden" (heavy) thought. Tired and heavy are slow-paced concepts, so it could sound odd to say them quickly. But trust Shakespeare not to leave the audience drowning in depression. Cassio picks up the pace first by saying the equivalent of "But forget about it" (lines 12–13) and then making a request (line 14). So within four lines the actor could vary his pace from slow to quick to average.

10	CASSIO	Pardon me, *Bianca*:
11		I have this while with leaden thoughts beene prest,
12		But I shall in a more continuate time
13		Strike off this score of absence. Sweet *Bianca*
14		Take me this worke out.

Now, because Cassio is carrying the intimate possession (a handkerchief) of a woman whom she immediately assumes is her rival, when he asks her to copy the embroidery on the handkerchief, Bianca gets angry. What's her pace going to be? Look at the *O*s on line 15–those might sound woeful and heartbroken said slowly. But then, having decided she's been betrayed, the actress could pick up the pace again.

15	BIANCA	Oh *Cassio*, whence came this?
16		This is some Token from a newer Friend,
17		To the felt-Absence: now I feele a Cause:
18		Is't come to this? Well, well.

CASSIO	Go too, woman:	19
	Throw your wilde gesses in the Divels teeth,	20
	From whence you have them. You are jealious now,	21
	That this is from some Mistris, some remembrance;	22
	No, in good troth *Bianca.*	23
BIANCA	Why, who's is it?	24
CASSIO	I know not neither:	25
	I found it in my Chamber,	26
	I like the worke well; Ere it be demanded	27
	(As like enough it will) I would have it coppied:	28
	Take it, and doo't, and leave me for this time.	29
BIANCA	Leave you? Wherefore?	30
CASSIO	I do attend heere on the Generall,	31
	And thinke it no addition, nor my wish	32
	To have him see me woman'd.	33
BIANCA	Why, I pray you?	34

When you see many vowel sounds, like in line 34, you can be sure the line carries emotion and is paced slower. The line also has a comma in it, another clue to elongate the first word "whyyy," a choice that allows you to relish the moment and slow the pace.

CASSIO	Not that I love you not.	35
BIANCA	But that you do not love me.	36
	I pray you bring me on the way a little,	37
	And say, if I shall see you soone at night?	38
CASSIO	'Tis but a little way that I can bring you,	39
	For I attend heere: But Ile see you soone.	40
BIANCA	'Tis very good: I must be circumstanc'd.	41

As you can see, if you scan the meter of the text, there is plenty of room to play physical business, such as on line 18 ("Is't come to this? Well, well."), which is an incomplete line–and there's a second clue in the repeated word–and line 30 ("Leave you? Wherefore?"), which is a half-line. Remember that a half-line can be stretched to fill ten counts, or the words can be followed by silence. If I were playing Bianca, I'd perform one quickly and the other slowly for variety. There are other incomplete lines in the remainder of the scene, and choices must be made.

The section of the scene extending from line 34 to line 40, where nearly every word is monosyllabic (the exceptions are "little" and "attend"), is also interesting. Monosyllables could indicate a shift in the pace–perhaps slowing down the delivery of the words, as Bianca might if she was attempting to seduce Cassio. Maybe she could stroll around him and use the handkerchief as a device to tease him, or she could whisper her lines in his ear. Of course, by the end Cassio agrees to come back and meet her, or go with her (offstage) so they can make out. They exit together.

During rehearsals with a scene partner the speed of your responses is dependent to a degree on how your partner says his or her lines to you. It's not so exciting to see two actors constantly using the same rhythms as each other. If one is fast, it can be interesting for the other to be slow. Or visa versa. Remember: A slow pace should never result in a low-energy performance! You need to be vital no matter what speed you're going. Your scene partner's energy is your launching pad just as your energy is your partner's launching pad. Be accountable for your own pace and energy, but keep it flowing.

Ultimately, to determine pace you must use all the clues you've been given by Shakespeare and found in the preceding days of rehearsal. These include meter, rhymes, punctuation, consonants and vowels, capital letters, verbs, descriptive words and phrases (adjectives, adverbs, metaphors), and whether or not the words are monosyllabic (simple) or polysyllabic (complicated). Then, make a choice. Do something only you could have done based on your imagination. Commit, concentrate, and be courageous.

—— Your Task—Mixing Up the Pace ——

Vary your pace as you perform your lines in order to make discoveries. For instance, try saying one of your lines staccato (sharp and quick) and then saying another legato (slow and elongated). Then do the opposite. As much as possible, your ultimate pace should be based on the meaning of the words in the text—on clarity. But sometimes opposites work well on stage, so being perfectly literal is not necessarily the only or best choice. Find a clear choice. Your goal in this task is to find variations, so that your ultimate delivery of the speech will contain plenty of contrasting moments and colors. For this task, mix it up—a lot.

Play one sentence, or one part of a sentence (such as an aside) differently than the next. Then, see what happens when you play the same moment at two different paces. For instance, there's a two-count pause written in following the word "Why" in *Measure for Measure* (Act 3, Scene 1):

CLAUDIO	Now sister, what's the comfort?	1
ISABELLA	Why,	2
	As all comforts are: most good, most good indeede...	3

You may recall this scene from the Day 3 rehearsal, where we looked at how Claudio and Isabella continually finish each other's thoughts. Claudio's line here is incomplete and gets finished by Isabella, but, even so, the total of the two lines combined only achieves eight counts. As an actress, this presents you with a decision on line 2. Because of the two counts that naturally follow it, you could elongate the word why so that its duration is three counts (a slow pace), "Whyyyyyyy?" Or you could say it quickly on one count and then be silent for an interval of two counts.

Verbal Gymnastics

Let's agree that your goal when speaking is to paint verbal pictures. Until your physical instrument—your tongue, your lips, your jaw, your lungs, and so on—is properly conditioned, you won't have as many options of different paces as you'd like. Pace provides color. You can load more colors onto your palette by learning how to relax and open up your breathing apparatus, and by exercising your vocal muscles.

The Secret of Perfect Prefixes

If you want to reach the back row in any size theatre, you need to make the most out of your articulation of three prefixes: en-, in-, and un-. How? All you have to do is specifically emphasize that smallest part of a word. Really hit the N sound. Don't slow down, just make sure the listener hears it. In an audition setting, possessing this technical skill truly impresses casting directors, as it's a major clue that you know how to handle language well. This puts you in an elite category of actors.

EN-forc't thee? Art thou king and wilt be forc't?

> (Queen, *Henry the Sixth, Part Three*, Act 1, Scene 1)

...who (for the most part) are capeable of
nothing, but **IN**-explicable dumbe shewes, and noise

> (Hamlet, *Hamlet*, Act 3, Scene 2)

I live distain'd, thou **UN**-dishonoured.

> (Adriana, *The Comedy of Errors*, Act 2, Scene 2)

Looke, here is writ, kinde *Julia*: **UN**-kinde *Julia*...

> (Julia, *Two Gentlemen of Verona*, Act 1, Scene 2)

O that I were a man! what, beare her in hand untill they
come to take hands, and then with publike accusation
UN-covered slander, **UN**-mittigated rancour?

> (Beatrice, *Much Ado about Nothing*, Act 4, Scene 1)

—— Your Task—Tuning Your Tongue ——

To become a more adroit articulator, I highly recommend that you practice tongue twisters every day. Before you begin the vocal work, I suggest you give the sides of your jaw a quick massage. Put your hands flat on your cheeks and open your mouth wide without straining, and then let everything go slack. Dig into tense muscular areas with your thumbs and fingertips, using small circular motions. Gently massage your temples, along the jaw hinges in front of your ears, and around the lower edge of your chin. Continue for about two minutes. It should feel good. Finish by sticking your tongue out as far as it can go and holding it there for five seconds.

When you're done, read some of the following tongue twisters aloud. This list includes old, familiar stalwarts that I've collected over the years from different sources, in addition to some newer favorites. Repeat each tongue twister at least ten times, starting gradually and slowly increasing the pace, until you're tripping up your tongue. Push yourself past the current level of your abilities. At the end, make note of which ones were the most challenging for you. Those deserve extra attention in future warm-up sessions.

A
Alice asks for axes
Able Andrew arced an arrow accurately at an amazing angle

B
Bad black bran bread
Bluebeard's blue bluebird
Bland Bea blinks back

C
Cheap sheep soup
Cinnamon aluminum linoleum

D
Does the doctor who doctors doctors doctor them diligently?
Did dumb Dora dip her thumb down deeply?

E
The enemy eats eight anemones
The epitome of femininity

F

Friendly fleas and huffy fruit flies

A fat-free fruit float

G

Greek grapes

Gig-whip

Cows graze in groves on grass that grows in grooves

H

The hare's ear heard ere the hair heeded

Hot Hottentots' tots hold hands wholesomely

I

Ike ships ice chips in ice chip ships

Why does my eye spy the wise guy I despise?

J

The jubilant jester jumped joyful jumping jacks

K

Keenly cleaning copper kettles

Kris Kringle carefully crunched on candy canes

L

Lemon lime liniment

Listen to the local yokel yodel

M

Much-mashed mushrooms are marvelous

Many mumbling mice are making merry music in the moonlight

My dame hath a lame tame crane

N

Any noise annoys a noisy oyster

Nine nice night nymphs nibbled nuggets

O

Awful old Ollie oils oily autos often

Under the mother otter uttered the other otter

P

Poor pure Pierre pissed off a pack of pesky pixies

Please pay Peter Peterson promptly

Q

The Queen coined quick clipped quips

Quick kiss, quicker kisser

R

Rigid rugged rubber baby buggy bumpers

Round and round the rugged rocks the ragged rascal ran

Rosco the rumrunner rubbed out Rudy the rat for ruining
    his rum receipts

S

The sixth Sheik's sixth sheep's sick

Strange strategic statistics

The sea ceaseth seething

T

Thrash the thickset thug

Tea for the thin twin tinsmith

A Tudor who tooted a flute tried to tutor two tooters to toot

U

Unique New York

Hugh used a used igloo to snooze

V

Valuable valley villas

Vincent vowed vengeance very vehemently

W

Real Swiss wristwatch straps

War weary warriors

Which witch wished which wicked wish?

X

"Extra, extra!" Exton exclaimed excitedly

Ezekiel exactingly axed the extra axioms

Y

Young Yankees yank yellow yo-yos

Z

Zithers slither slowly south

Zebras zig and zebras zag

—— Your Task—Relishing Your Reading ——

Now that you're properly warmed up, spend half an hour or so reading out loud from Shakespeare's plays. Read speeches or sections of speeches not because they were assigned to you for high school English class or because you have an audition looming on the horizon, but to see how well you can articulate the words and make them sound meaningful. Use them as if they were tongue twisters, to get you in the habit of wrapping your vocal instrument around rich, evocative language. Here are three particularly intriguing and complex passages, which I've chosen to help you improve your verbal dexterity with different vowel and consonant sounds.

HENRY   (*Henry the Sixth, Part Three*, Act 5, Scene 6)

1   I Dedalus, my poore Boy Icarus,
2   Thy Father Minos, that deni'de our course,
3   The Sunne that sear'd the wings of my sweet Boy.
4   Thy Brother Edward, and thy Selfe, the Sea
5   Whose envious Gulfe did swallow up his life:
6   Ah, kill me with thy Weapon, not with words,
7   My brest can better brooke thy Daggers point,
8   Then can my eares that Tragicke History.

QUEEN   (*Henry the Eighth*, Act 2, Scene 4)

1   Sir, I am about to weepe; but thinking that
2   We are a Queene (or long have dream'd so) certaine
3   The daughter of a King, my drops of teares,
4   Ile turne to sparkes of fire.

CHORUS   (*Henry the Fifth*, Act 3, Scene 1)

Now entertaine conjecture of a time,	1
When creeping Murmure and the poring Darke	2
Fills the wide Vessell of the Universe.	3
From Camp to Camp, through the foule Womb of Night	4
The Humme of eyther Army stilly sounds;	5
That the fixt Centinels almost receive	6
The secret Whispers of each others Watch.	7
Fire answers fire, and through their paly flames	8
Each Battaile sees the others umber'd face.	9
Steed threatens Steed, in high and boastfull Neighs	10
Piercing the Nights dull Eare: and from the Tents,	11
The Armourers accomplishing the Knights,	12
With busie Hammers closing Rivets up,	13
Give dreadfull note of preparation.	14
The Countrey Cocks doe crow, the Clocks doe towle:	15
And the third howre of drowsie Morning nam'd,	16
Prowd of their Numbers, and secure in Soule,	17
The confident and over-lustie French,	18
Doe the low-rated English play at Dice;	19
And chide the creeple-tardy-gated Night,	20
Who like a foule and ougly Witch doth limpe	21
So tediously away. The poore condemned English,	22
Like Sacrifices, by their watchfull Fires	23
Sit patiently, and inly ruminate	24
The Mornings danger: and their gesture sad,	25
Investing lanke-leane Cheekes, and Warre-worne Coats,	26
Presented them unto the gazing Moone	27

28 So many horride Ghosts. O now, who will behold
29 The Royall Captaine of this ruin'd Band
30 Walking from Watch to Watch, from Tent to Tent;
31 Let him cry, Prayse and Glory on his head:
32 For forth he goes, and visits all his Hoast,
33 Bids them good morrow with a modest Smyle,
34 And calls them Brothers, Friends, and Countreymen.
35 Upon his Royall Face there is no note,
36 How dread an Army hath enrounded him;
37 Nor doth he dedicate one iot of Colour
38 Unto the wearie and all-watched Night:
39 But freshly lookes, and over-beares Attaint,
40 With chearefull semblance, and sweet Maiestie:
41 That every Wretch, pining and pale before,
42 Beholding him, plucks comfort from his Lookes.
43 A Largesse universall, like the Sunne,
44 His liberall Eye doth give to every one,
45 Thawing cold feare, that meane and gentle all
46 Behold, as may unworthinesse define.
47 A little touch of Harry in the Night,
48 And so our Scene must to the Battaile flye:
49 Where, O for pitty, we shall much disgrace,
50 With foure or five most vile and ragged foyles,
51 (Right ill dispos'd, in brawle ridiculous)
52 The Name of Agincourt: Yet sit and see,
53 Minding true things, by what their Mock'ries bee.

Some experts assert that William Shakespeare himself played the role of the Chorus in *Henry the Fifth* because the language is so complex and rhythmically variable that only he could have properly handled it. I don't know about that, but I do know that all the lines of the Chorus are worth practicing. If you like the preceding speech, try others.

Your Day 13 Rehearsal Checklist

Have you completed your tasks?

☐ Mixing Up the Pace

☐ Tuning Your Tongue

☐ Relishing Your Reading

What discoveries have you made?

DAY 14

Finding Your Focus

Because there were no directors in Shakespeare's day, he told the actors through his text where to look when they were on stage. You might say he was taking a cinematic approach. He thought in pictures and, so, informed the actor where to place the "camera." Audiences tend to imagine what the actor is seeing: that is the power of focus. A typical mistake that actors make is putting their complete attention permanently on the person to whom they are speaking or fixating their gaze entirely on the back wall of the theatre. This eye lock limits their range of choices, produces speech composed of fewer colors, and keeps them stuck in one spot. However, if actors purposefully shift their focal point during the course of a speech or scene, they can reflect different attitudes, opinions, and feelings about whatever they're debating–and it's much easier to move around the playing area.

When you change your point of focus, you change your point of view and also speak with greater vocal variety. Shifting focus helps you to form new thoughts, which then can be shared with the audience. You are allowing the audience to see what you see, think, and feel, as it is written on the screen of your face and body, and in your voice.

The Three-Sided or Thrusting Elizabethan Stage

The best seats in the house today are front and center, just as they were in 17th century theatres, as people sitting in that location have an unimpeded view of the actors on stage throughout the entire play. But no one wants to look at the actors' backs for too long. Shakespeare understood the commerce of theatre. He knew he had to be fair to the people in the less desirable seats or they wouldn't come to see his productions. Therefore he gave his actors plenty of opportunities to change the audience's picture of them. One of the strategies he relied upon was instructing the actors to change their focal points.

Plays in the Elizabethan era were presented during the daytime in open-air theatres because they were reliant upon natural lighting. Citizens from every economic class attended plays and paid prices for seating in various ranges of affordability. The least expensive tickets allowed someone to stand on the ground right in front of the stage. Less well-off people milled about in this courtyard and, therefore, were known as the groundlings. If you've ever attended a free out-door rock festival, you've experienced a similar scene. The groundlings would have walked back and forth to get closer to the action. They ate, talked, and heckled the actors. Nobility had reserved seats in the area known on contemporary seating charts as the "center orchestra." Producers' seats! The mid-priced seats were located on three sides of the stage—right, center, and left.

The stage at the Globe Theatre in London was thrust forward into the U-shaped bowl of the seating. Two big pillars held up a 28-foot high ceiling. Upon occasion these would be worked into a pro-duction—actors used them as hiding places or trees, for instance. The set at the Globe was permanent and it possessed a few special features. It had two levels, and the top level could be used to represent a balcony, the ramparts of a castle, or a secondary location. The stairs behind the scenes leading up to the second level were a great route for a dramatic entrance or exit. The floor of the stage had three built-in trap doors, which could be used as the gateway to a dungeon, as hiding places, or as an entrance/exit for demons and devils. The two main exits were big doors located far upstage. There were also two side exits, normally used as the entrance point for messengers and servants in the plays. Sometimes players entered through the audience, making it seem as though the audience was involved in the life on stage.

Visit **www.willpowerthebook.com** to see images of the Globe Theatre.

The action on stage never stopped. As one scene was ending and its characters were moving off through one exit, a new scene was beginning with characters entering from another direction. Like cross-fades in a movie, the action was fluid and overlapping. Blocking within scenes was also constantly being modified to draw in the audience.

A convention of Shakespearean theatre is that the downstage area is private space, like a bedroom, or intimate scene. In a movie, downstage scenes would be shot as closeups. The nearer the action is to the audience, the more the audience feels let in on a secret world. When you are doing a truly intimate scene, such as a love scene, you can make the scene go to a "closeup" by holding the gaze of the one person with whom you're acting. But the rest of the time you need to share your eyes with the audience. The convention also holds that the upstage area is public space, such as court, a throne room, or a banquet hall. In a movie these would be filmed as establishing images or long-range shots.

Downstage Markers

Downstage markers are specific people, places, images, and things that are not on stage with you but are referred to in your speech. You need markers to focus your gaze. If you don't have them your eyes may wander, leading to a network of dysfunction. As Scott Kaiser, author of *Mastering Shakespeare*, states, "When your eyes wander your physical energy is not focused. When your physical energy is not focused, you don't have enough breath support. When you lack appropriate breath, your voice lacks resonance. When your voice lacks resonance, your speech also lacks vocal variety." Everything you say comes out as one long, flat statement. Then a performance seems generalized and no one will want to pay attention to you! So pick your markers

If you select three downstage markers—and therefore you're facing forward, rather than sideways in profile—an additional benefit is that audience members in every part of the house can always see both of your eyes.

Blocking Using Strong Focal Points

The triangle is the strongest geometric figure. Stage directors have found that diagonal planes are more visually exciting to the audience than horizontal and vertical planes, because they cut through the playing space like a triangle. In addition, as the actors turn their bodies and heads to shift their gaze, the audience is afforded a different angle on the performance. The audience sees a profile, a front view, a back view, another profile, and so on, as the picture on stage is altered for their entertainment.

Here's an example of how you might work with this concept. It's Tamora's speech from *Titus Andronicus* (Act 2, Scene 3). What you need to know about the plot, for the purpose of understanding the following suggestions for her blocking, is that she's asking her two sons to kill a pair of young lovers, and all four of those other characters (sons and lovers) are on stage with her.

The Stage

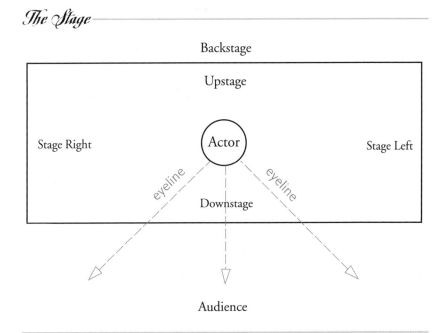

Imagine the points of Tamora's triangle as downstage right (the young lovers), downstage left (the two bad boys), and front and center, above the audience's heads (the forest). On line 1, the actress playing Tamora would look right on "reason" and left on "you." On line 2, she'd look right again on "these two" and then center on "this place."

Remember, the purpose of selecting downstage markers is to open the actor's face, especially the eyes (the windows of his or her world), to the audience so that they can see what's truly going on inside the character. What's the character thinking and feeling?

On line 6, Tamora might use a fourth location, perhaps pointing down at her feet, for special emphasis: "Heere never shines the Sunne, heere nothing breeds." On line 8, she'd shift her focus to the right again on "they shewed me..." And so it would continue. Her constant shifting from point to point would be highly dramatic.

If you were playing Tamora, where might you choose to shift your gaze again if you were using those same focal points?

TAMORA	Have I not reason thinke you to looke pale.	1
	These two have tic'd me hither to this place,	2
	A barren, detested vale you see it is.	3
	The Trees though Sommer, yet forlorne and leane,	4
	Ore-come with Mosse, and balefull Misselto.	5
	Heere never shines the Sunne, here nothing breeds,	6
	Unlesse the nightly Owle, or fatall Raven:	7
	And when they shew'd me this abhorred pit,	8
	They told me here at dead time of the night,	9
	A thousand Fiends, a thousand hissing Snakes,	10
	Ten thousand swelling Toades, as many Urchins,	11
	Would make such fearefull and confused cries,	12
	As any mortall body hearing it,	13
	Should straite fall mad, or else die suddenly.	14

15	No sooner had they told this hellish tale,
16	But strait they told me they would binde me here,
17	Unto the body of a dismall yew,
18	And leave me to this miserable death.
19	And then they call'd me foule Adulteresse,
20	Lascivious Goth, and all the bitterest tearmes
21	That ever eare did heare to such effect.
22	And had you not by wondrous fortune come,
23	This vengeance on me had they executed:
24	Revenge it, as you love your Mothers life,
25	Or be ye not henceforth cal'd my Children.

Now let's look at the focus and blocking in a scene from *The Tempest*. Ferdinand is one of several sailors shipwrecked on the shores of an island inhabited only by Miranda, her father Prospero, the slave Caliban, who is half-man and half-fish, and the magical spirit Ariel. In Act 3, Scene 2 Ferdinand, only the second man that Miranda has ever seen, is attempting to seduce her. Can you imagine how he might slowly approach her until line 10, at which point he is probably very, very close to her? His lines basically tell her, "Ooh, baby, baby, I want you."

1	FERDINAND Admir'd *Miranda*,
2	Indeede the top of Admiration, worth
3	What's deerest to the world: full many a Lady
4	I have ey'd with best regard, and many a time
5	Th' harmony of their tongues, hath into bondage
6	Brought my too diligent eare: for severall vertues
7	Have I lik'd severall women, never any

With so full soule, but some defect in her	8
Did quarrell with the noblest grace she ow'd,	9
And put it to the foile. But you, O you,	10
So perfect, and so peerlesse, are created	11
Of everie Creatures best.	12

For her part, with Ferdinand breathing down her neck, imagine that Miranda is intrigued, but responds chastely. She might look downstage right as she begins her speech—placing the search for an image of her mother there, as a memory. Then she might face center stage and address Ferdinand directly on line 15 "Nor have I seene…" And then turn downstage left—placing the image of her father Prospero there as a marker—on line 17, just for "And my deere father." Then she might turn right back to Ferdinand on line 17, after the colon.

MIRANDA	I do not know	13
	One of my sexe; no womans face remember,	14
	Save from my glasse, mine owne: Nor have I seene	15
	More that I may call men, then you good friend,	16
	And my deere Father: how features are abroad	17
	I am skillesse of; but by my modestie	18
	(The jewell in my dower) I would not wish	19
	Any Companion in the world but you:	20

On line 18, can you see how it might be effective for Miranda to literally walk away from Ferdinand—possibly upstage to a more public/less intimate zone of the stage—as she says, "but by my modestie (the jewell in my dower)"? Then, she might turn back and face Ferdinand again on line 19 "I would not wish…"? Miranda could turn again to the marker of her father (downstage left) on line 22, when she says, "but I prattle…"

21	Nor can imagination forme a shape
22	Besides your selfe, to like of: but I prattle
23	Something too wildely, and my Fathers precepts
24	I therein do forget.

The result of this conversation is that the couple pledges themselves to one another with Prospero looking on from the sidelines where they do not notice him.

——— Your Task—Establishing Three——— Primary Focal Points

Select three diverse downstage markers on varying angles from each other–perhaps far right, far left, and downstage center–and experiment with allowing yourself to perceive specific images in those locations. The idea is to create a variety of dramatic pictures for the audience, rather than eyelocking straight ahead on the back wall of the theatre behind their heads, and also to discover what kind of emotional life and color these focal points bring to your work.

Consider two questions while you're doing this task. Is one group of focal points exactly the same as another? Why does it matter where you look on a specific line?

Once you have established your three primary focal points it will be critical to maintain them in performance. Today, however, you're going to move your three primary focal points around the space. Pick one set of three and do the speech. Pick another three and do the speech. Pick a third set of focal points and do the speech again. How does one triangle of focal points color your speech and behavior differently than another?

If you were playing Lady Percy in *Henry the Fourth, Part Two,* and you had to deliver her famous speech from Act 2, Scene 3, where she begs Lord Northumberland, her father-in-law, not to go to war, you would notice that your focal point can change your internal action—the verb you are playing as an actor on a specific line. (We'll explore this concept in greater detail on Day 20, "Your Doings.") Prior to the speech, Northumberland had failed to join her husband in the battle where he, Harry Percy, died.

LADY PERCY Oh yet, for heavens sake, go not to these Warrs;	1
The Time was (Father) when you broke your word,	2
When you were more endeer'd to it, then now,	3
When your owne Percy, when my heart-deere *Harry,*	4
Threw many a Northward looke, to see his Father	5
Bring up his Powres: but he did long in vaine.	6
Who then perswaded you to stay at home?	7

If Lady Percy looks directly at Lord Northumberland on the line 6 words "but he did long in vaine," the line become a challenge, an accusation that he abandoned his son and that she is very angry about it. But if Lady Percy looks forward—out towards the audience—at a focal point the actress has chosen to represent her memory of her husband, the line evokes sympathy and remorse for the fact that Northumberland failed to show up in the battle. It's a regretful mistake, a persuasion rather than a threat. The first focal point enables the actress to portray "I challenge him." The second enables her to portray "I remind him." As you can see, these choices support distinct actions.

Your Day 14 Rehearsal
Checklist

Have you completed your task?

☐ Establishing Three Primary Focus Points

What discoveries have you made?

DAY 15

Surely, You Jest

Humor is a dignified way of dealing with life's difficulties. Among the other qualities of humor, it helps to unlock and relieve the audience's pain. Shakespeare used humor a lot in his plays–even the tragedies. In a tragedy, humor provides momentary relief and contrast to the darker moments. No matter what character you're playing, there will always be verbal jokes and physical jokes. He gave his clowns lots of pratfalls and stage business, such as double takes and false exits. But he gave them to his leading actors, too. For those less familiar with the plays, it could come as a surprise that he also dearly loved dirty jokes and sexual innuendo. In today's rehearsal, we'll explore numerous facets of humor, including jokes meant to be heard, and jokes meant to be watched. Many jokes are meant to be both seen and heard.

It is imperative to know the kind of comedy you are playing so you can make the joke without diffusing its power. If your joke is purely verbal and you move a muscle, no one will laugh! Research has revealed that in face-to-face spoken communication 55 percent of the message comes across through body language, 37 percent comes from tone of voice, and only 8 percent comes from the words that are said. That's why your actions and voice must always suit the text. Strive to decode your comedy.

Verbal Jokes

When two characters are arguing or debating a point of interest, allow your character to enjoy each new moment. As we discussed on Day 2 when we talked about sound and word repetitions, Shakespeare's characters typically fall into three categories: clever, witty, or mwah-ha-ha mad. Characters can be intelligent without being laughing out loud funny. They also can be witty even if they're not too bright. He wrote many of his jokes for a silly sensibility—one that everyone could understand. But Shakespeare's characters love to play games. Even his murderous arch villains demonstrate a kind of terrible dark humor. So think of your speech or scene as being part of a game of one-upmanship. If they are amused by your antics, the audience will pay attention and keep score. If they are not amused, you can be sure you've disappointed them to a degree.

Some actors have an unfortunate tendency to make negative choices and play them into the ground. A negative choice is one that stops the plot from building and moving forward. In Act 2, Scene 1 of *The Taming of the Shrew* (the scene we looked at in detail on Day 1), a common pitfall for the actress playing Kate is to insult her Petruchio on every line. But if the actress starts out angry with Petruchio, she'll have nowhere to go, except to be even louder and angrier, and the audience will abandon her.

1 PETRUCHIO Good morrow *Kate*, for that's your name I heare.

2 KATE Well have you heard, but something hard of hearing:

We know right away, from the ha-ha-ha-ha sound repetition, that Kate could be laughing. (She could also be out of breath from running over to him.) She's a clever woman. Even though she's acting on the surface as though she doesn't like him, she probably does find him attractive, because she's spending time and energy sparring with him. If she was repulsed by Petruchio or found him dull the play would end right then. An actress in the role needs to make a positive choice, one that keeps the play moving forward. Positive in this context doesn't mean playing the role as all-smiles-all-the-time. It means that there's something built into the character's perception that leaves room for interaction. Unless Petruchio wins the game of wits, he won't win her heart.

Interestingly, women in Shakespeare's plays tend to get the clever jokes and men tend to get the "groaners." Although the legal, economic, and social status of women in Elizabethan England was subordinate to that of men, Shakespeare loved to show women outfoxing men and being funny in the process. From the cleverness of his female characters, it appears he loved women. But whether or not you think the jokes you're telling are good or bad ones, you have to treat them like they're the best ever told. Approach groaners with as much relish and commitment as you imagine David Letterman or Jay Leno would.

Let's look at a few more lines from the same scene in *The Taming of the Shrew*. Notice the words *moved, movable,* and *remove*, which are printed in **bold** type.

PETRUCHIO	Thy vertues spoke of, and thy beautie sounded,	1
	Yet not so deeply as to thee belongs,	2
	My selfe am **moov'd** to woo thee for my wife.	3
KATE	**Mov'd**, in good time, let him that **mov'd** you hether	4
	Remove you hence: I knew you at the first	5

6		You were a **movable**.
7	PETRUCHIO	Why, what's a **movable**?
8	KATE	A joyn'd stoole.

Just to be clear, Kate has made a dirty joke. She's referencing a three-legged stool ("a joyn'd stoole"), which means she's saying that when Petruchio wants to woo her for his wife he is only being guided by his male anatomy–lust–and she's not interested. How the repeated words sound can make or break the listener's appreciation of the wit. It's not the punch line so much as how the actors arrive at it that gives us our pleasure.

There is one other possible meaning for this sentence that I can think of, which wouldn't involve her making a sexual reference: Perhaps she is saying the first thing that pops into her mind. Shakespeare might have set it up that way so that Petruchio could make a bawdy joke on the next line:

9 PETRUCHIO Thou hast hit it: come sit on me.

If you were playing the role of Kate, you would have to settle upon an interpretation.

Words have different weights. The weight of a word can be defined as the distance between the first and last consonant. For instance, the word *move* might be said literally on one count, comically on three counts *mooove*, farcically on six counts *moooooove*, and absurdly on nine counts *moooooooooove*. In order to sustain a word for additional counts, technically you elongate the vowels or diphthongs.

Pause in your reading right now and try out the different styles. Listen. Changing the weight of a word changes its emotional level and fortifies the actor's intentions (we'll look at this again on Day 20, "Your Doings").

The Weight of a Word ———————————————————————

The Weight of a Word

Literal	Mov'd
Comical	Mooov'd
Farcical	Moooooov'd
Absurd	Moooooooooov'd

Only bold actors can pull off the broadest comedy because it requires confidence. You have it in you, now that you know the secret of weighting your words.

O Is for Overdone

Whenever you find the word "O" (or "Oh") in your lines, you have to at least consider the possibility that it's intended as a funny moment. There is a fine line between comedy and tragedy depending on the weight given to the vowel. For instance "O woe" might be said literally in a tragedy or farcically in a comedy. In *Henry the Fourth, Part One* (Act 2, Scene 3), perhaps there could be a tinge of femme fatale in Lady Percy when she finds her husband alone in the middle of the night. Maybe it's the way she leans up against the door-frame or seats herself in his lap like a kitten, as much as her tone of voice, that lets us all know for a moment what she's got in mind.

LADY PERCY O my good Lord, why are you thus alone?

Lovesick people seem to say "O" a lot. Berowne, for instance, says it six times in *Love's Labours Lost* (Act 3, Scene 1). Costard, on the other hand, says it only has once. His jokes have to do with money. Maybe he loves cash? And maybe he is teasing Berowne by emulating Berowne's way of lovesick speaking? Before this scene he received a half penny farthing as remuneration for his services. At the end of this scene he receives a guerdon, which is more valuable. That's when Costard says "O."

 1 BEROWNE   O my good knave *Costard*, exceedingly well met.
 2 COSTARD   Pray you sir, How much Carnation Ribbon
 3   may a man buy for a remuneration?
 4 BEROWNE   What is a remuneration?
 5 COSTARD   Marrie sir, halfe pennie farthing.
 6 BEROWNE   O, Why then three farthings worth of Silke.
 7 COSTARD   I thanke your worship, God be wy you.
 8 BEROWNE   O stay slave, I must employ thee:
 9   As thou wilt win my favour, good my knave,
10   Doe one thing for me that I shall intreate.
11 COSTARD   When would you have it done sir?
12 BERWONE   O this afternoone.
13 COSTARD   Well, I will doe it sir: Fare you well.
14 BEROWNE   O thou knowest not what it is.

COSTARD	I shall know sir, when I have done it.	15
BEROWNE	Why villaine thou must know first.	16
COSTARD	I wil come to your worship to morrow morning.	17
BEROWNE	It must be done this afternoone,	18
	Harke slave, it is but this:	19
	The Princesse comes to hunt here in the Parke,	20
	And in her traine there is a gentle Ladie:	21
	When tongues speak sweetly, then they name her name,	22
	And *Rosaline* they call her, aske for her:	23
	And to her white hand see thou do commend	24
	This seal'd-up counsaile. Ther's thy guerdon: goe.	25
COSTARD	Gardon, O sweete gardon, better then remuneration,	26
	a levenpence-farthing better: most sweete gardon.	27
	I will doe it sir in print: gardon, remuneration.	28
	[*Exit.*]	
BEROWNE	O, and I forsooth in love,	29
	I that have beene loves whip?	30

Witty Banter

When two characters are funny and feel like enjoying themselves, they both crack jokes and the comedy builds. The same formula is frequently used in situational comedies on television, such as *Seinfeld* or *Roseanne*, where everyone has a smart mouth and a quirky personality. Even when a brief scene serves to inform the audience of an advance in the plot, like the following encounter from *Two Gentlemen of Verona* (Act 1, Scene 1), where Speed finds out his boss has left town, Shakespeare takes time to slip in some humor.

1 SPEED   Sir *Protheus*: 'save you: saw you my Master?

2 PROTHEUS But now he parted hence to embarque for *Millain*.

3 SPEED   Twenty to one then, he is ship'd already,

4   And I have plaid the Sheepe in loosing him.

5 PROTHEUS Indeede a Sheepe doth very often stray,

6   And if the Shepheard be awhile away.

7 SPEED   You conclude that my Master is a Shepheard then,

8   and I Sheepe?

9 PROTHEUS I doe.

10 SPEED   Why then my hornes are his hornes, whether I

11   wake or sleepe.

12 PROTHEUS A silly answere, and fitting well a Sheepe.

13 SPEED   This proves me still a Sheepe.

14 PROTHEUS True: and thy Master a Shepheard.

15 SPEED   Nay, that I can deny by a circumstance.

16 PROTHEUS It shall goe hard but ile prove it by another.

17 SPEED   The Shepheard seekes the Sheepe, and not the

18   Sheepe the Shepheard; but I seeke my Master, and my

19   Master seekes not me: therefore I am no Sheepe.

20 PROTHEUS The Sheepe for fodder follow the Shepheard,

21   the Shepheard for foode followes not the Sheepe: thou

22   for wages followest thy Master, thy Master for wages

23   followes not thee: therefore thou art a Sheepe.

24 SPEED   Such another proofe will make me cry baa.

After 18 repetitions of the words *sheep* or *shepherd*, most audiences truly enjoy hearing Speed say "Baa" like a farm animal. They thoroughly appreciate the ridiculous logic of the proofs for and against

Speed being a sheep. It's a rhetorical debate, even if it's nonsense, and they are working hard to win. The men are playing a game for their own amusement, and listeners are allowed to participate. Speed is a regular, if slightly irresponsible guy who needs to get back on the job after taking a detour behind his boss' back. It's easy to relate to him and his circumstances as a working class rascal.

Watching a lower status person sassing someone of a higher rank and power over him or her can be funny. Insults in a play, insults that wouldn't be tolerated in real life, may be offered with humor, and the audience appreciates the social barrier being broken. The same scene gives us this example of Speed teasing Proteus:

PROTEUS	Beshrew me, but you have a quicke wit.	1
SPEED	And yet it cannot overtake your slow purse.	2

Similarly, it can be funny to see the nun Isabella stand up to the evil Angelo in *Measure for Measure* (Act 2, Scene 2) even though she's not a clown.

ISABELLA	...Oh, it is excellent	1
	To have a Giants strength: but it is tyrannous	2
	To use it like a Giant.	3

Straight Men and Funny Men

Another kind of verbal humor involves one character, the "straight man," feeding opportunities for humor–questions and naive comments–to another character, the "funny man." A classic comedy team that used this setup was George Burns and Gracie Allen, whose signature repartee was, "Say goodnight, Gracie." "Goodnight Gracie."

In *Twelfth Night* (Act 3, Scene 1), Viola–in disguise as a teenage boy–engages Feste, the Clown, in conversation while she's running an errand for the Duke. Although she doesn't pretend to be ignorant or dimwitted, as Allen charmingly did in the Burns-Allen sketches, she does feed him questions as if they are having a logical discourse. (Just so you don't have to wonder, a *tabor* is a small drum and "Live by" has double meaning: "way to earn money" or "reside next to.") The exchange begins when the Clown chooses to misinterpret Viola's question. She plays along with his game.

1	VIOLA	Save thee Friend and thy Musick: dost thou live
2		by thy Tabor?
3	CLOWN	No sir, I live by the Church.
4	VIOLA	Art thou a Churchman?
5	CLOWN	No such matter sir, I do live by the Church: For,
6		I do live at my house, and my house dooth stand by the
7		Church.
8	VIOLA	So thou maist say the Kings lyes by a begger, if a
9		begger dwell neer him: or the Church stands by thy Tabor,
10		if thy Tabor stand by the Church.
11	CLOWN	You have said sir: To see this age: A sentence is
12		but a chev'rill glove to a good witte, how quickely the
13		wrong side may be turn'd outward.
14	VIOLA	Nay that's certaine: they that dally nicely with
15		words, may quickely make them wanton.
16	CLOWN	I would therefore my sister had had no name Sir.
17	VIOLA	Why man?

CLOWN	Why sir, her names a word, and to dallie with	18
	that word, might make my sister wanton: But indeede,	19
	words are very Rascals, since bonds disgrac'd them.	20
VIOLA	Thy reason man?	21
CLOWN	Troth sir, I can yeeld you none without wordes,	22
	and wordes are growne so false, I am loath to prove reason	23
	with them.	24
VIOLA	I warrant thou art a merry fellow, and car'st for	25
	nothing.	26
CLOWN	Not so sir, I do care for something: but in my con-	27
	science sir, I do not care for you: if that be to care for no-	28
	thing sir, I would it would make you invisible.	29

Can you find the secret formula for rhetoric that we explored on Day 8 in this scene? In addition to using questions and answers, the pair of comedians involved in this Shakespearean interlude use agreements and disagreements to keep the banter flowing. They must maintain the word play and keep it aloft–like a ball they are tossing back and forth–until it reaches a conclusion or changes direction. Then it has to have a whole new build to another equals sign $(1 + 1 + 1 + 1 = 4)$.

———— Your Task—Playing the Verbal Jokes————

Look for your verbal jokes (puns and witty banter). Do you have the chutzpah, or the nerve, to play the comedy fully? Or are you going to iron out the text and make each line sound like every other line? Is your character the straight man to another character's funny man? Be courageous.

Jokes serve many purposes, such as being an icebreaker, getting people to like you, teasing, impressing, flirting, and begging for money or forgiveness. Could they even be a way of disguising your character's authentic character, such as a female character might do if she wanted to be perceived as one of the guys? Once you've identified your character's verbal jokes, determine what action you're playing on them.

Physical Jokes

As we've discussed elsewhere, Shakespeare incorporated stage directions in his speeches. He also often wrote verse lines that are several counts short of ten syllables. If another character in your scene does not have a line that completes yours (meaning that the character is not supposed to jump right in and speak at the end of your line), this half-line ending leaves space for you to do some funny stage business. You'll find space for humor by reexamining the punctuation, verbs, and word meanings in your lines.

Physical comedy produces laughter using visual behavior and sometimes props. For instance, Shakespeare clearly intended for the audience to watch as well as hear Launce in *Two Gentlemen of Verona* (Act 2, Scene 3). At 33 lines in length and written in prose, Launce's speech is filled with colons but only has two end stops. That means he is supposed to just say the lines and keep them moving along. They have to build without letting the debate of the rhetoric come to a conclusion. This performance piece was inserted purely to stop the play and entertain the audience. Here's a sample:

1 LAUNCE   This shooe is my fa-

ther: no, this left shooe is my father: no, no, this left   2

shooe is my mother: nay, that cannot bee so neyther: 3

yes; it is so, it is so; it hath the worser sole: this shooe   4

with the hole in it, is my mother: and this is my father:...5

Right away, he's funny. He's got his shoes off his feet to make an explanation. But he gets distracted. He can't make a decision about which shoe is in worse shape and merits to be which parent. We hear the pun of using the word *sole* to mean *soul.* The audience is getting a royal laugh at his expense. He's definitely not acting very smart in this passage, although he may be trying to be clever. But he *is* funny.

A potential clue that you're being given the permission and the freedom to act funny is that the text is written in prose.

Scenes in Shakespeare serve one of three purposes. They develop character, they advance the plot, or they entertain. Sometimes they serve two or three of these purposes. In *The Comedy of Errors* (Act 3, Scene 2), it could be argued that we are being given pure entertainment. When the servant Dromio comes running onstage fleeing a woman the audience hasn't seen yet, Antipholus asks him to describe her. Nell is so fat, answers Dromio, that she looks perfectly round like a globe. From there, the two men enter into a dialogue about the map that is her body. The physical jokes must match the words.

DROMIO   No longer from head to foot, then from hippe   1

                to hippe: she is sphericall, like a globe: I could find out 2

                Countries in her.   3

ANTIPHOLUS In what part of her body stands *Ireland?*   4

DROMIO   Marry sir in her buttockes, I found it out by   5

                the bogges.   6

7	ANTIPHOLUS	Where *Scotland*?
8	DROMIO	I found it by the barrennesse, hard in the palme
9		of the hand.
10	ANTIPHOLUS	Where *France*?
11	DROMIO	In her forhead, arm'd and reverted, making
12		warre against her heire.
13	ANTIPHOLUS	Where *England*?
14	DROMIO	I look'd for the chalkle Cliffes, but I could find
15		no whitenesse in them. But I guesse, it stood in her chin
16		by the salt rheume that ranne betweene *France*, and it.
17	ANTIPHOLUS	Where *Spaine*?
18	DROMIO	Faith I saw it not: but I felt it hot in her breth.
19	ANTIPHOLUS	Where *America*, the *Indies*?
20	DROMIO	Oh sir, upon her nose, all ore embellished with
21		Rubies, Carbuncles, Saphires, declining their rich Aspect
22		to the hot breath of Spaine, who sent whole Armadoes
23		of Carrects to be ballast at her nose.
24	ANTIPHOLUS	Where stood *Belgia*, the *Netherlands*?
25	DROMIO	Oh sir, I did not looke so low…

Dromio needs to show us all where the "countries" are. What is going on when he is talking about her buttocks, the "barrennesse" in the hand, the forehead and hair ("heire"), the "chalkle cliffes," her hot breath, and so forth? Does "the Netherlands" refer to Nell's private parts? You could use it as a pun. Perhaps the actor crosses his arms over his crotch to indicate extreme (and clearly false) modesty when he says line 25.

Casting choices can support a joke like this one—for instance, by casting Nell with a man who looks like a goliath in a fat suit with a funny wig and a bad shave. And if Dromio is a very skinny actor or an extremely short actor, the visual contrast of the two of them standing side-by-side gets a laugh later. We've heard so much about Nell by then that we really want to see her in the flesh. Clowns often look funny. Or they know how to let us see them as funny, like Chris Rock rolling his eyes or smiling sarcastically.

False Exits

As soon as Benedick realizes and proclaims his love for Beatrice in *Much Ado About Nothing* (Act 4, Scene 2) she sends him on an errand to restore the good name of her young cousin Hero. They concoct a scheme together, and then off he goes…or does he? An actor playing Benedick might use the colons in his parting speech as occasions for three false exits. Why would he turn back? Perhaps he's so infatuated with Beatrice at this point that he just can't tear himself away from her presence. False exits are shown in **bold** in this speech.

> BENEDICK   Enough, I am engagde, I will challenge him, I   1
> will kisse your hand, and **so leave you:** by this hand *Claudio* 2
> shall render me **a deere account:** as you heare of me,   3
> so **thinke of me:** goe comfort your coosin, I must say she 4
> is dead, **and so farewell.**   5

Now, to be fair, some directors don't like false exits and some actors can't pull them off. If you're of that ilk, you must find some other comedic behavior to insert here. On each colon Benedick might switch places to stand on a different side of Beatrice. Whatever places you decide to do be courageous. Commit 100 percent to the choice you make so you can see if it really buys you laughs from your audience. If it doesn't, try something else.

Part of the reason audiences find this bit of the scene so amusing is that Benedick is a romantic lead and a warrior, and his behavior has changed with his emotions. We laugh because he's out of control and we've all been there before ourselves.

Malapropisms and Blunders

Nothing makes an audience feel better than being smarter than someone on stage. We love it when we can pick out poorly used words, especially when someone embraces a misunderstood term, such as the Constable does in *Much Ado About Nothing* (Act 3, Scene 5), and tries to use it to impress. Here, we are in on the joke with Leonato. The Constable is unsophisticated and pompous. He believes he's received a compliment. He's clearly trying to flatter Leonato, his superior in social status, and therefore there is an opportunity for the actor portraying him to use ingratiating body language—perhaps bowing in a manner as overly flowery and equally unsuitable as his comments.

1	LEONATO	Neighbours, you are tedious.
2	CONSTABLE	It pleases your worship to say so, but we are
3		the poore Dukes officers, but truely for mine owne part,
4		if I were as tedious as a King I could finde in my heart to
5		bestow it all of your worship.
6	LEONATO	All thy tediousnesse on me, ah?
7	CONSTABLE	Yea, and 'twere a thousand times more
8		than 'tis, for I heare as good exclamation on your Worship

as of any man in the Citie, and though I bee but a   9

poore man, I am glad to heare it.   10

Exceedingly bad acting is something else the audience relishes, especially when some of the characters onstage make jokes about it, as they do in watching the infamous play within the play from *A Midsummer Night's Dream* (Act 5, Scene 1). Here a group of bumbling tradesmen, who have been rehearsing in the forest since Act 1, finally get to do their rendition of a romantic tragedy (not unlike *Romeo and Juliet,* except terrible) for the nobles. Remember that men in drag would have played all the parts in Elizabethan times. "Bad" costumes, "bad" words, and "bad" acting are being combined here–if you add "bad" casting to the mix, this "bad" production can be really wonderful to watch.

First Piramus, the hero, believes a lion has killed his beloved Thisby, and so he takes out his sword and stabs himself. His death scene is prolonged. Count the meter. It switches from iambic pentameter to another, more singsong rhyme scheme on line 5. The character playing Piramus breaks even that scheme when he adds an extra word to his last line before–finally–dying. Instead of taking six counts to "dye," which would fit, he says "dye" five times and he's two counts short. Each one is a ripe opportunity for melodrama. What in the world could he do while dying for so long? If you play this role, it's up to you.

PIRAMUS   O wherefore Nature, did'st thou Lions frame?   1

                        Since lion vilde hath heere deflour'd my deere: 2

                        Which is: no, no, which was the fairest Dame   3

                        That liv'd, that lov'd, that like'd, that look'd with cheere.4

5	Come teares, confound: Out sword, and wound
6	The pap of *Piramus*:
7	I, that left pap, where heart doth hop;
8	Thus dye I, thus, thus, thus.
9	Now am I dead, now am I fled, my soule is in the sky,
10	Tongue lose thy light, Moone take thy flight,
11	Now dye, dye, dye, dye, dye.

One of the comments made in response to the terrible overacting is:

DUKE   With the help of a Surgeon, he might yet recover…

Not much further on in Act 5, Scene 1, another tradesman comes on portraying Thisby, who is very much alive. She finds her beloved Piramus dead and also decides to take her life. The rhymes, the repetitions, the punctuation, and the malapropisms ("These Lilly Lips, this cherry nose," "His eyes were green as Leekes"), as well as the attempt at romantic sophistication by concluding her death scene in French ("Adieu, adieu, adieu") give an actor so many levels of humor with which to work. In addition, the character playing Thisby has got the body of Piramus as a prop for his activities. And…since the character playing Piramus is supposed to be a really bad actor…maybe he's not so good at playing dead either. You must invent your physical jokes.

1	THISBY	Asleepe my Love? What, dead my Dove?
2		O *Piramus* arise:
3		Speake, speake. Quite dumbe? Dead, dead? A tombe
4		Must cover thy sweet eyes.
5		These Lilly Lips, this cherry nose,

These yellow Cowslip cheekes	6
Are gone, are gone: Lovers make mone:	7
His eyes were greene as Leekes.	8
O Sisters three, come, come to mee,	9
With hands as pale as Milke,	10
Lay them in gore, since you have shore	11
with sheeres, his thred of silke.	12
Tongue not a word: Come trusty sword:	13
Come blade, my brest imbrue:	14
And farwell friends, thus *Thisbie* ends;	15
Adieu, adieu, adieu.	16

Situational Comedy

Shakespeare has built visual jokes into the plots of some of his plays. It's as though he's asking: What happens when you bring a group of men of diverse natures together under strange circumstances, such as in *The Tempest* (Act 2, Scene 2)? Maybe their misperceptions and habits will conflict, and maybe they will also propel the plot forward. This is the basis of situational comedy. Here the humor is absolutely determined by the character, and the visual joke fuels an erroneous understanding that leads to new actions.

After a storm Caliban has been sent out by his master Prospero to collect firewood when he sees Trinculo, a shipwrecked sailor, coming along the beach. Thinking Prospero has sent a spirit to torment him for being lazy, Caliban falls to the ground and attempts to hide under his coat. As another storm threatens Trinculo decides to seek shelter underneath Caliban's body. Caliban's legs are sticking out in one direction and Trinculo's legs are sticking out in the other direction.

Then the drunken Stephano enters the scene singing a bawdy tune–probably in a terrible voice. Caliban responds to stop the torment, thinking again that this is Prospero's way of punishing him. His twice repeated "oh" could sound like howls or groans–very animal. As a result Stephano believes he has met a four-legged monster. To tame the "monster," he schemes to get Caliban drunk.

1	CALIBAN	Doe not torment me: oh.
2	STEPHANO	What's the matter?
3		Have we divels here?
4		Doe you put trickes upon's with Salvages, and Men of
5		Inde? ha? I have not scap'd drowning, to be afeard
6		now of your foure legges: for it hath bin said; as proper
7		a man as ever went on foure legs, cannot make him
8		give ground: and it shall be said so againe, while *Stephano*
9		breathes at' nostrils.
10	CALIBAN	The Spirit torments me: oh.
11	STEPHANO	This is some Monster of the Isle, with foure legs;
12		who hath got (as I take it) an Ague: where the divell
13		should he learne our language? I will give him some reliefe
14		if it be but for that: if I can recover him, and keepe
15		him tame, and get to *Naples* with him, he's a Present
16		for any Emperour that ever trod on Neates-leather.
17	CALIBAN	Doe not torment me 'prethee: I'le bring my
18		wood home faster.
19	STEPHANO	He's in his fit now; and doe's not talke after the
20		wisest; hee shall taste of my Bottle: if hee have never

drunke wine afore, it will goe neere to remove his Fit: 21

if I can recover him, and keepe him tame, I will not take 22

too much for him; hee shall pay for him that hath him, 23

and that soundly.   24

CALIBAN   Thou do'st me yet but little hurt; thou wilt anon,   25

I know it by thy trembling: Now *Prosper* workes   26

upon thee.   27

—— Your Task—Playing the Physical Jokes ——

Look for opportunities for physical comedy (shtick). Your opportunities will come from the text and from the power of your own imagination. Look for these clues:

- Prose or verse? What kind of verse?

- Repeated sounds and words (building)

- Half-lines (room to move)

- Punctuation: colons, question marks, periods, commas (chances to move)

- Descriptive words and images (do they make sense?)

- Storytelling (maybe the character is exaggerating or entertaining)

- Situational comedy (built in conflicts and obstacles)

- Character traits (voice, walk, appearance, attitude, habits)

Some people are born clowns. They have naturally good timing. From years of entertaining their peers in the schoolyard so they won't get beat up, or so they can get away with mischief, they've worked out their own unique methods of getting attention and laughs. Others develop better skills as clowns by practicing. They watch role models like Charlie Chaplin and Buster Keaton from the old silent films. They watch people in the world around them. They study other funny people and mimic them. You can too.

Shakespeare's Naughty Humor

Shakespeare's characters are crude at times, sometimes even graphic. He wasn't a Puritan and he sometime even loved making jokes based on the attraction between men and women. In fact, he stuck them in almost every chance he got. You could go back through the excerpts in this chapter alone and would find many sexual implications. But today, unless you know an audience can appreciate them, it is best not to be too graphic. Perform them as though with a wink to the audience, so they know that you know they know what you mean.

Humor, especially sexual humor, releases tension. An example comes in *Anthony and Cleopatra,* Act 2, Scene 3. Cleopatra is waiting for a messenger to bring her news of Anthony with whom she's been having a passionate love affair. But he's back in Rome and has married a Roman woman. Cleopatra doesn't know this yet. Here, she is hanging out and joking around with a handmaiden, Charmian, and Mardian, a eunuch (a male slave who has had his genitals removed), while she waits for her beloved to return. This humor provides contrast to the following, darker scene when she gets the bad news.

1 CLEOPATRA Let it alone, let's to Billiards: come *Charmian.*

2 CHARMIAN My arme is sore, best play with *Mardian.*

3 CLEOPATRA As well a woman with an Eunuch plaide, as

4 with a woman. Come you'le play with me Sir?

MARDIAN	As well as I can Madam.	5
CLEOPATRA	And when good will is shewed,	6
	Though't come to short	7
	The Actor may pleade pardon. Ile none now,	8
	Give me mine Angle, weele to'th' River there	9
	My Musicke playing farre off. I will betray	10
	Tawny fine fishes, my bended hooke shall pierce	11
	Their slimy jawes: and as I draw them up,	12
	Ile thinke them every one an *Anthony*,	13
	And say, ah ha; y'are caught.	14
CHARMIAN	'Twas merry when you wager'd on your Ang-	15
	ling, when your diver did hang a salt fish on his hooke	16
	which he with fervencie drew up.	17
CLEOPATRA	That time? Oh times:	18
	I laught him out of patience: and that night	19
	I laught him into patience, and next morne,	20
	Ere the ninth houre, I drunke him to his bed:	21
	Then put my Tires and Mantles on him, whilst	22
	I wore his Sword Phillippan.	23

In ancient times, there were two kinds of civilizations. The first were warring cultures dominated by symbols resembling the male anatomy, like spears and swords. The second were agricultural societies that worshipped female deities and embraced fertility symbols resembling the female anatomy, like circles and cups. When you notice sexual humor, beyond references to specific behavior like "sit on me" or "in the hand," it usually appears coded in one of these images, as a long object or as a circular object.

Mardian's physical circumstances provide a contrast to Cleopatra's mention of Anthony's "sword." When she says "play with me" it has double meaning. He responds "As well as I can." She replies, "Though't it come to short," she'll pardon him. Charmian can't resist getting into the game as well. She tosses in a line about a fish on a hook. Now what might that refer to–a sexual act? It could have both an innocent meaning (Anthony is attached to Cleopatra; they're a couple) and a naughty meaning (the couple went to bed together). Cleopatra says she "wore" his sword, which could also have two meanings. As an actor or an actress, when you come across scenes like this one, you must decide how naughty or how literal and innocent an interpretation you would like to play.

Visit **www.willpowerthebook.com** to find more information on naughty humor in Shakespeare's plays.

Your Day 15 Rehearsal Checklist

Have you completed your tasks?

☐ Playing the Verbal Jokes

☐ Playing the Physical Jokes

What discoveries have you made?

DAY 16

Art Thou Parent, Child, or Adult?

Although Elizabethans predate the field of psychology, which developed in the nineteenth century under the influence of doctors such as Sigmund Freud, Shakespeare was an astute observer of human nature. Therefore, concepts borrowed from psychologists can sometimes add nuance to an actor's performance. University of California theatre department professor Arthur Wagner, Ph.D., shared an insight with me that he gained from the therapeutic techniques of Transactional Analysis (TA): "When your language changes, your character changes." His basic premise, which he derived from Eric Berne, M.D.'s classic TA handbook *Games People Play,* is that characters are always adopting one of three possible psychological statuses—parent, child, or adult—in relation to other characters. These roles can shift literally from line to line in Shakespeare's plays. If you can identify with at least one of them, it may give you a fresh approach to your script.

Throughout *Will Power,* my main intention is always to teach you how to find or to craft entertaining and original ways of playing individual moments. As you have explored many layers of the text by now, you may already feel you are squarely on track. However, if Wagner's premise fits your scene, it can give you another significant way to work on your character that may ultimately be quite productive and useful.

The Three Psychological Roles and Their Voices

When identifying psychological status, an adult calmly says things like: "I think you should…" and "I would prefer if…" as though they're speaking to an equal. A parent dictates and speaks in imperatives, such as "Do it *now*!" Whereas a child is resistant and wanting—dependent and needy—and says, "No, I won't!" or "I want!"

Have you ever noticed that when people approach you using one of these tones it triggers a certain type of response in you? Maybe a calm tone would be met in you by a matching calm tone. Perhaps scolding and finger wagging would be met by rebellion. Perhaps other people's ineffectuality transforms you into a controlling taskmaster and nag. The same thing is true for the characters you will play on stage.

An example of two characters role-playing with one another, and cycling through the psychological statuses of parent, child, and adult for each other, is Julius Caesar and his wife Calphurnia in *Julius Caesar* (Act 2, Scene 2). You need to know that it's raining and Julius plans to go outside in his nightshirt. Enter Calphurnia as "Strict Mom":

1 CALPHURNIA   What mean you *Cesar*? Think you to walk forth?
2   You shall not stirre out of your house to day.

He responds as the "Petulant Child" with a disagreement, before continuing.

CAESAR	*Cesar* shall forth; the things that threaten'd me,	3
	Ne're look'd but on my backe: When they shall see	4
	The face of *Caesar*, they are vanished.	5

Then on her next line, Calphurnia becomes the "Frightened Child," and Caesar switches to the adult voice in reply.

CALPHURNIA	Cesar, I never stood on Ceremonies,	6
	Yet now they fright me…	7
	O Cesar, these things are beyond all use,	8
	And I do feare them.	9
CAESAR	What can be avoided	10
	Whose end is purpos'd by the mighty Gods?	11

His wife and he then converse for several lines of the scene as two reasonable adults. Notice how the bold lines below balance.

CALPHURNIA	**When Beggers dye, there are no Comets seen,**	12
	The Heavens themselves blaze forth the death of Princes.	13
CAESAR	**Cowards dye many times before their deaths,**	14
	The valiant never taste of death but once:…	15

When you're working on a scene or a speech, always look for places to adopt a new approach, such as changing your psychological role. Shakespeare wanted actors to surprise the audience by having their characters frequently change the tactics they use to achieve their objectives and the style with which they express themselves.

Consider Helena when she is pursuing Demetrius in *A Midsummer Night's Dream* (Act 2, Scene 1). At first she acts like a needy child who fears abandonment, or perhaps like a lovesick teenager who's obsessed with a movie star or pop music icon.

1	HELENA	I am your spaniel, and Demetrius,
2		The more you beat me, I will fawne on you.
3		Use me but as your spaniel; spurne me, strike me,
4		Neglect me, lose me; onely give me leave
5		(Unworthy as I am) to follow you.

After chasing him around the forest, Helena shifts to another psychological role. Then she no longer speaks as a child, but takes on the poetic, rational voice of an adult.

1	HELENA	Your virtue is my priviledge: for that
2		It is not night when I doe see your face.
3		Therefore I thinke I am not in the night,
4		Nor doth this wood lacke worlds of company.
5		For you in my respect are all the world.
6		Then how can it be said I am alone,
7		When all the world is here to looke on me?

The adult voice doesn't usually last long on stage. It serves for trading information matter-of-factly, and for those special moments when characters have suddenly become likeminded or are sharing their most intimate thoughts and feelings. The following passage from *Romeo and Juliet* (Act 3, Scene 5) reveals how close the couple is once they are married. At this point in the play, they are so synchronized that their sentences even form a perfect rhyming couplet.

JULIET	O now be gone, more light and light it growes.	1
ROMEO	More light & light, more darke and darke our woes.	2

Please note, only use what works for you. The Parent-Child-Adult technique will not be 100 percent effective for every line of Shakespeare. However, the Bard was status conscious enough for it to support his characters' behavior and vocal patterns in many cases. Keep role-playing and pull it out as an ingredient in your cupboard of tricks and if you're seeking a certain *je ne sais quoi* flavor for the sauce.

—— Your Task—Identifying Your—— Psychological Role

Consider whether your character is speaking a specific thought in the voice of:

- A parent (imperative/master to servant/status quo)
- A child (resistant/needy/rebellious)
- An adult (courageous/rational/equal-minded)

Now do your speech, assuming the part of the parent, child, or adult to a high degree. How does it affect your voice? How does it affect your body? Remember, voices may switch from moment to moment. In fact, in Shakespeare, characters often go from one extreme to another from thought to thought or from end stop to end stop. This technique may unlock one or two special moments in a speech or a scene, or even an entire play, that would contrast nicely with your other planned moments.

Do Characters Have Underlying Psychological Ages?

In *Cymbeline*, Posthumus is a man who is mentally rather dull. His name is a joke. In Latin, post means "after." It tells us that he's slow. In the English language, the word posthumous also means "after death." So his name indicates he's a guy who is, as a coroner would say, D.O.A. ("dead on arrival"). That's how far behind everyone else he is. Jokes abound about how Posthumus has been duped and doesn't understand what's happening. How could you represent him? What if you played him as a naïve first grader, rather than a stupid grownup? Couldn't that be an interesting picture to paint for the audience on a couple of lines?

Here's a speech of his taken from Act 2, Scene 4. He believes that his wife has betrayed him by cheating on him with Iachimo—a lie that Iachimo told him. He's mad, and he's also trying to work out what happened and the significance of of it. You can tell that he's in the psychological role of a child because he is not taking responsibility for directly asking his wife what happened. Instead he's taking someone else's word about her behavior and blaming her. In fact, he blames all women. Blaming is childish. An adult would confront the situation and seek a solution.

1	POSTHUMUS	Is there no way for Men to be, but Women
2		Must be halfe-workers? We are all Bastards,
3		And that most venerable man, which I
4		Did call my Father, was, I know not where
5		When I was stampt. Some Coyner with his Tooles
6		Made me a counterfeit: yet my Mother seem'd

The *Dian* of that time: so doth my Wife 7

The Non-pareill of this. Oh Vengeance, Vengeance! 8

Me of my lawfull pleasure she restrain'd, 9

And pray'd me oft forbearance: did it with 10

A pudencie so Rosie, the sweet view on't 11

Might well have warm'd olde Saturne; 12

That I thought her 13

As Chaste, as un-Sunn'd Snow. Oh, all the Divels! 14

This yellow *Iachimo* in an houre, was't not? 15

Or lesse; at first? Perchance he spoke not, but 16

Like a full Acorn'd Boare, a Jarmen on, 17

Cry'de oh, and mounted; found no opposition 18

But what he look'd for, should oppose, and she 19

Should from encounter guard. Could I finde out 20

The Womans part in me, for there's no motion 21

That tends to vice in man, but I affirme 22

It is the Womans part: be it Lying, note it, 23

The womans: Flattering, hers; Deceiving, hers: 24

Lust, and ranke thoughts, hers, hers: Revenges hers: 25

Ambitions, Covetings, change of Prides, Disdaine, 26

Nice-longing, Slanders, Mutability; 27

All Faults that name, nay, that Hell knowes, 28

Why hers, in part, or all: but rather all. For even to Vice 29

They are not constant, but are changing still; 30

One Vice, but of a minute old, for one 31

Not halfe so old as that. Ile write against them, 32

Detest them, curse them: yet 'tis greater Skill 33

In a true Hate, to pray they have their will: 34

The very Divels cannot plague them better. 35

As you know, actors have to make decisions about the way their characters walk, talk, laugh, eat, and so forth. Anything anyone else among us would do in our lives, they also have a unique way of doing. Does a particular character limp, skip, wheeze, snort, glide, or slouch? Those are different playable choices. For now, consider that a truly broad range of options—various kinds of idiosyncratic and quirky behavior—is available to you if you can borrow it from what you see exhibited by the people of different ages around you, such as toddlers, teenagers, and the elderly.

—— Your Task—Acting Your "Age" ——

For this activity, pick an age (any age at all) and do your speech or scene as if you were that age. Maybe you and your scene partner could agree to interact as if you were two three-year-olds in the playground. You could stamp your feet, whine, give each other little shoves (but not too rough), lie down on the floor, giggle, jump up and down, sing to yourself, hold hands, or hide your face behind your hands. Notice how this age affects your body and your whole being.

Now try a different age...and another. A slight change can make a line that was once nearly uniform with the other lines come across as brilliantly read. You can measure your progress here by whether or not real and specific possibilities have arisen. Of course, you never have to reveal to the audience how you achieved your results; all they see is what shows up on the surface. So you can secretly act any age you like.

Making Clean, Distinctive Shifts

In my Playing Shakespeare class, I assigned an actor and actress the same scene between Brutus and his wife Portia from Julius Caesar

(Act 2, Scene 1) that we looked at for our Day 12 rehearsal. Remember, "Portia Prods, Brutus Blabs"? When Portia enters the garden and comes upon Brutus, he's just been conspiring against Caesar, but he won't tell her why he's upset. She wants him to come back inside to bed. I had explained the principles of today's rehearsal to the actress, who applied them well. The technique gave her clear delineations for three sections of the scene, and, due to the shifts, it was thoroughly engaging to watch her work to achieve her objective. This Portia chose to act as would a child looking for her favorite playmate from the moment she entered the garden until Brutus advises her:

BRUTUS	Kneele not gentle *Portia*.	1

In the very next moment, she clearly switched into acting as a reprimanding parent. Game over! No more play time for Brutus as his wife scolded him:

PORTIA	I should not neede, if you were gentle *Brutus*.	2
	Within the Bond of Marriage, tell me *Brutus*,	3
	Is it excepted, I should know no Secrets	4
	That appertaine to you? Am I your Selfe,	5
	But as it were in sort, or limitation?	6
	To keepe with you at Meales, comfort your Bed,	7
	And talke to you sometimes? Dwell I but in the Suburbs	8
	Of your good pleasure? If it be no more,	9
	`*Portia* is *Brutus* Harlot, not his Wife.	10
BRUTUS	You are my true and honourable Wife,	11
	As deere to me, as are the ruddy droppes	12
	That visit my sad heart.	13

After that respectful response, which assuaged the character's hurt feelings, the class saw the actress flipping clearly into a calmer mode of egalitarian communication. She became the epitome of a rational, advising adult:

14	PORTIA	If this were true, then should I know this secret.
15		I graunt I am a Woman; but withall,
16		A Woman that Lord *Brutus* tooke to Wife:
17		I graunt I am a Woman; but withall,
18		A Woman well reputed: *Cato's* Daughter.
19		Thinke you, I am no stronger then my Sex
20		Being so Father'd, and so Husbanded?

Having three specific ways of doing her scene, which she took on one after another as an evolution, gave her three different acting styles. Those distinct styles enabled her to dramatize Portia's gearshifts so the audience could observe her inner life. In addition, the actress had fun abruptly changing her status, as if she had multiple personalities living inside her. Afterward she told the class that deciding to do so gave her freedom and confidence. "Normally I get cast in serious roles, and I don't give myself the permission to play as much as I did at the beginning of this scene."

The parent, child, adult concept was mesmerizing in her performance because it made her unique and entertaining. (Most people find it entertaining to watch children at play.) When she flipped into the parent voice, we realized how serious the situation was, because the contrast was so stark. Then, when she flipped into the adult voice, we realized how truly powerful she was as an individual, as Portia was attempting to create solutions rather than being stuck on the problem. Her portrayal was full of danger and surprise.

Your Day 16 Rehearsal Checklist

Have you completed your tasks?

☐ Identifying Your Psychological Role

☐ Acting Your "Age"

What discoveries have you made?

DAY 17

Greeks Bearing Gifts

In Ancient Greece, theatrical performances were said to produce *ecstasis,* a state similar to the euphoric and motivational effect of listening to a Southern Baptist preacher or vibing to music performed by a rock star. People would fill the coliseums in the afternoons to attend play festivals where performing masked pantomimes of the sacred myths was a popular competitive event. Historians and archaeologists have clear evidence that audiences would often get so charged up that at times they would riot in the streets afterwards. Pretty impressive, isn't it?

So what did Shakespeare borrow from the ancient Greeks that could rile up an audience–impact the listener–to such a degree? In today's rehearsal, you'll find out.

The gift of the ancient Greeks is that they approached their lines in four ways, each with a connotation related to nature. Delivery of lines could be *dramatic, lyrical, epic,* or *antithetical.* Since Shakespeare liked to surprise his audience, the natural mode of his speeches frequently switches in mid-sentence, and sometimes mid-line. If you, as an actor, can unwrap the gift of a speech's mode technically, it will help you find the nuances.

This technique was brought to my attention several years ago by

Robert Taylor, a British director working with the Moscow Art Theatre, who was on the faculty of the Sedona Shakespeare Festival at the same time as me. His results were impressive. Part of the technique's purpose is to help you fine-tune your energy language.

Is there enough force—and the right kind of force—behind the delivery of each of your lines or pieces of a line? After today's rehearsal, you'll have found an answer.

Dramatic Lines

Dramatic lines (or parts of lines) always have a specific target: a person, a place, or a thing. In antiquity, actors would practice these types of lines while hurling javelins. Of the dramatic mode of delivery, Taylor told me it was said by the Greeks: "All the winds of the world will gather and funnel through your head." Actors should deliver dramatic lines decisively, as their energy travels from Point A to Point B. When we look for dramatic lines in Shakespeare, we find they're often filled with the letters *T* and *D* (dental sounds) and other sharp consonants.

Queen Anne's first line in Act 1, Scene 2 of *Richard the Third* is a perfect illustration of where a dramatic mode of delivery would be compelling. Porters are carrying the corpse of her father-in-law into the castle, and she wants them to put him down IMMEDIATELY! Thus the line is direct and commanding—dramatic.

QUEEN ANNE	**Set downe, set downe your honourable load,**	1
	If Honor may be shrowded in a Herse;	2
	Whil'st I a-while obsequiously lament	3
	Th' untimely fall of Vertuous Lancaster.	4

To rehearse dramatic lines, I ask actors to pick an actual spot on the wall and pretend to throw a javelin or spear at it as they deliver the line. The actresses in my classes rarely use enough dramatic force when they do their first presentation of Queen Anne's speech. Until I instruct them to do this throwing action they never make it as powerful as it can be. But they usually find their power when they perform the line for the second time. If they haven't found their power by then, I have them imagine a spot that's farther away. The trick is to unleash the energy that makes the line hit a target.

Stand up and do an experiment. Try reading Queen Anne's line aloud now while hurling an imaginary javelin. Play with different focal points, near and far. What happens if you don't focus on an actual spot? What happens if it is close to you? What happens if it is far from you? Can you visualize that javelin sticking out of the target you hit?

My all-time favorite dramatic line (of course) is the first line in *Henry the Fifth*. When it comes blasting at the audience after the pre-curtain darkness, it sets an influential tone:

1	PROLOGUE	**O for a Muse of Fire**, that would ascend
2		The brightest Heaven of Invention:
3		A Kingdome for a Stage, Princes to Act,
4		And Monarchs to behold the swelling Scene....

The energy of a dramatic line always accomplishes an action. The "spear" has got to be gone by the end of the line. Throwing occurs *on* the line.

Lyrical Lines

Lyrical lines (or parts of lines) are poetic and moody. The ancients said: "All the waterfalls in the world will gather and pour through your heart." It's as if the line is being gently carried from one place to another on the waves of a tranquil ocean. In Shakespeare, such lines easily stand out. For instance, in *Twelfth Night* (Act 1, Scene 5), Viola, while disguising her gender by pretending to be a youth named Cesario, goes to visit the lady Olivia. She expresses her views of love. The message is lyrical.

VIOLA	Make me a willow Cabine at your gate,	1
	And call upon my soule within the house,	2
	Write loyall Cantons of contemned love,	3
	And sing them lowd even in the dead of night...	4

Similarly, in *The Merchant of Venice* (Act 3, Scene 2) after Bassanio tells Portia that he loves her, she replies to him with a lyrical piece of a line.

PORTIA	**You see my Lord Bassiano where I stand,**	1
	Such as I am; though for my selfe alone	2
	I would not be ambitious in my wish,	3
	To wish my selfe much better, yet for you,	4
	I would be trebled twenty times my selfe,	5
	A thousand times more faire, ten thousand times	6
	More rich, that onely to stand high in your account...	7

Lines are made lyrical by the characters' circumstance and deep feelings—of love, of loss, and so forth. In Portia's speech, she is giving herself to Bassanio both emotionally and spiritually. Lyricism is the only mode of delivery that can encompass that deep wellspring of simple sentiment. It enables actors to embrace the mood and keep the energy in a circle around them without breaking a fragile impression. Lyricism is not piercing, it is nurturing, soothing, and draws you in toward a person.

Actors should deliver lyrical lines with emotional vulnerability. When they don't do so correctly, they either seem false and flowery, and we don't believe them, or they appear to lack humanity. That breaks the connection with the audience. We want to believe they feel deep feelings. It makes the character less likable if we feel they don't care.

To rehearse lyrical lines, I ask actors to do a motion that resembles tai chi. Try it now if you would. Stand up and keep your knees slightly bent. Imagine that you are waist deep in water. Skim your hands over the surface of that water, moving them slowly from right to left in a smooth, flowing circular motion.

For practice, now say Viola or Portia's lines lyrically as if you are using them to caress and embrace your listeners. You're touching the surface around you with a light, velvety touch. How does that affect you and transform the way you say the lines?

Epic Lines

Epic lines involve storytelling without editorializing or forming an opinion. They are balanced, objective, and factual. Of epic lines, it was said: "The oceans of the world are at peace and flow through your center in harmony." We find an example of an epic line in the Prologue to *Romeo and Juliet* (found in Quarto 1, rather than the First Folio).

CHORUS	Two housholds both alike in dignitie,	1
	(In faire *Verona*, where we lay our Scene)	2
	From civill broyles broke into enmitie,	3
	Whose civill warre makes civill hands uncleane.	4
	From forth the fatall loynes of these two foes,	5
	A paire of starre-crost Lovers tooke their life:	6
	Whose misadventures, piteous overthrowes,	7
	(Through the continuing of their Fathers strife,	8
	And death-markt passage of their Parents rage)	9
	Is now the two howres traffique of our Stage.	10
	The which if you with patient eares attend,	11
	What here we want wee'l studie to amend.	12

Shakespeare's plays weren't compiled until after his death. Quartos are alternate versions that vary subtly from the First Folio. Not only were they handwritten, the texts were also drawn from cue scripts of different productions and time periods. The Prologue to *Romeo and Juliet* was written for the original production of the play–required to explain the basic conflict between the Capulet and Montague families. But when the play became famous everyone in the audience knew the story already, and so it was dropped.

Another great example of an epic speech is the Prologue from *Henry the Fourth, Part Two*. In this case the narrator is a personification, Rumor, who reappears at the start of each act and at the conclusion of the play. His appearance here let's us know the nature of what's happening in England at the start of the action—that gossip and innuendo are spreading and war and dissent are already underway. Many scholars believe that William Shakespeare himself played this role in the original Globe Theatre production. Who else could have handled this magnificent language as well as him?

1 RUMOUR…Why is *Rumour* heere?
2   I run before King *Harries* victory,
3   Who in a bloodie field by Shrewsburie
4   Hath beaten downe yong *Hotspurre*, and his Troopes,
5   Quenching the flame of bold Rebellion,
6   Even with the Rebels blood. But what meane I
7   To speake so true at first? My Office is
8   To noyse abroad, that *Harry Monmouth* fell
9   Under the Wrath of Noble *Hotspurres* Sword:
10   And that the King, before the *Dowglas* Rage
11   Stoop'd his Annointed head, as low as death.
12   This have I rumour'd through the peasant-Townes,
13   Betweene the Royall Field of Shrewsburie,
14   And this Worme-eaten-Hole of ragged Stone,
15   Where *Hotspurres* Father, old Northumberland,
16   Lyes crafty sicke. The Postes come tyring on,
17   And not a man of them brings other newes
18   Then they have learn'd of Me. From *Rumours* Tongues,
19   They bring smooth-Comforts-false, worse then True-wrongs.

Playing epic lines is a balancing act. Therefore, I ask actors rehearsing such speeches to stand with their arms out to the sides, palms facing up, and holding two heavy books flat on top of each hand. The goal is not to drop the books. They should lean–tilt to a side–when they talk about one opposing point of view or another. The challenge is to deliver the information without seeming to judge it as good or bad, right or wrong, or judging people as winners and losers, likable or dislikable. They should be stately and still, like the scales of justice. If they get too excited, they might drop a book.

Spend a few minutes now, attempting the same exercise using one or both of the two prologues above. How well did you do? Did you sense the balance in the language? Were you able to embody it and let its qualities resonate through your vocal tones?

In my experience, when actors don't do this well, they get angry on simple lines. They try to do too much with the material. Shakespeare just wanted the facts presented. Epic lines engage the audience and make the audience decide the issues for themselves.

Antithetical Lines

Antithetical lines are oppositional. According to the Ancient Greeks: "They are the way of the erupting volcano." If good theatre is made up of surprise and danger, then Shakespeare was a master of creating such occasions. For instance, it is startling and exhilarating in *A Midsummer Night's Dream* (Act 2, Scene 1), when Oberon, the fairy king, erupts two antithetical lines at his estranged wife Titania:

| OBERON | Ill-met by Moone-light. | 1 |
| | Proud Tytania. | 2 |

Often, antithetical lines are comedic. Shortly afterward, in the same play, as his would-be lover Helena is chasing him, the character Demetrius erupts at her:

1 DEMETRIUS I love thee not, **therefore pursue me not,**
2   Where is *Lysander,* and faire *Hermia?*
3   The one Ile stay, the other stayeth me.

Generally used for moments of broad comedy or intense anger, Shakespeare normally follows an antithetical line with a contrasting mode to make a point. Done well by an actor I directed in an American Globe Theatre production of *A Midsummer Night's Dream,* Oberon came on stage snorting and fierce, filled with rage, and delivered his line as he caught Titania. She replied in a loving, lyrical mode, "What, jealous *Oberon?*" That made his anger comedic. It garnered a huge laugh. The more explosive and antithetical he was, the more lyrical she became—and the more the audience responded.

Another dangerous antithetical speech is found in *A Winter's Tale* (Act 3, Scene 2). There the accused Paulina asks Leontes:

1 PAULINA   **What studied torments (Tyrant) hast for me?**
2   What Wheeles? Racks? Fires? What flaying? Boyling
3   In Leads, or Oyles?...

The first question in her list is oppositional, courageous and frighteningly confrontational since she may be tortured and put to death just for asking. To rehearse lines like this one, I ask actors to explode on the line. They must jump up in the air suddenly, as if they're going to do a jumping jack, and extend their arms and legs, letting their erupting energy shoot out through their fingertips and toes. It is as though there were a short blast of TNT.

Again, please experiment. Make a little bit of room around you so you don't knock over valuable objects or sock someone in the eye. Then try this explosive rehearsal technique as you say one of the antithetical lines above. Be Oberon, Demetrius, or Paulina for a moment and really lose your cool. *Pow!*

—— Your Task—Embodying the—— Elements of Nature

No speech is written entirely in one mode. The point of today's rehearsal is to practice building contrast into the performance of your lines. We've talked about this during earlier rehearsals, but let's establish the contrast even more deeply now by drawing upon the Ancient Greek technique. Going to the scene or monologue you've been working on, please take a few moments to consider whether or not each individual line is dramatic, lyric, epic, or antithetical.

Afterward, I want you to play around with making them come across in the tones of the natural descriptions (wind, waterfall, ocean, volcano) given in earlier sections of this chapter. Hurl the javelin. Touch the water. Balance the scales. Erupt!

Revisit your punctuation and sound repetitions. If the lines switch from *T*s and *D*s to *M*s and *L*s, you could be shifting from the dramatic to the lyrical mode. What happens when you exaggerate such a shift? Partly this is a judgment call for you. Style of delivery can be subjective. Does it sound and feel right? For instance, in the following passage from *Othello* (Act 2, Scene 1), where does the shift from dramatic to lyrical occur?

1	IAGO	That *Cassio* loves her, I do well beleev't: [dramatic]
2		That she loves him, 'tis apt, and of great Credite.
3		The Moore (how be it that I endure him not)
4		Is of a constant, loving, Noble Nature,
5		And I dare thinke, he'le prove to *Desdemona*
6		A most deere husband. **Now I do love her too**...[lyrical]

I feel the major shift takes place on the bold-faced line segment. Do you agree?

Or what about the more frequent shifts that occur in this speech by Julia in *Two Gentlemen of Verona* (Act 1, Scene 2)? Julia is Proteus' girlfriend until he goes to Milan and becomes enamored of another woman. When Julia's maid brings her a letter, Julia tears it up. Then, in a fit of regret she attempts to read its torn fragments while enduring a veritable emotional roller coaster. The last line even uses contrasting vocabulary!

1	JULIA	Nay, would I were so angred with the same: [dramatic]
2		Oh hatefull hands, to teare such loving words; [antithetical]
3		Injurious Waspes, to feede on such sweet hony, [lyrical]
4		And kill the Bees that yeelde it, with your stings;
		[dramatic/antithetical?]
5		Ile kisse each seuerall paper, for amends: [lyrical/epic?]
6		Looke, here is writ, **kinde Julia: unkinde Julia**...[A contrast!]

A word of advice: In breaking down the shifts and contrast of your speeches, a sensible plan is to work in the following progression:

1. End stop to end stop (sentence by sentence)
2. Line by line
3. Punctuation mark to punctuation mark

As you dive deeper into the microcosm of the language you may find beautiful contrasts such as Julia's "kind" and "unkind," each of which can be delivered in a different mode. You can present such distinctions by changing your physical actions, your vocal sounds, your pace, or the direction of your focus.

At the end of the day, take what works for you-and leave the rest! The Greeks gave us a gift that may help you design a rhetorically clear and highly specific moment of great beauty and excitement that blows the socks off the next casting director you meet.

Your Day 17 Rehearsal Checklist

Have you completed your tasks?

☐ Embodying the Elements of Nature

What discoveries have you made?

PHASE 4

Staking Your Claim

Stanislavski's Approach

Words reveal character. So language does half your work as an actor for you. But you also need to find and reveal your character's heart and soul, and this is where the Stanislavski approach—known in America as method acting—comes in. The trap of emphasizing your emotional life is that emotions are basically non-active. They are transient and intangible, and not *actable* in the way that verbs are. Actors who try to play an emotion get stuck on that one note and fail to respond truthfully. They lose the ability to play scales and concertos. However, the most proficient method-acting teachers have established systems that avoid this pitfall. With them, your performance can be subtly, or vastly, different every night—and any emotions that arise will have fresh nuances.

In this section of the book, Phase Four, we'll explore the techniques that are the backbone of modern American theatre, and see how these may apply to Shakespeare. American theatre training is concerned with naturalism. It is concerned with living through moments and communicating a deep internal reality to the audience. It is concerned with tapping into your imagination and making a bridge between yourself and the character you're portraying. Some actors mumble their words and speak too softly to be heard on stage, and excuse this as "natural." Such behavior may play on camera, but it won't play in a 2,000-seat theatre. There's an adage: Method without technique is embarrassing, and technique without method is boring. We need both.

DAY 18

Your Given Circumstances

Being an actor means being a good detective. You need to know the who, what, why, where, and when of your character, as the playwright has provided them. These are not the back-story that you make up for yourself so that you can associate with your character's life. None are made up. Given circumstances exist in the text itself, and they include things that affect people's behavior, such as the time of day, the year, the season, the location, what surrounds you (furnishing, lighting, people, and so on), what has already happened, and even when you last ate or slept. Given circumstances, like being cold or hot, are playable.

Today, Day 18, we'll look at given circumstances. For instance, in Act 1, Scene 1 of *Othello*, right away we discover that Iago wants to be Othello's lieutenant, but Othello has kept him an ensign and promoted someone else: Cassio. Later on, Iago persuades Othello that his innocent wife Desdemona has cheated on him with Cassio.

1	IAGO	For certes, saies he,
2		I have already chose my Officer. And what was he?
3		For-sooth, a great Arithmatician,
4		One *Michaell Cassio*, a *Florentine*,

We also learn that:

- Iago is a soldier and has been fighting at Rhodes and Cyprus.

- He believes in service to himself rather than service to his leader, Othello.

- He wants to avenge himself on Othello for slighting him.

- He's in Venice, standing outside of Brabantio's house.

- It is nighttime.

- Othello is a Moor (i.e., a Muslim, not a Christian) and a black man.

- Othello has stolen away with Desdemona, Brabantio's daughter (a younger, white Christian woman).

- War is going on between Christians and non-Christians.

- He plans to trick Othello by pretending to be his friend.

- And much more.

When I directed *Othello*, Rick Faye, my Iago, told me, "Except for the character of Rodrigo, no one else in the play ever suspects Iago until it's too late, including his wife Amelia. And the only reason Rodrigo knows anything is because Iago has chosen to tell him certain things about himself, his motives, and his plans. He does this at the top of the play and, of course, it allows Shakespeare to give exposition to the audience: the only other "character" who is in on Iago's entire scheme. Only the audience, during his many monologues, gets to know the real Iago. He has complete confidence that he can manipulate his dupe, Rodrigo, to achieve his objective–and he succeeds."

⎯⎯ Your Task—What Are Your Given Circumstances?

Go through the play you are working on and make note of your character's given circumstances at the beginning of each scene (or speech). Given circumstances change from scene to scene in a play. Some remain constant. But others are relevant exclusively to the particular moment in which a scene occurs. Look at:

- Who am I? Male or female, married or single, young or old, rich or poor, educated or uneducated, and so on.

- What time is it? Year, season, month, date, and time of day. Does the time relate to your needs?

- Where am I?

- What surrounds me? Space (description of environment; the feel of the place; color, sounds, smell, taste of the place; physical necessities; furniture or objects)?

- What has already happened? What's the history?

- When was the last time I ate? When was the last time I slept?

- How do I greet people?

- What's my character's point of view about these given circumstances?

- What does my character's name mean? For instance, in *Two Gentlemen of Verona* Proteus is named after a character from Greek mythology who was a shapeshifter. Phebe, in *As You Like It*, signifies the moon—and she has "moon sickness" (she's nuts). Bottom, well, means Bottom—and the character in *A Midsummer Night's Dream* is transformed by fairy magic into an actual ass. Constance, in *King John*, is constant. For a handout on the meaning of these and other Shakespearean names, visit the website **www.willpowerthebook.com.**

You may discover that you have a longer list of given circumstances in a scene that takes place late in a play than in an earlier scene. This accounts for time elapsing and for the events that have taken place during the play. If you keep track of your givens, it can help you figure out the trajectory of your character's development.

The Many Masks a Character Wears

Actors often make assumptions about their characters. For instance, in *Romeo and Juliet,* actors playing Romeo often portray him as young and serious. But when you look at other character's perceptions of Romeo, you can see that he is sometimes feisty and funny, and isn't always just a moody, infatuated boy. Actors need to find the clues that reference how they might behave to give off various impressions.

When I interviewed Rick Faye and asked him how he builds characters, Rick agreed, "Numerous clues are located in the text." He added, "The key I've discovered for my own work is to come from the perspective that the character is choosing them, not the actor, director, or playwright. If the character chooses a particular word or phrase, it automatically becomes more organic for the actor."

He continued, "Several clues that I have found particularly useful are repeated words, the iambic pentameter and/or poetry versus prose, and the punctuation from the First Folio text. Each of these can be used to learn what others in the play would say about the character, how the character chooses to speak, and how he chooses to address someone."

When actors don't really know the nature of the characters they're playing they can fall into traps like playing Iago as an ugly, mean-spirited person that everyone can recognize as evil. However, the description "Honest Iago" is used numerous times by different people in the play. This repeated phrase was chosen by Shakespeare to tell the actor playing Iago (and the audience) how he is perceived.

Rick made his physical and vocal choices for Iago based on that phrase and others like it. "Everyone else in the play experiences 'Honest Iago,' a soldier's soldier, steadfast and loyal. This told me that the performance should not be one of 'playing the evil' and 'winking' at the audience while speaking with Othello, or using makeup and costume to elicit fear and loathing. Complete and utter sincerity coming from a 'regular guy' is what would make everyone trust 'Honest Iago.'"

The people on stage form their impressions of your character based on what he or she says and does in their presence, so often the same clues you looked for in your Phase One rehearsals that took place between Day 1 and Day 8 will answer the question: How is my character being perceived *here*? Look at all of the following when answering this question.

POETRY VERSUS PROSE

Are you eloquent, terse, talkative, or crude? Are you emotional? Are you funny or clever? Your character's choice of expression is a clue to others in the play as well as to the audience of your personality and current state of being.

REPETITION OF WORDS OR SOUNDS

When Petruchio says 17 *K*s in *The Taming of the Shrew* (Act 2, Scene 1), he is unlike anyone else. When Iago expresses himself with a preponderance of *S*s in *Othello*, he is reminiscent of a hissing snake. It's a subliminal message to the audience and to others in the play about his true nature.

What does it seem as though Viola (in disguise as a youth) and Orsino are saying in this short exchange from *Twelfth Night* (Act 2, Scene 4)? Oh, oh, oh, oh, oh. Viola is in love with Orsino and comes as close as she can to saying it, here, in doublespeak. "My Father's daughter" means, of course, she herself.

ORSINO	And that I owe Olivia.	1
VIOLA	I but I know.	2
ORSINO	What dost thou know?	3
VIOLA	Too well what love women to men may owe:	4
	In faith they are as true of heart, as we.	5
	My Father had a daughter lov'd a man	6
	As it might be perhaps, were I a woman	7
	I should your Lordship.	8

CAPITALIZED WORDS

Frequently the captiualized words are the most important words in a sentence or a thought, at times they also have ironic significance. Consider the following speech from *Romeo and Juliet* (Act 4 Scene 5), which takes place when the adults are persuaded that Juliet is dead– although she isn't yet. If you read only the capitalized words, you would see very clearly that Lord Capulet is a grieving parent.

FATHER	Despis'd, distressed, hated, martir'd, kil'd,	1
	Uncomfortable time, why cam'st thou now	2
	To murther, murther our solemnitie?	3

4   **O Child, O Child**; my soule, and not my **Child**,

5   Dead art thou, alacke my **Child** is dead,

6   And with my **Child**, my joyes are buried.

PUNCTUATION

Where commas, colons, and endstops are placed in the script can help you find your character's breathing patterns and rhythm, and produces a physiological effect. Punctuation is part of the roadmap to building a character. For instance, Ophelia's father Polonius in *Hamlet* (Act 2, Scene 2) can't seem to get to the point. It is his special personality to always use three words where one would suffice. From her comment, the Queen clearly perceives him as longwinded. Consider the following exchange in which he goes on and on and on.

1 POLONIUS This businesse is very well ended.

2   My Liege, and Madam, to expostulate

3   What Majestie should be, what Dutie is,

4   Why day is day; night, night; and time is time,

5   Were nothing but to waste Night, Day, and Time.

6   Therefore, since Brevitie is the Soule of Wit,

7   And tediousnesse, the limbes and outward flourishes,

8   I will be breefe. Your Noble Sonne is mad:

9   Mad call I it; for to define true Madnesse,

10   What is't, but to be nothing else but mad.

11   But let that go.

12 QUEEN   More matter, with lesse Art.

13 POLONIUS Madam, I sweare I use no Art at all:

VERBS

Your actions are the core of your personality. That and whatever you say are the main clues others have about your identity and what to expect from you.

ADJECTIVES, SIMILES, METAPHORS

The imagery your character typically uses tells others about your interests, attitudes, and personality. For instance, it may reveal that you are oriented toward money, war, or love.

STATUS

Derived from your givens, your status is part of the foundation of your character. It influences word choice, body language, and social conventions. As an actor, it can help you establish relationships and humanity.

RHETORIC

Questions, comparisons and contrasts, and agreements or disagreements are signs of motivation and ability to reason. If your character asks a lot of questions, others may perceive you as nosey, curious, or possibly dangerous—or stupid. When Silvius disagrees with Phebe in *As You Like It* (she tells him that she doesn't love him and he tells her he wants to pursue her love anyway), she knows he's under her spell and can be pushed around, as seen in an excerpt from Act 3, Scene 5.

PHEBE	And yet it is not, that I beare thee love,	1
	But since that thou canst talke of love so well,	2
	Thy company, which erst was irksome to me	3
	I will endure; and ile employ thee too:	4
	But doe not looke for further recompence	5
	Then thine own gladnesse, that thou art employed.	6
SILVIUS	So holy, and so perfect is my love,	7

8	And I in such a poverty of grace,
9	That I shall thinke it a most plenteous crop
10	To gleane the broken eares after the man
11	That the main harvest reapes: loose now and then
12	A scattered smile, and that Ile live upon.

Drawing from Rick's explanation again:

> Iago uses the tool of repetition when he tells Rodrigo to '...follow thou the Warres.' He constantly says, 'Put money in thy purse,' or some variant thereof. From reading the given circumstances in the story, we know that Iago has been conning Rodrigo out of his money. He may be using this repetition because he wants Rodrigo to follow him to Cyprus so he can continue to do so.
>
> Iago also chooses prose over verse when speaking to Rodrigo. Why prose? Maybe he chooses prose because Rodrigo is not the brightest of people and he wants to drive home the fact that if Rodrigo 'fills his purse,' he (Rodrigo) will get Desdemona.
>
> Within all of this we see different uses of punctuation from the First Folio. Sometimes Iago's repeated phrase begins the sentence. Sometimes it follows a colon. What does this all mean? I felt that although Shakespeare was not telling me to rush it, but he didn't want me to slow down my lines either. If we listen to everyday conversations, we realize people do not do a lot of pausing. They speak in a natural way to make their point at that very moment. They use variety and chosen emphasis to make that point. So does Iago here. He fills Rodrigo's ears with many

reasons why he should 'fill his purse,' using different tempos, different attacks, and different images, and he elicits different responses and reactions that all lead to Rodrigo's conclusion that he must, of course, make all the money he can for Iago so he can finally have Desdemona.

Rick concluded, "If the actor uses the Folio punctuation as a starting point, he can have fun discovering a playful and manipulative Iago."

At the end of Act 1, Scene 3, when Rodrigo exclaims, "Ile sell all my land" on his exit, the audience has seen Iago achieve his objective and have fun doing it. He then turns right to them and speaks in verse. Rick felt that this clue clearly meant that Iago respects the audience's intelligence and wants to let them in on what he will do next, which was a personal choice about Iago's internal life with which another actor may or may not agree. Read the following speech and decide for yourself. What do you think?

IAGO	Thus do I ever make my Foole, my purse:	1
	For I mine owne gain'd knowledge should prophane	2
	If I would time expend with such Snipe,	3
	But for my Sport, and Profit: I hate the Moore,	4
	And it is thought abroad, that 'twixt my sheets	5
	He ha's done my Office. I know not if't be true,	6
	But I, for meere suspition in that kinde,	7
	Will do, as if for Surety. He holds me well,	8
	The better shall my purpose worke on him:	9
	Cassio's a proper man: Let me see now,	10
	To get his Place, and to plume up my will	11

12	In double Knavery. How? How? Let's see.
13	After some time, to abuse *Othello's* eares,
14	That he is too familiar with his wife:
15	He hath a person, and a smooth dispose
16	To be suspected: fram'd to make women false.
17	The Moore is of a free, and open Nature,
18	That thinkes men honest, that but seeme to be so,
19	And will as tenderly be lead by'th' Nose
20	As Asses are:
21	I hav't: it is engendred: Hell, and Night,
22	Must bring this monstrous Birth, to the worlds light.

Here's a summation of Rick's analysis and approach to the speech you just read. Iago begins by talking about Rodrigo, but in the fourth line, after a colon, changes gears abruptly with the words: "I hate the Moor." Four simple, uncomplicated words. This is the closest the audience ever comes to a motive for all Iago's actions. Line 4 is also an 11-count line, which means there's a lot packed into it.

Indeed, two more lines down, in line 6, there is a midline ending—meaning that the next thought follows hard upon. After having talked about Othello being "twixt my sheets" with Amelia, he vows revenge and comes full stop. He has midline ending again in line 8 after basically asserting to the audience, "I don't care if my suspicion is true or not. I am going to hatch this scheme anyhow." He then immediately says, "He holds me well." This is a good thing, no? Maybe this is a clue to the actor to smile on the line. It's a certain contrast to what just came before, and injects humor out of nowhere. If the audience can laugh with Iago—go along with him—it makes for a good show.

Three lines from the end, after insulting Othello by saying he'll "as tenderly be led by'th'nose as asses are:" there is a six-count break on a half-line (line 20). It made Rick wonder: Maybe an opportunity for a cross, preparing for the exit? Iago has just sown the seed of an idea with the audience, so it seems like a good spot.

Iago then finishes his speech with contrasting images and a rhyme: "Hell Night, monstrous Birth," and then "the worlds Light." Bad, bad, awful...Good! Maybe another smile at the very end? It surely would inject a sense of fun between Iago and the audience–very important, what with all the evil that's yet to come.

A delicious aspect of Iago's several soliloquies is that they provide the audience with a chance to penetrate Iago's mask. When other characters are on stage we get to see what they see–mostly a smooth, friendly, steadfastly loyal soldier–and when they're not, we see the world from Iago's point of view. It makes his villainy doubly awful.

——— Your Task—How Are You Perceived?———

Go through the play you're working on for a second time, and make a list of what the other characters say about you. For instance, Othello constantly repeats, "Iago is good and true." Even though Iago's behind-the-scenes actions belie these statements, they indicate that he is coming across well publicly. As an actor, this information may provide you with a wider, more contrasting range of behavioral and vocal choices. If you were playing Iago, it would give you an opportunity to alternate between extremes. Put all your clues to work.

Working with Your Given Circumstances

In his book *Creating a Role*, Stanislavski describes the actor's job as developing the ability to feel (internalize) the reality of given circumstances (externals), which usually involves an association process. Of course, there is another step: actors must allow those feelings they discover or develop to be communicated to the audience.

In tomorrow's rehearsal we'll talk about forming clear and powerful associations to your character's life, and explore how to make substitutions that can be read from the back row of any theatre. All you've learned so far will gel and become integrated.

—— Your Task—Living a Day in the—— Life of Your Role

In the late '70s I was cast in an Off-Broadway play, *Innocent Thoughts and Harmless Intentions,* in the role of Walky, a cold-blooded killer. The director had me shave my head–a scary look on me. To get into character, I rode the New York City subway wearing sunglasses and staring directly into people's eyes without smiling. It was an odd and unfamiliar feeling to be perceived as menacing; everyone would look down at his or her newspaper or away from me. Of course, I never hurt anyone or made any overt threats of any kind. That wouldn't have been right or respectful of the strangers with whom I was coming into contact.

Just as I did in preparing to portray Walky, it is highly recommended that you spend a day or a part of a day living inside your character's skin. Here are three ways to help you unzip your character's skin and climb in:

- Do something as your character: for instance, ride the subway, go to the grocery store, eat in a diner, workout at the gym, or perform another daily task.

- Create a written biography of your character's life during the past five years. Don't share this with anyone else. It's just for you.

- Write a letter to a loved one or an enemy as your character.

Pay attention to how you feel when acting as the character would. Pay attention to how others behave differently toward your presence as your character than toward your normal presence. Also pay attention to how the way you as your character are being treated feels. Have fun. You may be surprised at how real you come across.

Your Day 18 Rehearsal Checklist

Have you completed your tasks?

☐ What Are Your Given Circumstances?

☐ How Are You Perceived?

☐ Living a Day in the Life of Your Role

What discoveries have you made?

DAY 19

Five Basic Human Needs

Mira Rostova, one of the "three sisters" of acting with whom I trained, taught that all human behavior is motivated by five underlying needs: survival, love, validation, happiness, and winning. Most characters pursue one of these basic human needs from the beginning to the end of a play. They rarely switch around. So once you figure out the category that your character falls into, you can layer the essence of that motivational need beneath the activities of every scene in which you participate. Knowing what motivates your character is important. Having determined your character's given circumstances in yesterday's rehearsal, you will use this technique to begin the process of making those bits of information feel real, and important to you.

The Need to Survive

Survival is a primal need that applies to life and death issues, such as having enough air, and water, food, and money. If someone or something in the play is threatening your character's life, your character might do anything to survive. Characters perceive levels of danger differently. What elicits an extreme response depends on personality.

In the turning point of *Othello* (Act 5, Scene 2), Desdemona begs her husband, "Please let me live." The stakes are high. She is highly motivated by the need to survive, as he tells her directly that he is about to choke her to death. Nothing she says can sway him to believe in her innocence, he is so blinded by jealousy. As he is a warrior, killing is a characteristic action that his rage brings out in him.

OTHELLO	Sweet Soule, take heed, take heed of Perjury,	1
	Thou art on thy death-bed.	2
DESDEMONA	I, but not yet to dye.	3
OTHELLO	Presently.	4
	Therefore confesse thee freely of thy sinne:	5
	For to deny each Article with Oath,	6
	Cannot remove, nor choake the strong Conception	7
	That I do grone withall. Thou art to dye.	8
DESDEMONA	O Heaven have mercy on me.	9
OTHELLO	I say, Amen.	10
DESDEMONA	And have you mercy too. I never did	11
	Offend you in my life: never lov'd *Cassio*,	12
	But with such generall warrantie of Heaven,	13
	As I might love. I never gave him Token.	14
OTHELLO	By Heaven I saw my Handkerchiefe in's hand.	15
	O perjur'd woman, thou do'st stone my heart,	16
	And makes me call, what I intend to do,	17
	A Murther, which I thought a Sacrifice.	18
	I saw the Handkerchiefe.	19
DESDEMONA	He found it then:	20
	I never gave it him: Send, for him hither:	21
	Let him confesse a truth.	22

23	OTHELLO	He hath confest.
24	DESDEMONA	What, my Lord?
25	OTHELLO	That he hath us'd thee.
26	DESDEMONA	How? unlawfully?
27	OTHELLO	I.
28	DESDEMONA	He will not say so.
29	OTHELLO	No: his mouth is stopp'd:
30		Honest *Iago* hath 'tane order for't.
31	DESDEMONA	Oh, my feare interprets. What is he dead?
32	OTHELLO	Had all his haires bin lives, my great Revenge
33		Had stomacke for them all.
34	DESDEMONA	Alas, he is betray'd, and I undone.
35	OTHELLO	Out Strumpet: weep'st thou for him to my face?
36	DESDEMONA	O banish me, my Lord, but kill me not.
37	OTHELLO	Downe Strumpet.
38	DESDEMONA	Kill me to morrow, let me live to night.
39	OTHELLO	Nay, if you strive.
40	DESDEMONA	But halfe an houre.
41	OTHELLO	Being done, there is no pawse.
42	DESDEMONA	But while I say one prayer.
43	OTHELLO	It is too late. [*Smothers her.*]

The historical plays of Shakespeare are also filled with survival conflicts. For example, in Act 1, Scene 4 of *Richard the Third*, two assassins have been sent by Richard to kill his brother Clarence, who is being held prisoner in the Tower of London. The guard is persuaded to leave Clarence unprotected. When he awakes, a conversation ensues between him and his murderers in which he begs for his life.

CLARENCE	Relent, and save your soules:	1
	Which of you, if you were a Princes Sonne,	2
	Being pent from Liberty, as I am now,	3
	If two such murtherers as your selves came to you,	4
	Would not intreat for life, as you would begge	5
	Were you in my distresse.	6
MURDERER 1	Relent? no: 'Tis cowardly and womanish.	7
CLARENCE	Not to relent, is beastly, savage, divellish:	8
	My Friend, I spy some pitty in thy lookes:	9
	O, if thine eye be not a Flatterer,	10
	Come thou on my side, and intreate for mee,	11
	A begging Prince, what begger pitties not.	12
MURDERER 2	Looke behinde you, my Lord.	13
MURDERER 1	Take that, and that, if all this will not do, [*Stabs him.*]	14
	Ile drowne you in the Malmesey-But within. [*Exit.*]	15

The Need to Love and Be Loved

In the classical sense, needing love involves mutuality, sensuality, intimacy, and romance. It's about the union of two people and the desire for reciprocity of good feeling. Without the beloved, the lover feels incomplete. In plays, this basic need encompasses relationships between siblings, and between parents and their children, in addition to sexual and romantic relationships.

Romantic union motivates Cressida in *Troylus and Cressida* (Act 3, Scene 2). She takes a risk in this conversation, because her desire to be intimate with Troylus is intense.

CRESSIDA	Boldnesse comes to mee now, and brings mee	1

2		heart: Prince _Troylus_, I have lov'd you night and day, for
3		many weary moneths.
4	TROYLUS	Why was my _Cressid_ then so hard to win?
5	CRESSIDA	Hard to seeme won: but I was won my Lord
6		With the first glance; that ever pardon me,
7		If I confesse much you will play the tyrant:
8		I love you now, but not till now so much...
9		But I might maister it; infaith I lye:
10		My thoughts were like unbrideled children grow
11		Too head-strong for their mother...

The love of a daughter for her father is the underlying need that Cordelia demonstrates in _King Lear,_ Act 4, Scene 7. For her, this is a motivating factor throughout the play, although the King hasn't acknowledged his daughter's love until this moment.

1	CORDELIA	O looke upon me Sir,
2		And hold your hand in benediction o're me,
3		You must not kneele.
4	LEAR	Pray do not mocke me:
5		I am a very foolish fond old man,
6		Fourescore and upward,
7		Not an houre more, nor lesse:
8		And to deale plainely,
9		I feare I am not in my perfect mind.
10		Me thinkes I should know you, and know this man
11		Yet I am doubtfull: For I am mainely ignorant
12		What place this is: and all the skill I have
13		Remembers not these garments: nor I know not

	Where I did lodge last night. Do not laugh at me,	14
	For (as I am a man) I thinke this Lady	15
	To be my childe *Cordelia*.	16
CORDELIA	And so I am: I am.	17

The Need for Validation

Being validated means receiving acknowledgement for one's worth, receiving support and respect, and belonging. The desire is: "I want and deserve respect because I'm a human being." The need grows stronger when it is frustrated. A perfect example of a character motivated by validation is Edmond in *King Lear*. Let's look again at his famous speech from Act 1, Scene 2, that we evaluated on Day 8.

BASTARD	Thou Nature art my Goddesse, to thy Law	1
	My services are bound, wherefore should I	2
	Stand in the plague of custome, and permit	3
	The curiosity of Nations, to deprive me?	4
	For that I am some twelve, or fourteene Moonshines	5
	Lag of a Brother? Why Bastard? Wherefore base?	6
	When my Dimensions are as well compact,	7
	My minde as generous, and my shape as true	8
	As honest Madams issue? Why brand they us	9
	With Base? With baseness Bastardie? Base, Base?	10
	Who in the lustie stealth of Nature, take	11
	More composition, and fierce qualitie,	12
	Then doth within a dull stale tyred bed	13
	Goe to th' creating a whole tribe of Fops	14
	Got 'tweene a sleepe, and wake? Well then,	15

Legitimate *Edgar*, I must have your land,	16
Our Fathers love, is to the Bastard *Edmond*,	17
As to th' legitimate: fine word: Legitimate.	18
Well, my Legittimate, if this Letter speed,	19
And my invention thrive, *Edmond*, the base	20
Shall to' th' Legitimate: I grow, I prosper:	21
Now Gods, stand up for Bastards.	22

In *Twelfth Night*, Malvolio, the steward of Lady Olivia's household, wants to elevate his status by marrying Olivia. Of course, he's not really her equal and so his desire for validation makes him the target of everyone's jokes. Because he is a pompous buffoon, other characters play a trick on him by planting a fake letter from Olivia where he will find it. The letter identifies all sorts of things that Olivia supposedly loves, such as yellow, cross-gartered stockings—when actually she hates them. Throughout the rest of the play, he annoys Olivia and makes a complete fool of himself—to our amusement. In Act 2, Scene 5, Malvolio gives a prose speech of self-validation as he reads the letter.

1 MALVOLIO M. O. A. I. This simulation is not as the former:
2 And yet to crush this a little, it would bow to mee, for e-
3 very one of these Letters are in my name.

The shipwrecked Ferdinand in *The Tempest* also validates himself as he woos Miranda (Act 3, Scene 1). But he's not a buffoon. He seduces her in verse, wanting her to know the reality of his nature and noble status despite his current situation.

| FERDINAND | I am in my condition | 1 |
| | A Prince (Miranda) I do thinke a King | 2 |

The Need for Happiness

Many characters are motivated either by the need for pleasure or the need to relieve suffering–their own or someone else's. Some of them want to cultivate harmony in the world, and others want to resolve pain. In fact, the pain–pleasure polarity is always involved in actions that derive from this underlying motivation.

Consider the monologue spoken by the Jailor's Daughter in *Two Noble Kinsman* (Act 2, Scene 4). She is not yearning for a mutual love so much as for happiness and a good husband. Most importantly, she genuinely wants to restore harmony in the world by relieving the prince's suffering through setting him free.

JAILOR'S DAUGHTER

Why should I love this Gentleman,	1
'Tis odds he will never affect me. I am base,	2
My Father the meane Keeper of his Prison,	3
And he a Prince; To marry him is hopelesse;	4
To be his whore, is witles; Out upon't;	5
What pushes are we wenches driven to	6
When fifteene once has found us? First I saw him,	7
I (seeing) thought he was a goodly man;	8
He has as much to please a woman in him,	9
(If he please to bestow it so) as ever	10
These eyes yet lookt on; Next, I pittied him,	11

12	And so would any young wench o'my Conscience
13	That ever dream'd, or vow'd her Maydenhead
14	To a yong hansom Man; Then I lov'd him;
15	And yet he had a Cosen, faire as he too.
16	But in my heart was *Palamon,* and there
17	Lord, what a coyle he keepes? To heare him
18	Sing in an evening, what a heaven it is?
19	And yet his Songs are sad-ones; Fairer spoken,
20	Was never a Gentleman. When I come in
21	To bring him water in a morning, first
22	He bowes his noble body, then salutes me, thus:
23	Faire, gentle Mayde, good morrow, may thy goodness,
24	Get thee a happy husband; Once he kist me,
25	I lov'd my lips the better ten daies after,
26	Would he would doe so ev'ry day; He grieves much,
27	And me as much to see his misery.
28	What should I doe, to make him know I love him,
29	For I would faine enjoy him? Say I ventur'd
30	To set him free? what saies the law then? Thus much
31	For Law, or kindred: I will doe it,
32	And this night, or to morrow he shall love me.

In *The Merchant of Venice,* Jobbe the Clown works for Shylock, a mean spirited man who doesn't treat him well. He yearns for relief from the pain of serving Shylock. That relief would bring him happiness. During this comic prose speech from Act 2, Scene 1, Jobbe is talking to the angel on one shoulder telling him to be good and stay, and to the demon on the other telling him to be bad and flee for his own

pleasure. His boss Shylock is Jewish, which is why Jobbe keeps referring to "the Jew my maister."

CLOWN   Certainely, my conscience will serve me to run   1
from this Jew my Maister: the fiend is at mine elbow,   2
and tempts me, saying to me, *Jobbe, Launcelet Jobbe,* good 3
Launcelet, or good *Jobbe,* or good *Launcelet Jobbe,* use   4
your legs, take the start, run awaie: my conscience saies 5
no; take heede honest *Launcelet,* take heed honest *Jobbe,* 6
or as afore-said honest *Launcelet Jobbe,* doe not runne,   7
scorne running with thy heeles; well, the most coragi-   8
ous fiend bids me packe, *fia* saies the fiend, away saies   9
the fiend, for the heavens rouse up a brave minde saies 10
the fiend, and run; well, my conscience hanging about   11
the necke of my heart, saies verie wisely to me: my ho- 12
nest friend *Launcelet,* being an honest mans sonne, or ra- 13
ther an honest womans sonne, for indeede my Father did 14
something smack, something grow too; he had a kinde of 15
taste; wel, my conscience saies *Lancelet* bouge not, bouge 16
saies the fiend, bouge not saies my conscience, conscience 17
say I you counsaile well, fiend say I you counsaile well, 18
to be rul'd by my conscience I should stay with the *Jew* 19
my Maister, (who God blesse the marke) is a kinde of di-20
vell; and to run away from the *Jew* I should be ruled by 21
the fiend, who saving your reverence is the divell him- 22
selfe: certainely the *Jew* is the verie divell incarnation, 23
and in my conscience, my conscience is a kinde of hard 24
conscience, to offer to counsaile me to stay with the *Jew;*25

26	the fiend gives the more friendly counsaile: I will runne
27	fiend, my heeles are at your commandement, I will
28	runne.

The Need to Win and Be at the Top of the Heap

On stage, needing to win is always handled in the extreme. It is an all-or-nothing motivation. In the theatre, winning power or wanting to succeed involves killing. It is a struggle to rise above everyone at any cost—even the ultimate cost. Where have we seen this before? Although her husband strangles Desdemona as the turning point in *Othello*, Iago really murders her, because he is motivated by the need to beat Othello and so turns Othello against her. Iago sets up the fatal outcome in Act 1, Scene 1, when he says:

1 IAGO	I follow him, to serve my turne upon him.
2	We cannot all be Masters, nor all Masters
3	Cannot be truely follow'd...

In *Richard the Third*, Richard wants to be king of England at all costs, and kills loads of people to achieve his goal. In fact, the end of the play is a blood bath. Knowing he will murder her, he coerces Lady Ann to marry him, an act he describes in this *mwah-ha-ha* mad speech from Act 1, Scene 2. Richard is driven by his insatiable hunger for power.

1 RICHARD	Was ever woman in this humour woo'd?
2	Was ever woman in this humour wonne?
3	Ile have her, but I will not keepe her long.
4	What? I that kill'd her Husband, and his Father,

To take her in her hearts extreamest hate,   5

With curses in her mouth, Teares in her eyes,   6

The bleeding witnesse of my hatred by,   7

Having God, her Conscience, and these bars against me, 8

And I, no Friends to backe my suite withall,   9

But the plaine Divell, and dissembling lookes?   10

And yet to winne her? All the world to nothing.   11

Hah!   12

In Act 4, Scene 5 of *Coriolanus,* the Roman top general Coriolanus turns traitor and joins with his enemies, the Volces (a Germanic people), motivated by the desire to beat his countrymen. His power usurped, he's been exiled; so he is eager for revenge.

CORIOLANUS…Now this extremity,   1

Hath brought me to thy Harth, not out of Hope   2

(Mistake me not) to save my life: for if   3

I had fear'd death, of all the Men i'th' World   4

I would have voided thee. But in meere spight   5

To be full quit of those my Banishers,   6

Stand I before thee heere: Then if thou hast   7

A heart of wreake in thee, that wilt revenge   8

Thine owne particular wrongs, and stop those maimes 9

Of shame seene through thy Country, speed thee straight 10

And make my misery serve thy turne: So use it,   11

That my revengefull Services may prove   12

As Benefits to thee. For I will fight   13

Against my Cankred Countrey, with the Spleene   14

Of all the under Fiends…   15

In *Macbeth* (Act 3, Scene 1), Macbeth indicates that he would kill to win. He has already murdered the king, Duncan, to become king, and fears that Banquo may figure it out. That's a threat with which he feels he cannot live.

1 MACBETH To be thus, is nothing, but to be safely thus
2   Our feares in *Banquo* sticke deepe,
3   And in his Royaltie of Nature reignes that
4   Which would be fear'd.

—— Your Task—Naming Your Basic Human Need ——

In a realistic way, go through the speech or scene you are working on, and identify which of the five basic human needs most highly motivates your character. Make your decision based upon the givens you found in your Day 18 rehearsal. How high are the stakes for your character? Is this a motivation that you, as an actor in a role, could pursue with passion throughout this play?

Daydream about the need you have decided upon. Make notes in a journal. Can you personally associate with this need in your own life? Maybe there was a time you felt you would do anything to win, or to survive, or to create harmony. Can you imagine a situation in which your behavior would be compelled by one of the five basic needs?

Find a role model for your character. Have you ever seen anyone in the real world who was motivated by the need you've chosen? How did they behave? For example, Iago in *Othello* lusts for power just as much as any Enron executive ever lusted to earn money. Enron was an energy company whose leadership cheated consumers on the West Coast out of billions of dollars. Iago is willing to lie, cheat, steal, play the fool, and plant handkerchiefs implicating people to get ahead. His every action and speech is designed to manipulate people and maneuver around them by persuading them that he loves them and is honest. He constantly repeats: "I think you know I love you." He does not care who dies, or how many people die as long so he wins and ends up as king of the hill.

Have you seen an Enron executive, such as CEO Jeffrey Skilling, in action on tape or in person? Watch the documentary released in 2005 called *Enron: The Smartest Guys in the Room.* You could adopt Skilling's characteristics. Another model could be someone else whose public persona is charming and attractive, but who he is dastardly in secret, such as the serial killer Ted Bundy. Because Bundy was a good-looking, clean-cut guy, he was able to lure numerous young women to their deaths. You could play Ted Bundy's known characteristics as a substitution for inventing fictitious ones.

Of course, your role might be as a character in a comedy. Look around until you locate someone in the real world to study that has givens like your character's. How does this individual behave? What notable features might you borrow for your portrayal?

Living a Genuine Life on Stage

Acting means you are living through a genuine moment-to-moment reality on stage even though you are using scripted words. To bring your character to life on stage, whatever your character is going through has to be evident in your body and voice. The stage is literally no place to hide. The audience can see the truth of whatever you are or are not feeling, so it is important to find ways to arouse true feelings that you can freely express and share. Perhaps the most important method-acting tool is your imagination, because your body doesn't distinguish between memories, daydreams, and reality. Once you plant a seed of reality inside your mind, it will color and influence your body language and vocal styles. Everyone, fortunately, can see it.

You have to serve the requirements of the play and you need to give other actors appropriate energy to work off of. Some days feeling energized and emotional will be easy and other days achieving the right state will be hard, depending on how closely you can relate to the given circumstances of the plot. Each actor has to find the special triggers that are his or her own keys to arousing genuine life. My wife, Elizabeth Keefe, played Lady Macbeth in *Macbeth*, so I asked her to describe her emotional preparation process.

Lady Macbeth shifts her personality drastically from scene to scene. As the play progresses, her guilt at murdering Duncan, his guards, and Banquo causes her to deteriorate emotionally, until she is sleepwalking in Act 5, Scene 1, while imagining that she has blood on her hands that she cannot wash off. Here, a physician and a lady of the court are observing her. Lady Macbeth enters carrying a lit candle.

1 GENTLEWOMAN Lo you, heere she comes: This is her very guise, and upon
2 my life fast asleepe: observe her, stand close.
3 DOCTOR How came she by that light?
4 GENTLEWOMAN Why it stood by her: she ha's light by her continually,
5 'tis her command.

DOCTOR	You see her eyes are open.	6
GENTLEWOMAN	I, but their sense are shut.	7
DOCTOR	What is it she do's now?	8
	Looke how she rubbes her hands.	9
GENTLEWOMAN	It is an accustom'd action with her, to seeme	10
	thus washing her hands: I have knowne her	11
	continue in	
	this a quarter of an houre.	12
LADY MACBETH	Yet heere's a spot.	13
DOCTOR	Heark, she speaks, I will set downe what comes	14
	from her, to satisfie my remembrance the more	15
	strongly.	
LADY MACBETH	Out damned spot: out I say. One: Two: Why	16
	then 'tis time to doo't: Hell is murky. Fye,	17
	my Lord, fie,	
	a Souldier, and affear'd? what need we feare?	18
	who knowes	
	it, when none can call our powre to accompt:	
	yet who	19
	would have thought the olde man to have had so	
	much	20
	blood in him.	21
DOCTOR	Do you marke that?	22
LADY MACBETH	The Thane of Fife, had a wife: where is she now?	23
	What will these hands ne're be cleane?	24
	No more o'that	
	my Lord, no more o'that: you marre all with	25
	this starting.	

26	DOCTOR	Go too, go too:
27		You have knowne what you should not.
28	GENTLEWOMAN	She ha's spoke what shee should not, I am sure
29		of that: Heaven knowes what she ha's knowne.
30	LADY MACBETH	Heere's the smell of the blood still: all the perfumes
31		of Arabia will not sweeten this little hand.
32		Oh, oh, oh.
33	DOCTOR	What a sigh is there? The hart is sorely charg'd.
34	GENTLEWOMAN	I would not have such a heart in my bosome,
35		for the dignity of the whole body.
36	DOCTOR	Well, well, well.
37	GENTLEWOMAN	Pray God it be sir.
38	DOCTOR	This disease is beyond my practise: yet I have
39		knowne those which have walkt in their sleep, who have
40		dyed holily in their beds.
41	LADY MACBETH	Wash your hands, put on your Night-Gowne,
42		looke not so pale: I tell you yet againe *Banquo's* buried;
43		he cannot come out on's grave.
44	DOCTOR	Even so?
45	LADY MACBETH	To bed, to bed: there's knocking at the gate:
46		Come, come, come, come, give me your hand: What's
47		done, cannot be undone. To bed, to bed, to bed.
		[*Exit Lady.*]

When we spoke, Elizabeth reported,

The audience's perceptions were most important to me when I did Lady Macbeth's mad scene. Were they being entertained? I felt like I cracked the role, and the scene, because I did everything specifically and didn't mush all the moments together. I wanted to take a journey with Lady Macbeth as she was coming undone, to arrive where her mind is unhinged. Personally, I don't know what that feels like, so it was an illusion that I created. But I thought about it and decided that craziness would probably look like a combination of anxiety, mood changes, and frustration.

My belief is that it is best not to 'play' a character's state of being, such as Lady Macbeth's madness. I prefer to really do something. So I didn't act mad. Instead I took almost everything from the text. Yes, I began by doing my homework. I made up a story about what happened to her and how she got to this place. Then I forgot about it. When I'm in performance, hopefully it's been so solidified by then that I can trust it.

When we ran the play in rehearsal, I got a sense of how much time I needed to put on the mad makeup, so I could put them on at the last moment. I would blacken my eyes and make my skin grayer, and I wore a weird wig. As I put these on, I allowed them to take me to a certain place inside me where everything seemed askew. Then I would literally listen to the last scene in Act 4 while rocking back and forth in my mad makeup like a child. Physicalizing it helped immensely! I would rock and rock and rock.

From the text I took that she's rubbing her hands. So on stage I rubbed my skin as though I was rubbing it off. I really did it. One time I actually rubbed my skin raw, I was so focused on rubbing. Of course, nothing was happening, as there is no real blood, so a sense of frustration and anxiety would come up. Those were real feelings. I trusted that my instrument–my body and voice–would respond to the reality of what I was doing and put me in a different frame of mind. From the text I also took my gearshifts, which were like 90-degree angles. And I changed my point of focus each time. I made sharp movements on the punctuation. There were many, many colons and end stops.

Another possibility would have been for me to mimic specific behavior patterns, such as those of a clinically diagnosed schizophrenic, borrowing observed body language and speech patterns from actual individuals. As actors we can do research and watch documentary film to select the kind of behavior patterns we prefer and believe serve the script. Sometimes this gives us options we wouldn't invent on our own.

In different plays I have used personal substitutions to evoke tears and emotion. My dad had cancer and one of our dear family friends had died just before I did a play with a farewell scene in it, and substituting these people for the character to whom I was saying goodbye worked as a trigger. After awhile different triggers fade. When those weren't as rich, I picked a new one. You have to know yourself well enough to know when a trigger has become dull so you can find something else to evoke true feeling.

Depending on the day, the well may also feel dry. But the show must go on. On those days, I have to give myself an extra half hour to work on myself emotionally. Other days I am more fully present with my given circumstances and I am triggered quickly.

────── Your Task—Making Substitutions ──────

Anything in a script, including your own character's behavior, may have a prototype or parallel in the real world or in the realm of your imagination. If your character says the name of a place, a person, or a thing, in your mind you can substitute something personal that evokes strong feelings in you that are aligned with what the playwright intended for your character. For instance, when Lady Macbeth says "Banquo," whom would you imagine? Is there anyone you regret having offended or harmed accidentally or on purpose? When the Jailor's Daughter talks about the kiss the prince gave her, you could substitute the memory of a sweet kiss you once experienced. When Jobbe talks about being torn between remaining with Shylock and running away, what comes to mind? Maybe you have had a similar experience of being unable to decide between two opposite actions.

Use this list of questions to find possible substitutions for circumstances you've discovered in the text:

- Have you or has anything in your life ever been like this?

- Have you ever seen anyone or anything like this in the real world?

- If your character were an animal, what animal would you be? Are you a panther, a snake, a puppy? What animals do you perceive in other characters?

- If this were a game, what game would you be playing? Are you playing hopscotch, tag, hide-and-go-seek, poker, or dodge ball?

Can you decode the rules of the game that your character is playing?

- If this were a dance, what style of dance would it be? Are you doing the tango, swing dancing, tap dancing, or performing in a ballet?

A great thing about your preparation is that it is invisible. The audience doesn't perceive your substitution or what you have done to create a genuine life for them, all they see is what they see: hopefully, an excellently crafted scene filled with emotion.

Your Day 19 Rehearsal Checklist

Have you completed your tasks?

☐ Naming Your Basic Need

☐ Making Substitutions

What discoveries have you made?

DAY 20

Your Doings

Today's rehearsal builds upon the work of creating a role from the inside out that you did in your last two rehearsals. At this phase of performance, it is important to focus on your character's goals. These drives influence your emotional state and physical behavior. On Day 18, you identified given circumstances as provided by the script. You explored how these might feel if they were true for your life. On Day 19, you named the underlying human need that motivates your character. You began forming a genuine connection to this basic need as an overarching objective. Now your work will center on breaking down your script (a speech or scene) into smaller playable units. For each unit—a portion of the script that could be a sentence, a line, or a line fragment—you will assign a verb that describes what your character is doing at that moment in order to achieve his or her objective right then. This technique is precise and personal.

Identifying Your Beats (Units of Action)

Character is established by the actions pursued during speeches, scenes, acts, and entire plays. Each end stop (period, exclamation mark, or question mark) encompasses a complete thought and at least one playable objective. Every verb you play to achieve this objective, whether it lasts for one line, ten lines, or only for a fragment of a line, is considered a *beat*. You must choose one verb for each beat—that's a doing. You can find new beats by looking at Shakespeare's idiosyncratic punctuation. With commas, semicolons, colons, and end stops he is telling you where you should shift gears. A beat lasts as long as you can play the same action, or doing. Continue pursuing the same action until something changes in the script—your lines or your partner's lines. In other words, continue until your strategy has led you to succeed or fail to accomplish your objective.

A doing is any verb that can be actively pursued. It must affect, change, or fix another person on stage. Galvanizing verbs are those intended to stimulate or excite someone, like bioelectricity running through a muscle and making it twitch. Predicating verbs are intended to trigger events and responses (if *this*, then *that*). They are the first link in a chain of events. Such verbs set the plot in motion or move it forward.

A trap that many actors fall into is evaluating their doings in terms of what the verbs do to them personally (e.g., "I want," "I adore," "I laugh"). Playable verbs should actually be doings done to others (e.g., "I tease," "I intimidate," "I seduce").

Be mindful that Shakespeare loved surprises. In a long speech, you may believe that your character is building to a specific conclusion, only to discover halfway through that Shakespeare has your character switch gears and entertain the audience for a while with a digression, and then picks up the first point later. You might go in a whole new direction just to please the audience. Be ready: Gearshifts are beat changes.

STRONG, PLAYABLE ACTION VERBS

What makes some verbs hot and strong while other verbs are cool and weak? According to William Ball, author of *A Sense of Direction*, a main quality of an actable verb is that it is a commonplace activity that a person should be able to pursue with gusto for at least ten minutes. It shouldn't be intellectual. It should have an emotional tangible feel to it. The example Ball uses is "castigate." An actable equivalent might be "give him hell."

Open yourself to the richly diverse power and expression of words. Give them careful consideration. Romance them. Marina Calderone and Maggie Lloyd-Williams, coauthors of *Actions*, state that choosing strong action verbs "heightens an actor's spontaneity." Choosing compelling doings will enable you to respond honestly to the truth of your onstage circumstances, because your doings will be instinctive, and thus your body and voice will have freedom and color.

Don't confuse the playable verbs I'm describing here with the verbs that are a part of the script (see Day 5, "Revving Up Your Verbs"). Playable verbs express a character's internal life and behavior patterns. As an example, let's say that your objective is to drink from a glass of water sitting near you on a table. One given circumstance is that you are dying of thirst—so your underlying need is survival. It's urgent. Another given is that someone is standing between you and the table. Your lines and playable verbs are:

YOU	I'm so thirsty. I need that water.	[Admit]
	Won't you please get out of my way?	[Request]
	If you don't move I'm going to make you.	[Threaten]
	I said to move!	[Demand]
	This is delicious.	[Brag]

In this situation, do you see how none of the playable verbs are ever mentioned in the lines? Rather, the verbs describe your character's doings: his or her ways of overcoming an obstacle (getting past the other person) and achieving the goal (drinking the glass of water). For simplicity, I've written each line as a single unit of the script–one line, one doing.

Notice that there are many different ways each of these doings can be done. For instance, a threat could include a stern look, a raised fist, a loud voice, or another set of physical and vocal choices that you invent that make the moment uniquely yours. As long as you know that your doing is "to threaten," you could probably come up with an infinite stream of options to offer a director until an ideal approach is chosen. Perhaps, if this were a comedy, you would be threatening to tickle the other person with a feather. How you decide what is appropriate depends in part on who your character is, who the other person is, your relationship to that individual, and what the stakes are.

Picking a strong action verb is an art. But there are only a few rules to follow:

1. It has to be something you can do to another person. To test this, sandwich it between the words "I" and "you" to see if it functions (e.g., "I tempt you").
2. Phrase it in the present tense.
3. Phrase it in the positive. The word "not" cannot be played.
4. Be precise.
5. It must be a singular action. You cannot play two things at one time.
6. The verb has to matter to you–search until you find one that does. You want it to arouse your gut instincts and emotions.

────── Your Task—Picking Your "Doings" ──────

To establish your doings, break your speech into sections that terminate with end stops or other pieces of punctuation, and write a verb next to each of these smaller units of text— your beats. How long can you sustain the first action verb? You can test your chosen doings by playing each one for as long as you can until you are forced by the script to change to the next doing.

Once you've chosen your doings, perform your speech. With every fiber of your being suit your doing to your need. Solve your problems. Be mindful to avoid playing pain, as that is an unproductive choice. In this process, something magical will occur—you'll discover that you don't have to generate feeling. The flow of life will move through you of its own accord, because you are really doing what you're doing, not faking it.

You may already be playing doings instinctively after all the text work you've done up to this point in your rehearsal process. By labeling this energy with a verb, you have the freedom to strengthen the choice, commit more fully to it, or change the verb.

When in Doubt: Eight Major Categories of Doings

There are eight main categories of doings, which encompass almost all other playable verbs. If you're ever in doubt about what verb to play, you can always fall back upon one of these never-fail archetypal doings. When I was a student these were always my starting place to make sense of complicated language. Twenty-five years later, I still find them useful, although I have discovered exceptions, such as simple lines, which don't fall under their rubric, and I encourage actors in my productions to use many more verbs than these. Let's look at the list of eight fundamental playable verbs now.

TO ADMIT

A unique internal action, with admission you are giving out information without editorializing. Simple. Powerful. Calm. And reminiscent of the epic style from the Ancient Greeks. The Prologue to *Romeo and Juliet* is a good example of "admit":

1	CHORUS	Two housholds both alike in dignitie,
2		(In faire *Verona*, where we lay our Scene)
3		From civill broyles broke into enmitie,
4		Whose civill warre makes civill hands uncleane.

TO CONVINCE/PERSUADE

An attempt to change or fix someone else's thinking or feeling. In *All's Well that End's Well* (Act 1, Scene 3), Helen asserts her love for the Countess' son. Although the Countess would like the pair to marry, she wants to have proof of Helen's true feelings. Helen's doing is "persuade." She says:

1	HELEN	Then I confesse
2		Here on my knee, before high heaven and you,
3		That before you, and next unto high heaven, I love your Sonne.

TO DEFY

Total disagreement. If one character says yes, the other says no. It's a polar opposite. We see defiance occur in *King John* (Act 3, Scene 3).

Interestingly, in this example the doing matches the verb in Constance's line. Sometimes defiance may be harder to spot.

FRANCE	Patience good Lady, comfort gentle Constance.	1
CONSTANCE	No, I defie all Counsell, all redresse	2

TO SCOLD

Chastising someone for wrongdoing or misbehavior, such as the Queen does to her husband in *Henry the Sixth* (Act 1, Scene 1), because he gave away his crown:

QUEEN	Ah wretched man, would I had dy'de a Maid?	1

And a little later in the same scene:

QUEEN	Enforc't thee? Art thou King and wilt be forc't?	1
	I shame to hear thee speake: ah timorous Wretch	2

TO LAMENT

A rare, but interesting internal action that arises when a character feels that everything is out of his or her hands. It's a spoken expression, usually beginning with the word "Well." Don't confuse the word lament with grief or mourning. In this context it can be an opportunity for humor, which is often a more plot-propelling choice.

In *Henry the Fourth, Part One*, Falstaffe utters five laments in Act 2, Scene 4. The disreputable Prince Harry and his friend Poins have been getting drunk at the Boar's Head Tavern with the locals when a messenger arrives with bad news from the prince's father, King Henry. As Falstaffe, the Prince's friend and mentor in the ways of vagabonds and criminals, describes the Scotsman Douglas, a leader of the revolution, he says:

FALSTAFFE   Well, that Rascall hath good mettall in him…

                 Well, hee is there too, and one Mordake, and…

                 Well, thou wilt be horrible chidde to morrow…

                 Well, and the fire of Grace be not quite out of thee…

                 Well, here is my legge.

All these lines are laments. It's as if Falstaffe is repeating, "It's out of our hands. That's the way it is." Serious matters are intruding on their fun.

TO FIND OUT

In Act 2, Scene 1 of *Titus Andronicus,* Tamora finds Aaron alone working out a stratagem to cope with an enemy. She wants to figure out what he's thinking and feeling, and possibly cheer him up. Tamora says:

1 TAMORA   My lovely *Aaron,*

2   Wherefore look'st thou sad,

3   When every thing doth make a Gleefull boast?

We can think of this internal action as investigating, questioning, seeking the truth or answers, asking, or discovering. It is speech aimed at eliciting information.

TO UNDERSTAND

Wrestling with an idea is in the realm of this internal action. Even if you're on stage alone involve the audience in the process. Otherwise this becomes self-involved navel gazing and disinteresting to watch. For example, consider the speech that Henry gives in Act 4, Scene 1 of *Henry the Fifth.* The king has gone out among his men in disguise the night before a big battle. He wants to be a regular man and his goal is to understand the difference between an ordinary man and a king.

HENRY	What infinite hearts-ease must Kings neglect,	1
	That private men enjoy?	2
	And what have Kings, that Privates have not too,	3
	Save Ceremonie, save generall Ceremonie?	4
	And what art thou, thou Idoll Ceremonie?	5
	What kind of God art thou?...	6

TO DEMONSTRATE
(ANGER, DELIGHT, SCORN, DISGUST, SURPRISE, AND SO ON)

In the acting sense, demonstrations are either larger-than-life expressions or they are masks or facades that characters put on to fool others. We see a huge demonstration of anger and disgust in Act 2, Scene 1 of *The Merry Wives of Windsor*. Mistress Page, a married woman, has received a love letter from an admirer, and is aflutter with excitement until she reaches the signature: John Falstaffe. Then she demonstratively says:

MISTRESS	What a Herod of Jurie is this? O wicked, wicked world:	1
PAGE	One that is well-nye worne to peeces with age	2
	To show himselfe a yong Gallant?	3

Imagine two actors are up for the same role and one of them gets chosen. The one who wasn't cast turns with a smile to the other and enthusiastically says, "I'm sooo happy for you." That's probably a white lie, a demonstration of support, if the actor who says it is trying to hide disappointment. Of course, there can be dangerous pretenses and malicious lies, but often demonstrations are for enter-tainment. An example in a play by Shakespeare is Act 2, Scene 4 of *Henry the Fourth, Part One*, a few minutes before the news arrives about the start of the civil war.

Earlier in the day, Sir John Falstaffe and three other scoundrels robbed a coach. Prince Harry and Poins saw it, and decided to trick the highwaymen. They disguised themselves and threatened the group of four, who promptly dropped the bootie and ran away. To hide their cowardice, they cut off their clothes to make it look as though they had fought back. Falstaffe tells the Prince whopper after whopper. His tall tale only gets more elaborate under scrutiny. When the Prince asks: "Where is the money?" Falstaffe replies, describing an increasing numbers of marauders; a dozen, sixteen, and more.

1	FALSTAFFE	Where is it? taken from us, it is: a hundred
2		upon poore foure of us.
3	PRINCE	What, a hundred, man?
4	FALSTAFFE	I am a Rogue, if I were not at halfe Sword with
5		a dozen of them two houres together. I have scaped by
6		miracle. I am eight times thrust through the Doublet,
7		foure through the Hose, my Buckler cut through and
8		through, my Sword hackt like a Hand-saw, *ecce signum.*
9		I never dealt better since I was a man: all would not doe.
10		A plague of all Cowards: let them speake; if they speake
11		more or lesse then truth, they are villaines, and the sonnes
12		of darknesse.
13	PRINCE	Speake sirs, how was it?
14	GADSHILL	We foure set upon some dozen.
15	FALSTAFFE	Sixteene, at least, my Lord.

A little bit further in the scene, the numbers of attackers increases yet again.

PRINCE	What, fought yee with them all?	1
FALSTAFFE	All? I know not what yee call all: but if I	2
	Fought not with fiftie of them, I am a bunch of Radish.	3

Later on, the Prince remarks astutely:

| PRINCE | These Lyes are like the Father that begets them, | 1 |
| | grosse as a Mountaine, open, palpable. | 2 |

How to Choose Doings for a Scene

Let's dissect the Nurse and Juliet's scene from Act 2, Scene 4 of *Romeo and Juliet* to identify the two characters' doings. What might an actor be thinking when making a decision? When are they admitting, persuading, scolding, and so on? In this 23-line scene, Juliet has been waiting for news from the Nurse. Her preceding soliloquy is a conversation with the audience about how impatient she feels. But when the Nurse finally arrives, she drags out telling Juliet the news of her impending marriage to Romeo. So there is a conflict built in between the pair.

For our current purpose, every few lines I'll interrupt the scene and give my explanation (≈~) of the doings. Then the scene will be continued. (When a doing is a line fragment, it is underlined in the text.)

| JULIET | <u>O God she comes</u>, O hony Nurse what newes? | 1 |
| | Hast thou met with him? <u>send thy man away</u>. | 2 |

᠅ As the Nurse arrives, "O God she comes" is a demonstration of Juliet's urgency to get the information. It is not said to the Nurse, but to the audience as the tag line to the soliloquy that preceded this scene. So the first beat is: Demonstrate (urgency).

᠅ The remainder of line 1 and the first part of line 2 are a single action: Find out.

᠅ The second half of line 2 is a separate beat: Command.

3 NURSE   *Peter* stay at the gate.

᠅ Line 3 is a simple line, with a simple action: Command. The playwright's purpose here as to establish that Juliet and the Nurse are in private. It is an intimate scene.

4 JULIET   Now good sweet Nurse:
5   O Lord, why lookest thou sad?
6   Though newes, be sad, yet tell them merrily.
7   If good thou sham'st the musicke of sweet newes,
8   By playing it to me, with so sower a face.

᠅ If Juliet's underlying goal in the scene is to find out the information, she may have to play several other actions to accomplish that goal. Each one of those actions is a separate beat. As an actor, you must stay on the beat you're on–it's like a stepping-stone taking you across a river of life. Don't play ahead of your character.

᠅ On line 4, the actress playing Juliet begins by flattering the Nurse. But how long can she sustain this action? When she hits the colon, she's got to shift gears. The new beat "Oh Lord, why lookest thou sad?" could be played as: Comfort or soothe. What verb will get Juliet closer to her goal? What verb might truly impact the Nurse if it were played 100 percent? She can only sustain that verb to the question mark.

∼ Next she makes a rhetorical argument for three lines, during which the verb convince may be sustainable. This is a digression. She has to cheer up the Nurse in order to hear the news that she has been anticipating, which is her overarching objective. Juliet's basic human need here and elsewhere in the play is to love and be loved. An actress might also play these two lines as two separate beats, each a complete sentence. The first, line 6, might be: Cheer up or Bolster. The second, lines 7 and 8, might be: Scold.

∼ An actress should be wary of playing negative (plot-stopping) choices. Her given circumstances reveal a great affection between Juliet and the Nurse. She probably would not berate the Nurse harshly. Scolding could be done in fun or teasingly. Maybe it's an established form of communication between the two characters. Much depends on the interpretation the individual performers give their portrayals, and the relationship.

NURSE	I am a weary, give me leave awhile,	9
	Fie how my bones ake, what a jaunt have I had?	10

∼ Here the Nurse appears to be demonstrating her exhaustion for Juliet's sake. What's the reason? Her little girl has grown up and will be leaving home. Now the Nurse won't be able to give and receive affection from Juliet anymore. Possibly, she's dragging out the news for as long as she can so she can get just one more dose of attention.

◈ Remember that doings are always done to or for others. So the actress playing the Nurse needs to be doing to Juliet even though she's making self-centered remarks.

11 JULIET   I would thou had'st my bones, and I thy newes:
12   Nay come I pray thee speake, good good Nurse speake.

◈ Line 11 is a beat that ends with a colon. Juliet's goal is to find out, but that may not be playable here as an action. Her obstacle to overcome here is to get the Nurse to stop thinking about her aching body and start telling about the news she's got. How can Juliet solve this problem? Perhaps the actress could play Commiserate, or maybe it's Remind. Or quite possibly it is Demonstrate. Juliet could be demonstrating her frustration or impatience to the Nurse in order to get her back on track towards revealing her secret information.

◈ Line 12 is a new beat. Perhaps Beg or Plead would be stronger playable verbs at this juncture than Ask. As a performer you need to choose a doing that revs your motor.

13 NURSE   <u>Jesu what hast?</u> can you not stay a while?
14   Do you not see that I am out of breath?

◈ The Nurse could be perceived as scolding Juliet on the three sentences of lines 13 and 14 (each is a question). In seeking variety, an actress would benefit from selecting three different playable verbs. Maybe it's a sandwich of actions: two demonstrations surrounding a scolding. How the Nurse plays it depends on characterization—elements of performance that come from the givens (Day 18) and personal substitutions (Day 19). Maybe Juliet has always been an impatient child, so it's easy to torment her. How put on is the Nurse's exhaustion? Is her fatigue real or is it a white lie?

JULIET   How art thou out of breath, when thou hast breth 15
      To say to me, that thou art out of breath?   16

∾ Juliet contradicts the Nurse on lines 15 and 16. Then continues:

      The excuse that thou dost make in this delay, 17
      Is longer then the tale thou dost excuse.   18

∾ An actress could rely upon the verb Scold for the beat on lines 17 and 18.

      <u>Is thy newes good or bad</u>? answere to that, 19
      Say either, and Ile stay the circumstance: 20
      Let me be satisfied, ist good or bad?   21

∾ "Is thy news good or bad?" is a direct question. You could rely upon the verb Ask or Find Out to handle it. Make it as simple line with no frivolous excesses. How the next two beats are played depends on how the actress wants Juliet to come across—how impatient, how good natured, and so forth. The first doing might be: Tease. There's a colon, so you also could be making a physical choice. What is this "circumstance" to which she refers that she will stop ("stay")–is she tickling the nurse?

◄ On line 21, Juliet could Beg or Plead. If she won the contest with the Nurse on the preceding line, maybe she's playing this triumphantly: Triumph.

22 NURSE   Well, you have made a simple choice, you know
23   not how to chuse a man:…

◄ Can you guess what the verb for the Nurse is above? Line 22 begins with "Well." You'd be in good shape going with the verb Lament. In the remainder of the speech she describes how fabulous Romeo is, so we know this would be lighthearted lamenting. The nurse is essentially saying "It's out of my hands that you, Juliet, have so stupidly chosen such a man. What can I do? He is only…perfect, handsome, and so on."

When you are choosing your doings consider the given circumstances, your human needs, your substitutions, your relationship to the other characters, and how best you can serve the script in this moment–what is happening in the story, the plot? Draw upon your earlier language exploration. Your strongest choices are those that advance your character toward his or her intended goal (or could have–some characters don't succeed). Every conflict is a contest, a game.

Playing to Win

Remember that you are playing to win because the stakes are high. Once you have chosen an action to play, you must pursue it fervently,

at risk of failure. Conflict is built into the plays, so the assertive character says lines in anticipation of receiving a denial or an objection. This
speaker says, "See it my way!" That's a positive acting choice since it
moves the play forward; it changes another character, if it succeeds.

When my friend Rainard was preparing the role of Lord Capulet
for the Orlando Shakespeare Festival in 1992 he decided to approach
the role based on the idea that Capulet is a powerful, passionate man
who has always been in complete control of his family. Now that
Capulet is getting older, he starts to see this control slipping away. It
is the conflict between his need to protect and hold on to his family
and his family's apparent disregard for his authority that drives him
to heights of emotion.

The pivotal scene (Act 3, Scene 5 where Juliet tells her father that
she will not marry Paris (the boy her parents intend for her) is the
final straw that sends Lord Capulet over the top. An actor playing
Capulet might be pursuing a goal, such as "making an unruly child
see it my way" (doing: convince) or "submit to my authority" (doing:
dominate).

CAPULET	And why my Lady wisedome? hold your tongue,	1
	Good Prudence, smatter with your gossip, go.	2
NURSE	I speak no treason,	3
	Father, O Godigoden,	4
	May not one speake?	5
CAPULET	Peace you mumbling foole,	6
	Utter your gravitie ore a Gossips bowles	7
	For here we need it not.	8
LADY CAPULET	You are too hot.	9
CAPULET	Gods bread, it makes me mad.	10

In order to reach the level of emotion necessary when Capulet explodes with "God's bread, it makes me mad," Rainard needed to find a preparation that would make him furious. He decided to look at the words that Shakespeare had given him to see if they could help in any way. He always looks for patterns of speech to help him build a character, and in this case the exercise was rewarded. He noticed an unusual amount of words beginning with the letter *G* in the lines leading up to his explosion.

From this he deduced that Shakespeare was giving him a visceral tool to help build the anger to a climax inside him. In a rehearsal, by hitting every *G* leading up to "God's bread" he found that the emotion, even if it wasn't present at the beginning, would arise through the physical, guttural effort of speaking the *G*s. He used this discovery as an offstage warm-up before he entered the scene. Then he was confident that, by a Pavlovian response, he would reach the same level of fury on the *G*s. It worked for every performance.

When performing Shakespeare, actors never need to worry about playing a feeling if they are clear about their objective and doings, and commit fully to the music of the language.

Your Day 20 Rehearsal Checklist

Have you completed your task?

☐ Picking Your Doings

What discoveries have you made?

DAY 21

Presto, $\mathcal{P}$ASTO!

In the Western world, plays are often based upon a classical five-part structure that represents a dramatic arc of increasing tension and ultimate resolution of conflict. The acronym for this arc is PASTO, which stands for preparation, attack, struggle, turning point, and outcome. Shakespeare's plays usually embody these elements in five acts, with each act serving one of the purposes. Furthermore, as the parts of a play are microcosms of a macrocosm, each scene within an act serves a purpose. Each speech and each line within a scene also serves a purpose. All of these textual fragments move us toward the same outcome. As an actor, understanding the concept of PASTO may add another layer of clarity to your role—and your rhetoric. It can help you play moments more specifically. In today's rehearsal, we'll look at each element of PASTO in turn.

Preparation

Preparation is the set up of a speech or a scene. It includes any background information that the audience requires to be kept up to speed. Typically, it also sets up the characters' rhetorical debate. In individual speeches, there's usually a sentence or two of establishment that lets you know where the character is coming from. For instance, in *The Two Noble Kinsman* (Act 2, Scene 4), the Jailor's Daughter begins a monologue:

JAILOR'S DAUGHTER

1	Why should I love this Gentleman,
2	'Tis odds he will never affect me. I am base,
3	My Father the meane Keeper of his Prison,
4	And he a Prince...

When we previously explored this monologue on Day 19, it was suggested that this character is driven by the need to create happiness. She hopes to evoke love in the prince by setting him free. Here she establishes that his social rank is above hers, and so she cannot naturally expect his love. Her preparatory comments seem intended to help us understand the thought process that leads her to decide to liberate him.

In *The Merchant of Venice* (Act 5, Scene 1), Lorenzo prepares Jessica, his bride, for a night of lovemaking. They have just eloped. His comments set the scene for seduction. What will the outcome be? He is playing to win his chosen objective.

1	LORENZO	How sweet the moone-light sleepes upon this banke,
2		Heere will we sit, and let the sounds of musicke
3		Creepe in our eares soft stilnes, and the night
4		Become the tutches of sweet harmonie:

Attack

In the arc of PASTO, attack is how characters begin to pursue their actions. It may last for only one beat (the duration of the first playable action) in a monologue, or it may represent the initial development of a longer theme. In a scene, it may represent how one character actively tries to persuade another until it is necessary to shift tactics.

As an example, the Jailor's Daughter in *The Two Noble Kinsman* goes into her attack phase in the middle of line 4. It's her first effort to rise to her challenge of winning the prince's love and being happy. Let's look at that section together.

JAILOR'S DAUGHTER

...To marry him is hopelesse;	4
To be his whore is witles; Out upon't;	5
What pushes are we wenches driven to	6
When fifteene once has found us?...	7

In *Henry the Sixth, Part Three* (Act 1, Scene 4) York is a captive of Queen Margaret, who is mocking him before having her men put him to death. He begins his speech in an attack mode. His goal is to shame her for her actions.

YORK

Shee-Wolfe of France,	1
But worse then Wolves of France,	2
Whose Tongue more poysons then the Adders Tooth:	3
How ill-beseeming is it in thy Sex,	4
To triumph like an Amazonian Trull,	5
Upon their Woes, whom Fortune captivates?	6

In *Comedy of Errors* (Act 3, Scene 1), Shakespeare similarly begins the scene between Luciana and Antipholus with Luciana already in an attack mode. She is adamantly telling him how to treat her sister well. She wants him to be nice and lie by omission.

1	LUCIANA	And may it be that you have quite forgot
2		A husbands office? shall *Antipholus*
3		Even in the spring of Love, thy Love-springs rot?
4		Shall love in buildings grow so ruinate?
5		If you did wed my sister for her wealth,
6		Then for her wealths-sake use her with more kindnesse:
7		Or if you like else-where doe it by stealth,
8		Muffle your false love with some shew of blindnesse:
9		Let not my sister read it in your eye:
10		Be not thy tongue thy owne shames Orator:
11		Looke sweet, speake faire, become disloyaltie:
12		Apparell vice like vertues harbenger:
13		Beare a faire presence, though your heart be tainted,
14		Teach sinne the carriage of a holy Saint,
15		Be secret false: what need she be acquainted?

Struggle

Struggle is a debate in full force. In a scene, it may depict two characters with conflicting agendas or opinions interacting. In a monologue, it may depict someone on the horns of a dilemma: "On the one hand, *this*...On the other hand, *that*..." Struggle can involve many beats and many permutations of the specific theme that's being discussed. It involves building up the dramatic tension.

Love's Labours Lost, Act 3, Scene 1, shows the bachelor Berowne contemplating the kind of woman who is appropriate for him. He's struggling to articulate her nature.

BEROWNE	What? I love, I sue, I seeke a wife,	1
	A woman that is like a Germane Clocke,	2
	Still a repairing: ever out of frame,	3
	And never going a right, being a Watch:	4
	But being watcht, that it may still goe right.	5

If we return to the Jailor's Daughter again in *The Two Noble Kinsman,* we can see how she moves into the struggle phase of her speech on the second half of line 7. She tells us she saw and liked the man in the jail, pitied him, fell for him, saw he was sad, and then interacted with him pleasantly. It's a history of the evolution of her compassionate feelings for the prince. But it has reached no conclusion yet.

JAILOR'S DAUGHTER

...First I saw him,	7
I (seeing) thought he was a goodly man;	8
He has as much to please a woman in him,	9
(If he please to bestow it so) as ever	10
These eyes yet lookt on; Next, I pittied him,	11
And so would any young wench o'my Conscience	12
That ever dream'd, or vow'd her Maydenhead	13
To a yong hansom Man; Then I lov'd him;	14
And yet he had a Cosen, faire as he too.	15
But in my heart was *Palamon,* and there	16
Lord, what a coyle he keepes? To heare him	17

18		Sing in an evening, what a heaven it is?
19		And yet his Songs are sad-ones; Fairer spoken,
20		Was never a Gentleman. When I come in
21		To bring him water in a morning, first
22		He bowes his noble body, then salutes me, thus:
23		Faire, gentle Mayde, good morrow, may thy goodness,
24		Get thee a happy husband;…

Notorious for breaking the rules of classical playwriting, Shakespeare often combines elements of PASTO. In *Julius Caesar*, for instance, he begins the famous "tent scene" (Act 4, Scene 3) already in struggle, skipping preparation and attack. In such a case the audience experiences an immediate sensation of danger and surprise.

1	CASSIUS	That you have wrong'd me, doth appear in this:
2		You have condemn'd, and noted *Lucius Pella*
3		For taking Bribes heere of the Sardians;
4		Wherein my Letters, praying on his side,
5		Because I knew the man was slighted off.
6	BRUTUS	You wrong'd your selfe to write in such a case.
7	CASSIUS	In such a time as this, it is not meet
8		That every nice offence should beare his Comment.
9	BRUTUS	Let me tell you *Cassius*, you your selfe
10		Are much condemn'd to have an itching Palme,
11		To sell, and Mart your Offices for Gold
12		To Undeservers.
13	CASSIUS	I, an itching Palme?
14		You know that you are *Brutus* that speakes this,
15		Or by the Gods, this speech were else your last.

Turning Point

The turning point should always be the most dramatic or exciting moment in the arc. It sometimes coincides with the most physical moment (a slap, a kiss, a death). In a scene, it's where one character tops another. In a monologue, it represents a discovery or a conclusion reached. In *King Lear* (Act 1, Scene 2), for instance, after questioning the unfairness of his illegitimate status as compared to his brother's, Edmond decides:

| BASTARD | …Well then, | 1 |
| | Legitimate *Edgar*, I must have your land,… | 2 |

The Jailor's Daughter from *The Two Noble Kinsman* comes to a conclusion, her turning point, when she recalls how the prisoner kissed her. Ever since, her heart grieves for him as much as he grieves. That leads her to make the decision to set him free.

JAILOR'S DAUGHTER		
	…Once he kist me,	24
	I lov'd my lips the better ten daies after,	25
	Would he would doe so ev'ry day; He grieves much,	26
	And me as much to see his misery.	27

In *Henry the Sixth, Part Three* (Act 5, Scene 5), when Richard stabs Henry and Henry dies, we are at a major turning point in the scene and in the play. The outcome is that Richard is set up in a competition with his brothers to become king.

| RICHARD | Ile heare no more: | 1 |

2		Dye Prophet in thy speech, [*Stabbes him.*]
3		For this (among'st the rest) was I ordain'd.
4	HENRY	I, and for much more slaughter after this,
5		O God forgive my sinnes, and pardon thee. [*Dyes.*]

Outcome

Outcome is either the resolution of a turning point, or it is what's going to happen next in the conflict—and it could set you up again, becoming the next preparation. For the Jailor's Daughter, the outcome of her speech is her plan to free the man she loves. That serves to develop the plot, and subsequently leads to a stream of future actions.

JAILOR'S DAUGHTER

28	What should I doe, to make him know I love him,
29	For I would faine enjoy him? Say I ventur'd
30	To set him free? what saies the law then? Thus much
31	For Law, or kindred: I will doe it,
32	And this night, or to morrow he shall love me.

In *A Midsummer Night's Dream*, which is a play that involves young men and women chasing each other around in the woods until the right matches are made, the outcome of Act 3, Scene 2 is Hermia's exit on line 17, and also Demetrius giving up on following Hermia (lines 18-23). Hermia is in love with Lysander, not Demetrius.

| 1 | HERMIA | Out dog, out cur, thou driv'st me past the bounds |
| 2 | | Of maidens patience. Hast thou slaine him then? |

Henceforth be never numbred among men.   3

Oh, once tell true, even for my sake,   4

Durst thou a lookt upon him, being awake?   5

And hast thou kill'd him sleeping? O brave tutch: 6

Could not a worme, an Adder do so much?   7

An Adder did it: for with doubler tongue   8

Then thine (thou serpent) never Adder stung.   9

DEMETRIUS You spend your passion on a mispris'd mood,   10

I am not guiltie of *Lysanders* blood: 11

Nor is he dead for ought that I can tell.   12

HERMIA I pray thee tell me then that he is well.   13

DEMETRIUS And if I could, what should I get therefore?   14

HERMIA A priviledge, never to see me more;   15

And from thy hated presence part I: see me no more 16

Whether he be dead or no.   [*Exit*] 17

DEMETRIUS There is no following her in this fierce vaine,   18

Here therefore for a while I will remaine.   19

So sorrowes heavinesse doth heavier grow: 20

For debt that bankrout slip doth sorrow owe,   21

Which now in some slight measure it will pay,   22

If for his tender here I make some stay. [*Lie downe.*] 23

Putting the Stages of PASTO together

Working on PASTO will help you complete the roadmap you began creating for yourself on Day 1. In yesterday's rehearsal you learned to break a scene into beats. This technique overlaps with that one. It is an additional method of compartmentalizing a scene–chopping it into manageable bites. At the most basic level, it helps you answer the question: Is my character moving toward the goal, or has the goal been passed? Preparation, attack, and struggle precede the goal. Turning point and outcome follow it.

Pasto

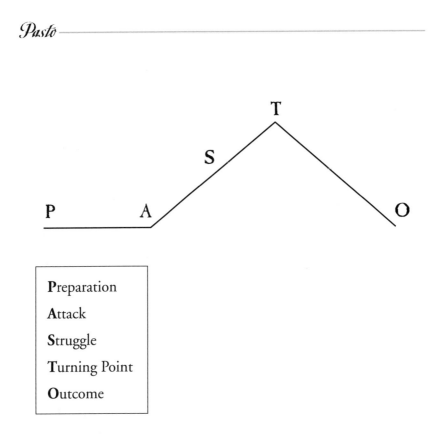

Preparation
Attack
Struggle
Turning Point
Outcome

Shakespeare's plays usually embody the elements of PASTO in five acts, with each act serving one of the purposes.

Of course, the resolution of an objective (a win or a loss) is the bridge to the next Preparation. Night comes, so we go to sleep. But the next morning when the sun rises, we get up again and a new day starts. Life doesn't stop on stage until the curtain falls.

Different characters are frequently moving through the stages of PASTO at different places in a scene. One character's attack may overlap another's preparation. That keeps the action interesting for the audience, as they want to know everyone's unique agenda. It is fun to watch characters working in opposition, conflicting and competing.

Towards the end of *The Taming of the Shrew* (Act 4, Scene 5), Petruchio plans to bring Kate home to her father's house for a visit. But he speaks nonsense to test her first, in order to determine whether or not she will back him up or contradict him in public. Are they a team now, even if he does something that she could potentially ridicule? Has she been tamed? This is Kate and Petruchio's moment of truth. A companion named Hortentio accompanies them. At first Kate disagrees with her husband, which is her half of the struggle. He explains what he wants her to do, which is his half of the struggle. Hortentio contributes to the action by pleading with Kate to give in and let Petruchio win.

If you cast your mind back to the couple's first meeting, which we looked at on Day 3, you can see that their relationship has evolved considerably, yet there's still a spark of the original conflict that was established in that preparation scene. This scene is the play's turning point. Between the two scenes a prolonged struggle has ensued: a highly entertaining and comedic battle of the sexes. The play's outcome is yet to be determined. Even though the scene is the play's turning point, it contains a full PASTO arc.

Here is the preparation:

1	PETRUCHIO	Come on a Gods name, once more toward our
2		fathers:
3		Good Lord how bright and goodly shines the Moone.
4	KATE	The Moone, the Sunne: it is not Moonelight
5		now.

Here is the attack (and a counterattack):

6	PETRUCHIO	I say it is the Moone that shines so bright.
7	KATE	I know it is the Sunne that shines so bright.

And here is the struggle:

8	PETRUCHIO	Now by my mothers sonne, and that's my selfe,
9		It shall be moone, or starre, or what I list,
10		Or ere I journey to your Fathers house:
11		Goe on, and fetch our horses backe againe,
12		Evermore crost and crost, nothing but crost.
13	HORTENTIO	Say as he saies, or we shall never goe.

The struggle continues even when Kate agrees to play along with Petruchio. Petruchio tests her agreement with his sun-moon paradigm even further by switching his opinion (line 20) to the opposite of what he originally said. Kate holds her ground. She agrees to agree, no matter what he says and how ridiculous she might seem (lines 22–25), which is the scene's turning point.

KATE	Forward I pray, since we have come so farre,	14
	And be it moone, or sunne, or what you please:	15
	And if you please to call it a rush Candle,	16
	Henceforth I vowe it shall be so for me.	17
PETRUCHIO	I say it is the Moone.	18
KATE	I know it is the Moone.	19
PETRUCHIO	Nay then you lye: it is the blessed Sunne.	20
KATE	Then God be blest, it is the blessed sun,	21
	But sunne it is not, when you say it is not,	22
	And the Moone changes even as your minde:	23
	What you will have it nam'd, even that it is,	24
	And so it shall be so for *Katherine*.	25

The outcome is reached when Hortentio gets Petruchio to admit that he won the struggle and they can move forward on their journey.

HORTENTIO	*Petruchio*, goe thy waies, the field is won.	26
PETRUCHIO	Well, forward, forward, thus the bowle should run,	27
	And not unluckily against the Bias:	28
	But soft, Company is comming here.	29

The outcome turns to a new preparation when they move forward, as an old man approaches (line 29) and the essence of the scene is repeated: Kate will agree that she's meeting a young girl–even though it's really an old man–just because Petruchio says so. That's the ultimate proof; they are now a team.

—— Your Task—Working with PASTO——

When working with PASTO, I recommend asking yourself the following series of questions about the speech or the scene you are currently working on. Keep an open mind as you do.

- *Does this act (and scene, speech, and sentence) pertain to P, A, S, T, or O?* Remember that Shakespeare sometimes jumps ahead. For dramatic purposes he doesn't always start with a preparation.

- *Do the end stops in the text show me where shifts in the arc occur?* A single end stop can be a beat. A line fragment can be a beat. Several end stops may make up one beat. And there may be more than one beat in each of the phases of a scene.

- *How does this information feed my other acting processes?* For example, ask: What verb could I play on this beat? What repeated words or sounds do I say?

- *What makes Beat A in this scene different from Beat B?* If you've decided that your character is in struggle mode for three beats, ask: What are the different strategies and tactics that are involved in the struggle? Aim for variety.

Breaking Down Your Roadmap

A former student swears to me that at auditions PASTO regularly wins him roles. He has performed at my company, American Globe Theatre, and also did *Nunsense and Torch Song Trilogy* for a regional summer theatre. He said, "I don't know if where I break my scenes into pieces is 100 percent correct. Even so, looking for PASTO helps me be specific and spontaneous, and to act in the moment. It makes my tasks bite sized, so I find them easier and more doable. If I'm in preparation mode, for instance, and I notice three end stops in the text, it makes me aware that I have to find three (or possibly more) gearshifts. So it's a formula for reading the text that I appreciate because it's simple. It gives me clarity and it gives me confidence."

As you rehearse your own speeches and scenes, it's a good idea to keep in mind that you're creating a roadmap for a journey through the text. After you accomplish one line, you can focus on the next. Each line is a stepping-stone. Anything that can help you in breaking down a speech into smaller steps makes your journey easier. Of course, like learning any other technical skill, it may take you a while to use PASTO effectively. People usually aren't fully proficient at it until they've tried it half a dozen times or so. But as you learn to dissect the plays using PASTO, anything that originally seems like a mountain ultimately resembles a collection of tiny hills. Problems are diminished.

Your Day 21 Rehearsal Checklist

Have you completed your tasks?

☐ Working with PASTO

What discoveries have you made?

SHAKESPEARE
in Action

ON DAY 22...

Congratulations! You've reached the end of your 21-day journey and you're ready to give a performance or go on an audition. Before you consider your rehearsal process complete, it is vital for you to "take the show on the road." Finding out whether or not your interpretation of a script is effective can only occur in the field. If you have taken advantage of the rehearsal steps in this book, I guarantee you'll have something to show off. But if you left this process a mental exercise–chair acting–when you stood up it wasn't embedded in your body memory. In that case, you're likely to have anxiety as well as pleasure when you finally get around to sharing your work with an audience.

In many ways, this day's activities are your golden reward. As an actor, it's the moment when your work pays off and you're entitled to celebrate and enjoy your artistry. You can trust that the various layers drawn from your rehearsals live within you. The rehearsal process has enabled you to integrate meaningful choices within your body, mind, and heart. I've seen poor actors become competent ones and good actors become excellent ones doing the same exercises. You're ready, if you've done the work fully.

Remember the seven Cs of acting? The first is commitment. A student of mine went to an audition and blanked on her lines. The director generously gave her a second chance…and her mind went blank again. When she told me about it, I asked, "Did you follow all the steps I taught you in class?" She said no. Her experience in that audition resulted from under preparation. No surprise. She had lacked commitment. But the experience wasn't wasted on her. She learned an important lesson from the frustration of forgetting her lines in the face of opportunity. She renewed her commitment to rehearsing and after her next audition she got called back twice by a respected casting director.

The other six Cs are concentration, conditioning, control, confidence, courage, and clarity. If you committed to the rehearsal process on Day 1, these Cs should work in your favor when you get up to perform on stage, or in a classroom, an acting studio, or a casting director's office. Every audition should be considered a performance. The caliber of your work needs to reach the highest standard if you want a shot at getting hired.

Realistically, you either know what you're doing by now–or you don't. If you have a performance or an audition scheduled today, it's too late for major revisions in your interpretation. But you can always change your approach to the script in future rehearsals. For now you simply have to let go and be present to the moment being freshly-minted on the stage. Although you'll focus on what you're doing–the specific moments and bits you've planned–your performance may yet hold a series of surprises. As best as you can, remain open to the sense of genuinely living through your lines for the first time.

The audience is the last part of the learning process for any role. They will show you where the funny moments and the dramatic moments are. They will teach you where to breathe and give them a pause to catch up with you. If you lose their attention, you'll hear them rustling around and reading their programs. Feedback is essential. So go to the next Shakespeare audition you see announced and try out your piece. At least do it for a group of friends or for someone you trust to give honest, objective criticism (probably not an emotionally involved person, such as a significant other or a competitor).

Preparing for Your Performance

When it's show time, that's it. You have to be ready, willing, and able to give your performance your all. It doesn't matter if you feel sad, tired, or have a head cold that day. You still have to give your every appearance on stage your best. You want your audience to get their money's worth. You want casting directors to be impressed. You want to get the best feedback from your classmates, teacher, or coach. Here's how you can raise your energy, gather your focus, and come across like a radiant star.

CREATE AN ENVIRONMENT OF SUCCESS

Put yourself into positive surroundings today. Avoid personal dramas and conflicts if you can. Let your answering machine or voice mail pick up phone calls from friends and relations. Be successful at something before you go to the theatre so that you can experience yourself as powerful and competent. This will establish a successful frame of mind and give you a "can-do" attitude.

Accomplish a physical task. For instance, earlier in the day take a bike ride or go swimming, rather than allowing routine interactions, your nerves about performing, and other people's problems distract you from concentrating and getting ready. As you get closer

to the time of your audition or performance, use the following steps
to prepare.

RELAX AND FOCUS

Lay down on the floor for a few minutes and surrender to your natural breathing pattern. As you do, pay attention to the flow of air in
and out of your lungs on each inhalation and exhalation. Succumb to
the force of gravity weighing down your arms and legs. If you have
any tension, send the air to that place.

WARM UP YOUR BODY

You'll need to limber up your entire body. This can be done before
you arrive at performance site. From a standing position, bend forward and let your head and arms be floppy. This stretches the spine,
hamstrings, and shoulders. Raise your arms overhead and stretch
upwards as high as you can go. Alternate stretching your right and
left sides. Roll your head in circles a few times to the right and a few
times to the left. Raise your shoulders and then let them drop. Do
whatever else feels good that releases the tension in your body.

If you're performing in a theatre, be sure to find a place backstage
where you can do jumping jacks or another aerobic activity before
your entrance without disrupting anyone else. If you're in class, step
outside during the scene before yours to warm up. If you're on an
audition, go into the bathroom to get some privacy. Your goal should
be to get your blood pumping and your airways open to circulate flu-
ids and oxygen throughout your body. If you're breathing hard, the
body responds by becoming more alert.

WARM UP YOUR VOICE

In the same way you warmed up your body, you also need to limber
up your vocal apparatus. You need to free the voice, so it has lots of

color and dynamics (e.g., high and low, loud and soft, legato and staccato). You need to open the breath, so you are able to sustain and accomplish any type of speech or onstage effort. You want to loosen your tongue, so it's dexterous and can wrap around Shakespeare's most complex language. And you want to raise your energy–by receiving sufficient oxygen and sending vibrations of sound throughout your body. Use different tasks from past rehearsals for these purposes and others, like having fun. For instance:

- "Playing with Accents" (Day 1): Frees the voice and raises energy

- "Can-Do Kazoo" (Day 3): Frees the voice, opens the breath, and raises energy

- "Singing Your Lines" (Day 10): Opens the breath and raises energy

- "Tuning Your Tongue" (Day 13): Limbers the tongue and opens the breath

Also practice a quick breathing exercise: Place a small straw, such as a coffee stirrer, between your lips. Then, inhale for ten counts and exhale for ten counts. Next increase your inhalation and exhalation to 15 counts each. Then go to 20/20. Keep increasing the length of the flow of air. Go up to a 60/60 breathing pattern if you can. In time, this will improve your breath control enormously. It is an excellent warm-up.

QUICKLY RECONNECT TO YOUR SCRIPT

In order to give a high caliber performance, you may also have to start your emotional motor. Spend a few minutes daydreaming about your given circumstances before you set foot on stage. Borrow other tasks from the preceding days of rehearsal to help keep your performance fresh, vulnerable, and intuitive (not to make it conform to your static expectations). For example, you might:

Reread your script, making note of repetitions (Day 1), capitalized words (Day 2), and punctuation (Day 4)

Reconnect to your "doings" by taking a glance at the newspaper headlines you drafted on Day 12

Visualize your imaginary focal points (Day 14)

Mentally review your basic human need and personal substitutions (Day 19)

RAISE THE STAKES AND INSPIRE YOURSELF

Imagine that you're a warrior putting on your armor on the day of battle. You're conditioned from rehearsing. Now you need to tap into your commitment by remembering the high stakes involved. Ask yourself, "Am I going to get hired today so I can pay my rent, my health insurance premiums, and my other bills?"

Each time you perform a particular role you might give yourself a new task to work on (e.g., to discover all the humor, to play more off of a specific actor, to make your consonants stand out) to make the event of the performance stand out.

Perhaps altruism is more of a motivation for you than bills or improving your craft. On an off night or on every night, try dedicating your performance to someone who is sick, such as an ailing parent, or to a worthy cause, such as kids with HIV/AIDS. That keeps the work special and sacred, more than just a job. You are making a unique gift to at least one person in the audience—somehow—every time you perform.

Find your own particular reason to give it 110 percent. Then, be courageous. Be willing to fail knowing that you've done your best. If you've done the work, you need to claim and own it now, in this moment. You needn't second-guess the choices you've made, as they're not mistakes. Human behavior is surprising, weird, and spontaneous. You are here to represent all of that for us. You must learn to trust your instincts.

Tips for Auditions

1. Get there with plenty of time to spare. Early is on time. On time is late.

2. Stay focused. Let others chitchat and socialize. Conversation diffuses mental and emotional energy, and disrupts concentration.

3. Don't be thrown if a casting director doesn't look at you while you audition. Casting directors sometimes need to write notes, prefer to listen rather than watch, or might be testing you to see what you do when you're under pressure.

4. Give yourself a new task to work on each time you audition—to keep the piece fresh.

5. Use a piece that gets good results. Discard pieces that aren't working in your favor.

6. Seize the day and have as much fun as you are able.

7. Remember that you may be the solution to their problems, a valuable commodity.

8. Be grateful and polite to everyone you meet.

A Final Note:
Follow Shakespeare's Explicit Advice for Actors

I want you, the reader, to know that the work of preparing a life for the stage can never truly be finished. That's why your aim must be to grow through a part, rather than go through a part–to find more nuances and unique choices. At the race track the announcer reports, "The horse won by a nose!" What's the something extra that makes your work special and unique? If you haven't put the extra work into it, your result is going to be ordinary–copycat.

Before you set this book down, read a final scene from *Hamlet* (Act 3, Scene 2). Always heed this brilliant acting wisdom–Hamlet's famous speech to the Players–with which Shakespeare surely intended to instruct his own company of actors. The Bard knew what he was talking about, clearly. Let's give him the last word.

1	HAMLET	Speake the Speech I pray you, as I pronounc'd
2		it to you trippingly on the Tongue: But if you mouth it,
3		as many of your Players do, I had as lieve the Town-Cryer
4		had spoke my Lines: Nor do not saw the Ayre too much
5		your hand thus, but use all gently; for in the verie Tor-
6		rent, Tempest and (as I may say) the Whirle-winde of

Passion, you must acquire and beget a Temperance that   7

may give it Smoothnesse. O it offends mee to the Soule,   8

to see a robustious Pery-wig-pated Fellow, teare a Passi-   9

on to tatters, to verie rages, to split the eares of the   10

Groundlings: who (for the most part) are capeable of   11

nothing, but inexplicable dumbe shewes, and noise: I could 12

have such a Fellow whipt for o're-doing Termangant: it 13

out-*Herod's Herod*. Pray you avoid it.   14

PLAYER 1   I warrant your Honor.   15

HAMLET   Be not too tame neyther: but let your owne   16

Discretion be your Tutor. Sute the Action to the Word, 17

The Word to the Action, with this speciall observance: 18

That you ore-stop not the modestie of Nature: for any 19

thing so over-done is from the purpose of Playing, whose 20

end both at the first and now, was and is, to hold as 'twer 21

the Mirrour up to Nature: to shew Vertue her owne   22

Feature, Scorne her owne Image, and the verie Age and 23

Bodie of the Time, his forme and pressure. Now, this   24

over-done, or come tardie off, though it make the unskil- 25

full laugh, cannot but make the Judicious greeve; The   26

censure of the which One, must in your allowance o're- 27

way a whole Theater of Others. Oh, there bee Players   28

that I have seene Play, and heard others praise, and that 29

highly (not to speake it prophanely) that neyther having 30

the accent of Christians, nor the gate of Christian, Pagan, 31

or Nor man, have so strutted and bellowed, that I have   32

thought some of Natures Journey-men had made men,   33

and not made them well, they imitated Humanity so ab- 34

35   hominably.
36 PLAYER 1 I hope we have reform'd that indifferently with us, Sir.
37 HAMLET O reforme it altogether. And let those that
38   play your Clownes, speake no more then is set downe for
39   them. For there be of them, that will themselves laugh,
40   to set on some quantitie of barren Spectators to laugh
41   too, though in the meane time, some necessary Question
42   of the Play be then to be considered: that's Villanous, and
43   shewes a most pittifull Ambition in the Foole that uses
44   it. Go make you readie.

RECOMMENDED READING

TEXT

The Arden Shakespeare (various eds.). New York, NY: Arden, different years. Each of the 36 plays, individually bound.

The First Folio and Early Quartos of William Shakespeare. University of Virginia. Website: http://etext.lib.virginia.edu/shakespeare/folio/

Freeman, Neil, ed. *The First Folio of Shakespeare in Modern Type: Comedies, Histories, and Tragedies.* New York: Applause Books, 2001.

Freeman, Neil, ed. *Shakespeare's First Texts: Folio Scripts.* New York, NY: Applause Books, 1999. Each of the 36 plays, individually bound.

The New Variorum Editions of Shakespeare (various eds.). Different publishers, including Dover, J. B. Lippincott, and the Modern Language Association of America. Each of the 36 plays, individually bound.

PERFORMANCE

Ball, William. *A Sense of Direction: Some Observations on the Art of Directing.* Brooklyn, NY: Drama Publishers, 1984.

Barton, John. *Playing Shakespeare: An Actor's Guide.* London: Methuen, 1984.

Berry, Cicely. *The Actor and the Text.* New York: Applause, 2000.

Calderone, Marina and Maggie Lloyd-Williams. *Actions: The Actor's Thesaurus.* Brooklyn, NY: Drama Publishers, 2004.

Harold, Madd. *Performing Shakespeare: For Film, Television, and Theatre.* Los Angeles, CA: Lone Eagle, 2002.

Kaiser, Scott. *Mastering Shakespeare: An Acting Class in Seven Scenes.* New York: Allworth Press, 2003.

Rodenburg, Patsy. *Speaking Shakespeare: Voice and the Performer.* New York: Palgrave Macmillan, 2002.

Scheeder, Louis and Shane Ann Younts. *All the Words a Stage: A Pronunciation Dictionary for the Plays of William Shakespeare.* Manchester, NH: Smith and Kraus, 2002.

Stanislavski, Konstantin. *Creating a Role.* New York: Theatre Arts Books, 1961.

REFERENCE

Barker, H. Granville. *Prefaces to Shakespeare.* Multiple editions of individual plays. London, UK: Batsford, 1958.

Berne, Eric. *Games People Play.* New York: Grove Press, 1964.

Boyce, Charles. *Encyclopedia of Shakespeare A-Z: The Essential Reference to His Plays, His Poems, His Life and Times, and More.* New York: Roundtable Press, 1990.

Davis, J. Madison and Frankforter, A. Daniel. *The Shakespeare Name Dictionary.* Oxford, UK: Routledge, 2004.

Espy, William R. *The Garden of Eloquence: A Rhetorical Bestiary.* New York: Harper & Row, 1983.

Graves, Robert. *Greek Gods and Heroes.* New York: Laurel Leaf, 1965.

Hamilton, Edith. *Mythology: Timeless Tales of Gods and Heroes.* New York: Warner Books, 1999.

Kökeritz, Helge. *Shakespeare's Names: A Pronouncing Dictionary.* New Haven, CT: Yale University, 1974.

Mahood, M.M.. *Shakespeare's Wordplay.* London, UK: Methuen, (1957) 1979.

RECOMMENDED READING

Merriam-Webster Online Dictionary. Website: www.m-w.com

Moston, Doug, ed. *The First Folio of Shakespeare 1623.* New York: Applause Books, 1995, out of print.

Partridge, Eric. *Shakespeare's Bawdy.* New York: Routledge, 1968.

Roberts, Philip Davis. *How Poetry Works.* New York: Penguin, 1986.

Rubinstein, Frankie. *A Dictionary of Shakespeare's Sexual Puns and Their Significance.* New York: Palgrave Macmillan, 1996.

Schmidt, Alexander. *Shakespeare Lexicon and Quotation Dictionary: A Complete Dictionary of All the English Words, Phrases, and Constructions in the Works of the Poet,* Volume 1 (A-M) and Volume 2 (N-Z). Mineola, NY: Dover Publications, 1971.

Spark Notes: Shakespeare Study Guides (various authors) Website: wwwSparkNotes.com/Shakespeare/

Spurgeon, Carolyn F. E. *Shakespeare's Imagery and What It Tells Us.* Cambridge, UK: Cambridge University Press, 1935.

Styan, John L. *Shakespeare's Stagecraft.* Cambridge, UK: Cambridge University Press, 1967.

LIFE AND TIMES OF SHAKESPEARE AND THE GLOBE THEATRE

Beckerman, Bernard. *Shakespeare at the Globe.* New York: Macmillan, 1962.

Gurr, Andrew. *William Shakespeare: The Extraordinary Life of the Most Successful Author of All Time.* New York: HarperCollins, 1995.

Laroque, Francois. *Shakespeare: Court, Crowd, and Playhouse.* New York: Thames and Hudson, 1993.

Rutter, Carol, ed. *Documents of the Rose Playhouse.* Manchester, UK: Manchester University Press, 1984.

INDEX

✦ INDEX ✦

About the Author

JOHN BASIL is Producing Artistic Director and co-founder of American Globe Theatre, an Off-Off-Broadway theatre company located in the heart of Times Square in Manhattan. Through his independent acting studio, the American Globe Theatre Conservatory, he teaches the Playing Shakespeare Series. Will Power is his first book.

Basil's professional career in theatre has spanned three decades. After receiving an M.F.A. in Acting from Temple University in 1975, he worked as an actor while also training in method acting with Stella Adler, Uta Hagen, and Mira Rostova. Following several seasons at the Williamstown Theatre Festival, he explored the art of direction at the Writer's Theatre and the Ensemble Studio Theatre. He then became a principal director and teacher at the Riverside Shakespeare Company, where he remained until 1987, when he founded the American Globe Theatre and Conservatory.

As a director, Basil has worked as a guest artist at venues such as the American Stage Festival, the Sarasota Opera Company, the Raft Theatre, the Asolo Conservatory at Florida State University, Bradley University, Long Island University, and the University of Wyoming, among others. In addition, he has served as casting director for the Writer's Theatre, and as a speech and text consultant to Frank Langella. He has directed seventeen of Shakespeare's plays at American Globe Theatre.

As a teacher, Basil's Playing Shakespeare Series has enlightened and inspired actors and college students across the nation, including those at the Sedona Shakespeare Festival, Montclair State University, Columbia University Teachers College, Bradley University, Pennsylvania State University, the University of Colorado, the University of Wyoming, Long Island University, Oklahoma State University, the Asolo Conservatory, and the American Globe Theatre Conservatory. Basil has also taught teens in public and private junior high schools, high schools, and youth programs located throughout New York and New Jersey.

Mr. Basil resides in New York City with his wife, actress Elizabeth Keefe.

STEPHANIE GUNNING is an author, editor, and publishing consultant with over 20 years' experience in the book business. Her A-list clientele includes bestselling authors, major publishing firms, top caliber literary agencies, and innovative self-publishers. She has coauthored and ghostwritten sixteen books, including Easy Homeopathy, Total Renewal, The Passion Principle, Exploring Feng Shui, and Creating Your Birth Plan. She is the author of an audio program entitled Partner with Your Publisher.

After graduating with a B.A. from Amherst College in 1984, Gunning launched her publishing career in New York City, rapidly rising through the editorial ranks at HarperCollins Publishers, then being recruited as a senior editor at Bantam

Doubleday Dell, and ultimately establishing an independent business, Stephanie Gunning Enterprises LLC, in 1996. Currently, she resides in Manhattan, where in addition to her writing, she teaches teleseminars and workshops. To find out more about Ms. Gunning, and her products and services, visit: www.stephaniegunning.com.